AF531537

ENTREPRENEURSHIP IN TINY SECTOR INDUSTRIES

AN INDIAN SCENARIO

ENTREPRENEURSHIP IN TINY SECTOR INDUSTRIES

AN INDIAN SCENARIO

By

Dr. P.LOURDES POOBALA RAYEN

SELECTION GRADE LECTURER
ST.XAVIER'S COLLEGE (AUTONOMOUS)
PALAYAMKOTTAI-627 002
TAMIL NADU

&

Dr. X. ANTONY THANARAJ

READER IN COMMERCE
SCOTT CHRISTIAN COLLEGE (AUTONOMOUS)
NAGERCOIL
KANYAKUMARI DISTRICT
TAMIL NADU

DISCOVERY PUBLISHING HOUSE PVT. LTD.
NEW DELHI-110 002

First Published-2010

ISBN 978-81-8356-655-1

Published by:
DISCOVERY PUBLISHING HOUSE PVT. LTD.
4831/24, Ansari Road, Prahlad Street
Darya Ganj, New Delhi-110002 (India)
Phone: +91-11-23279245, 43764432 • Fax: +91-11-23253475
E-mail: parul.wasan@gmail.com
info@discoverypublishinggroup.com
web: www.discoverypublishinggroup.com

Printed at:
Mehra Offset Press
Delhi

PREFACE

The winds of Liberalization and Globalisation have opened new vistas for the large as well as small and micro enterprises. The small and micro units have the flexibility and adaptability to switch over to low volume specialized markets and diversify in to different products with appropriate manufacturing processes. Small and Micro enterprises are expected to gain through linkages with a medium and large enterprises or export houses.

In the emerging scenario of a liberalized regime, unrestricted competition from multinationals entering the consumer durables and non-durables market segments with their internationally known brand names, technological superiority and intensive marketing efforts would offer formidable challenge to the small and micro enterprises.

Indian industry is in the cross roads where on the one hand it has to integrate itself with the global markets, while on the other, it has to face competition in the domestic market from the international suppliers. Technology, product quality, factor productivity and competitive marketing techniques and management practices alone seem to hold the key for the future of Indian small scale industry. On moving from a protected economy to a market-oriented economy, some amount of transitional problems seems unavoidable to it, the sector can look forward to a level of sustained development in the coming years.

The small and micro enterprises must be developed along with the large units. From the view point of long term perspective, however, the capacity of small manufacturers to become economically viable, technically progressive and efficient and to develop competitive strength shall be the only justification for their continuance. In the intervening period, the government should help create conditions to facilitate their smooth growth.

The small and micro enterprises have a distinct advantage of low investment with a high potential for employment generation. It is also expected to bring about the dispersal of industries in the rural and semi-urban areas with the concomitant advantage of equitable distribution of national income.

Empirical evidence indicates that small and micro enterprises can be an important vehicle for meeting the growth and equity objections of developing economies. The government would therefore, be fair to foster entrepreneurship and should help create conducive environment to facilitate rapid growth of efficient small and micro enterprises in the country.

The book earnestly attempts to present the various aspects of entrepreneurship as a result of research work carried out by the authors. It is hoped that the readers will not only gain a perspective of the entrepreneurial function, but also be able to pursue research in the area of entrepreneurship for gaining in depth knowledge.

I feel great pleasure in expressing my profound gratitude to my Ph.D. guide and co-author of this book Dr. X. Antony Thanaraj, Reader, Research Department of Commerce, Scott Christian College, Nagercoil, Tamil Nadu for his incessant guidance and encouragements in my academic endevours. I am grateful to Shri Tilak Wasan, Director of Discovery Publishing House Pvt. Ltd., New Delhi for having come forward to publish this book.

LOURDES POOBALA RAYEN

Contents

List of Abbreviations

DI	-	Directorate of Industries
DIC	-	District Industries Centre
IDBI	-	Industrial Development Bank of India
IFCI	-	Industrial Finance Corporation of India
KVIB	-	Kadhi Village Industries Board
NABARD	-	National Bank for Agricultural and Rural Development
NSIC	-	National Small Industries Corporation
SIDBI	-	Small Industrial Development Bank of India
SIDO	-	Small Industries Development Organisation
SIPCOT	-	State Industries Promotion Corporation of Tamil Nadu
SISI	-	Small Industries Service Institute
SSI	-	Small Scale Industries
SSIDC	-	Small Scale Industries Development Corporation
TIIC	-	Tamil Nadu Industrial Investment Corporation

1

Introduction and Design of the Study

INTRODUCTION

The development of human resources constitutes the central objective of all development efforts of any country. The proper utilization of human resources is the key to economic and social development. In a labour–surplus Indian economy, the role of human resource development in the form of creation of job avenues thereby increasing earnings and productivity of unemployed or partially employed persons is a challenge to the planner. Rapid industrial development contributes to the process of accelerated economic growth. In a country like India, where unemployment and underemployment prevail, where most of the entrepreneurs are capable of only small investment and where there is dearth of sophisticated machinery and modern technology, the tiny and small-scale industry, which is labour-intensive and capital-saving, plays a vital role in the overall economic development.

TINY SECTOR INDUSTRIES

A unit is treated as a tiny enterprise where investment in plant and machinery does not exceed Rs. 25 lakhs irrespective of the location of the unit[1]. Enterprise in the tiny sector is labour-intensive, requires low capital investment and uses locally available skill and technology in manufacture. They are mostly household types and village based. As tiny industrial units could be started anywhere and everywhere, they would help for balanced regional development throughout the country. Tiny industrial units are owned, controlled and managed by individual entrepreneurs or partners with the help of family members. Success or failure depends upon the entrepreneur and he alone gets all the profits and bears all the business risks. The entrepreneur of a tiny industrial unit only manufactures those consumer items and components which are required by the customers in the same or neighboring localities. The entrepreneurs of the tiny sector also take advance order from known customers. After some time, the tiny industrial units grow and become small, medium and even large scale units due to the efforts of the entrepreneur. Not all tiny industries have attained the highest growth level. Some industries reach the peak level, some of them maintain the same level, some of them prove to be sick and some of them go out of business.

The concept of the tiny sector came to vogue by the passing of the Industrial Policy Resolution 1977 of the Government of India. The emergence of the tiny sector and the setting up of the District Industries Centre to provide services and support enabled the rural entrepreneurs to set up tiny industrial units. The main thrust was on an effective promotion of cottage and small industries which were widely dispersed in rural areas and small towns. With this end in view, the new sector 'tiny' was created for the first time in the year 1977. All the industries, with a capital investment of Rs. 1 lakh in plant and machinery and located in rural areas and small towns with a maximum population of up to 50000 as per the 1971 census were included in the tiny sector. The industrial policy resolution 1980 redefined the investment limit in plant and machinery for tiny units and the limit was increased from Rs. 1 lakh to Rs. 2 lakhs to cover cottage industries in rural and semi urban areas. The enhancement of the limit of investment in plant and machinery helped the genuine tiny units, particularly those which were set up by young and technically qualified entrepreneurs. In the

1988-89 budget the investment limit was further raised from Rs. 2 lakhs to Rs. 2.5 lakhs. Later, according to the SSI policy statement in the year 1991, the investment limit in plant and machinery for the tiny units was increased from Rs. 2.5 lakhs to Rs. 5 lakhs and the location specific condition was removed. Once again in the year 1997 the definition of tiny sector industries was redefined to increase the investment limit in plant and machinery and the limit was raised from Rs. 5 lakhs to Rs. 25 lakhs. The investment limit of Rs. 25 lakhs was retained in the newly passed Micro, Small and Medium Enterprises Development Act, 2006 which came into force on 2nd October 2006.

The Government of India gives special assistance for the promotion of tiny industrial units by providing technical advice, marketing assistance, margin money assistance, purchase of the products of the tiny industrial units, extension of the credit guarantee scheme, export assistance, package assistance and the like. Moreover, the Government of India and the Government of Tamil Nadu have established Industrial Estates exclusively for tiny industrial units. The Government measures enabled many rural entrepreneurs to establish tiny industrial units and utilized the local resources of both men and materials for the economic betterment of the individuals and the country as a whole. The tiny industrial units strive to bring in a social emancipation of villagers in rural India. Though the tiny sector was created through the Industrial Policy Resolution of 1977 itself, till today the tiny sector has been kept under the small scale industries sector. As per the final results of the Third All India Census of Small Scale Industries released in January 2004, the size of the registered SSI sector was reported as 13,74,974 units and the number of tiny units among the SSI was estimated as 97.9 per cent[2]. It reveals the dominance of the tiny sector industries in the SSI sector. The tiny sector consists of manufacturing, processing and service activities which are carried on with relatively simple tools and techniques. The capital investment in plant and machinery is much lower than in the small scale industries.

In India, small scale industry is not a single connotation terminology. The small-scale industrial sector includes a wide range of activities with different specific sizes and other parameters. This sector is a bundle of small units with huge variations in investment on the one hand and the nature of technology on the other.

The small-scale industrial sector in India is primarily divided into two categories namely:

(i) traditional sector; and

(ii) modern sector.

The traditional sector is divided into six categories, namely:

(i) khadi;

(ii) village industries;

(iii) handlooms;

(iv) sericulture;

(v) handicrafts; and

(vi) coir.

The traditional sector industries are mostly carried out as household or cottage activities. They are family based enterprises and employ little or no hired labour and use traditional methods and skills that are hereditary and move from one generation to another. The modern industries in the small-scale industrial sector mainly comprises of two sets of industries namely, the powerloom sector and the small-scale industry sector. The small scale industry primarily consists of four sets of industrial enterprises namely:

(i) tiny sector;

(ii) service establishments;

(iii) small-scale units; and

(iv) ancillary units.

The small-scale industry has made its significant contribution to the economy by increasing its share in exports, generating large scale employment opportunities, dispersing industrial activities and reducing concentration of economic power. Its contribution in different areas enabled it to get priority treatment both from the Central and the State Government.

ROLE OF SMALL SCALE INDUSTRIES IN ECONOMIC DEVELOPMENT

Small and tiny industries contribute significantly to social and economic development objectives such as labour absorption, income distribution, rural development, poverty eradication, regional balance and promotion of entrepreneurship. In fact they play an important role in the process of a country's industrial development. In the Indian context, they play a key role in the economic development of the country. More importantly, they are a stepping stone for entrepreneurs to grow from small to big. They provide in-plant training to millions of entrepreneurs and motivate them to become innovative entrepreneurs to improve the economy. Promotion of small and tiny industries has been one of the main strategies for economic development in the developing countries since the1950s. The special feature of planning in India is that it does not stop at giving conceptual emphasis to the growth of small and tiny industries, but it has in particular drawn up a concrete and constructive planned programme to attain the planned objectives. The development of small and tiny industries as the focal point of industrial development is the evidence of the awareness of the Government to propagate and develop this sector for the ultimate objective of tackling the all prevailing and ever growing problem of unemployment.

The performance of the small-scale sector in India during the last five years is presented in Table 1.1.

Table 1.1 shows the performance of the small-scale sector. During 2000-01 to 2004-05, the SSI sector registered a continuous growth in the number of units, production, employment and exports. The average annual growth during this period, in the number of units was 4.1 per cent, while employment grew by 4.4 per cent annually. Further, the average annual growth in production at current and constant prices was 10.6 per cent and 7.6 per cent respectively.

Table 1.1: Performance of the Small-scale Industries Sector in India India

Year	No. of Units (Lakhs)			Production (Rs. in crore)		Employment in Lakhs	Exports (Rs. crore)
	Regd.	Un-regd.	Total	At current prices	At constant prices (1993-94)		
2000-01	13.10	88.0	110.10 (4.1)	261289 (11.5)	184428 (8.0)	239.09 (4.4)	69797 (28.8)
2001-02	13.75	91.46	105.21 (4.1)	282270 (8.0)	195613 (6.1)	249.09 (4.2)	71244 (2.1)
2002-03	14.68	94.81	109.49 (4.1)	311993 (10.5)	210636 (7.7)	260.13 (4.9)	86013 (20.7)
2003-04	15.54	98.41	113.95 (4.1)	357773 (11.6)	228730 (8.6)	271.36 (4.3)	97644 (13.5)
2004-05	16.57	102.02	118.59 (4.1)	418263 (16.9)	251511 (10.0)	282.91 (4.3)	NA

Figures in parenthesis indicate percentage growth.

Source: Development Commissioner, SSI, Ministry of SSI, Government of India.

Comparison of the SSI Sector with the Overall Industrial Sector

The growth rate of the SSI sector in comparison with that of the overall industrial sector is presented in Table 1.2.

Table 1.2: Comparison of the SSI Sector with the Overall Industrial Sector in India

Year	*Growth Rate of the SSI Sector (per cent)*	*Growth Rate of the Overall Industrial Sector (per cent)*
2000-01	8.0	5.0
2001-02	6.1	2.7
2002-03	7.7	5.7
2003-04	8.6	6.9
2004-05	9.96	8.4

Source: http://ssi.gov.in/SSIArReport2005-06. pdf.
Government of India, Ministry of SSI, AR 2005-06, Chapter II, p. 40-41.

During 2000-01 to 2004-05 the SSI sector growth rate showed an increasing trend except in the year 2001-02. The same trend could be seen in the overall industrial sector too. But the average rate of growth of the SSI sector is more (8.072 per cent) compared to the overall industrial sector's average growth rate of 5.74 per cent during 2000-2005.

Contribution of SSI to the Gross Domestic Product (GDP)

The small-scale industry's contribution to the Gross Domestic Product is shown in Table 1.3.

Table 1.3 reveals that on an average of around 39.61 per cent of the total industrial production was contributed by the small-scale industries sector during 2000-01 to 2003-04. In the same period the SSI's average contribution to gross domestic product was around 6.8 per cent.

Table 1.3: SSI Contribution to the Gross Domestic Product

(per cent)

Year	*Contribution of SSI to Total Industrial Production*	*Gross Domestic Product (GDP)*
2000-01	39.91	6.86
2001-02	39.63	6.67
2002-03	39.48	6.82
2003-04	39.42	6.71

Source: http://ssi.gov.in/SSIArReport2005-06. pdf.
Government of India, Ministry of SSI, AR 2005-06, Chapter II, p. 40-41.

Flow of Credit to the SSI Sector from Public Sector Banks

Credit is one of the critical inputs for the promotion and development of small scale industries. To ensure timely and adequate credit to the SSI sector the Government is implementing several schemes.The Small Industries Development Bank of India (SIDBI) is the apex refinance bank. Term loans are provided by State Financial Corporations (SFCs), Scheduled Commercial Banks and Small Industries Development Corporations (SIDCs). Direct and indirect credit is also undertaken to some extent by NABARD, NSIC etc. Measures for improving the flow of credit to the SSI sector are taken through announcements made in the Union Budget and Comprehensive Policy Packages.

It is evident from Table 1.4 that the net bank credit to SSI has increased from 45788 crores to 67634 crores over a period of 6 years from 2000 to 2005. But the percentage of net bank credit to SSI has declined during the same period. The percentage declined from 15.6 per cent to 9.4 per cent during the period 2000 to 2005.

Table 1.4: Flow of Credit to the SSI Sector from Public Sector Banks

(Rs. in crores)

Credit to the Small-scale Sector from Banks in the Public Sector	*March 2000*	*March 2001*	*March 2002*	*March 2003*	*March 2004*	*March 2005*
Net Bank Credit	292943	340888	396954	477899	558849	718722
Credit to the Small-scale Sector	45788	48445	49743	52988	58278	67634
No. of Small-Scale Sector Accounts (in lakhs)	22.72	22.80	22.23	16.95	16.33	17.71
Small-Scale Sector Credit Percentage of net bank credit	15.6	14.2	12.5	11.1	10.4	9.4

Source: http://ssi.gov.in/SSIArReport 2005-06.pdf.
Credit and Fiscal concession to SSI Sector. Chapter III, p. 41.

Status of Credit to Tiny Sector

The credit extended to the tiny sector industries by the public sector banks is presented in Table 1.5.

Table 1.5: Status of Credit to the Tiny Sector

Credit to the Tiny Sector	*At the end of March 2000*	*At the end of March 2001*	*At the end of March 2002*	*At the end of March 2003*	*At the end of March 2004*	*At the end of March 2005*
Net bank credit to the Tiny Sector (Rs. in crores)	24742	26019	27030	26937	30826	28063
Tiny Credit as a	54.0	53.7	54.3	50.8	52.9	41.5

Source: http://ssi.gov.in/SSIArReport 2005-06.pdf.
Credit and Fiscal concession to SSI Sector. Chapter III, p. 41.

Table 1.5 reveals that the net bank credit to the tiny sector increased from Rs. 24742 crores to Rs. 28063 crores during the period 2000-2005. The percentage increase is 13.42 per cent. Tiny credit as a percentage of net SSI credit declined from 54 per cent to 41.5 per cent during the same period.

SMALL SCALE INDUSTRY IN TAMIL NADU

Small-scale industries made an early start in Tamil Nadu with the Government stepping in to create major industrial estates at Guindy and Ambattur in Chennai. In 1973, Tamil Nadu had the largest number of SSIs in the country with 18,500 registered units and it has maintained this leadership by and large when the second All India Census of SSIs was carried out in 1987-88.

Between 1993-94 and 2002-03, the state has recorded an annual growth rate of 10.69 per cent in the number of registered units, 13.10 per cent in the investment deployed, 16.34 per cent in output and 9.38 per cent in employment. The state accounts for 12.6 per cent registered SSI units in the country, 12.1 per cent of output and 15.7 per cent of employment during 2002-03.

The trend in growth from 2000-01 may be seen from the table below.

Table 1.6: Trend in the Growth Units in SSI Units in Tamil Nadu

Year	*Number of Permanent Registered Units*	*Investment (Rs. in crores)*	*Production (Rs. in crores)*	*Employment (in Number)*
2000-01	387597	11567.22	78281.66	2902122
2001-02	419524	12466.19	83904.80	3104477
2002-03	448905	12569.34	89781.00	3142335
2003-04	474699	13291.50	94939.80	3417832
2004-05	489782	14397.31	99496.77	3525582

Source: www.tn.gov.in/spc/annualplan/ap2005-06/ch_10_2.pdf. Directorate of Industries and Commerce, Chennai.

It is evident from Table 1.6 that the number of registered SSI units has increased from 387597 in the year 2000-01 to 489782 in the year 2004-05 registering 20.86 per cent increase over a period of 5 years. As regards the investment in SSI units, it increased from Rs. 11567.22 crores to Rs. 14397.31 crores between 2000-01 and 2004-05. The percentage increase in investment during the period is 19.66 per cent. SSI units' production has increased from Rs. 78281.66 crores to Rs. 99496.77 crores between 2000-01 and 2004-05. The percentage increase during this period is 27.10 per cent. Employment provided through the SSI units increased from 2902122 in the year 2001-01 to 3525582 in the year 2004-05 registering 21.48 per cent increase over a period of 5 years.

STATEMENT OF THE PROBLEM

The quality of life of the people depends on the availability of goods and services alike at affordable prices. The position of a country in the body of nations is determined by its ability to industrialise and progress economically. The interplay of these two sets of compelling factors provides the space for productive entities to exist and operate. Though from a subjective and stand alone position, both demand altogether opposite and varied requirements. In the real world of existence-consumption, these factors throw open a whole range of challenges and opportunities. One such opportunity is the case for sustaining and developing the tiny sector.

While the emergence of the tiny sector as a corollary to mankind's urge to organize and produce is well documented and discussed, the search for finding ways to sustain and promote the same is still on. In this modern era of technology driven, mass producing big business, globalization and quality consciousness dimensions, is there a case for the tiny sector? An answer in the affirmative emerges at least on two major counts: one in the socio-economic context of the thickly populated developing countries like India and the other in the realm of compulsions in the big business itself.

The viability of a nation to hold itself together depends a great deal on its ability to offer gainful employment to its population on continued basis. Apart from other initiatives, nations that have found methods in this direction have flourished with minimum distortions and disturbances. The tiny sector clusters across the length and breadth of India seem to be making appreciable contributions to massive employment generation. A study of the ratio of capital invested to employment generated is bound to throw answers that would put the tiny sector on top of the production entities list.

The other favourable argument for the propagation of the tiny sector in India arises due to the scenario in the industrialization spectacle that is witnessed today. Wooing foreign direct investment into their countries to achieve better economic growth is the order of the day for developing countries. India is no exception. A multi-pronged strategy to accelerate the Foreign Direct Investment flows involves ensuring a well oiled supply chain for the proposed investment projects in the industrial sector. Here an inevitable role is assured for the tiny sector. Medium and large sized industries by nature would not like to play second fiddle to prospective foreign business projects. Rewards in yield would not match the effort in capital and organization. With minimum of adaptation and modification, existing and new units in the tiny sector could cater to the supply chain requirements with ease. The proliferation of tiny units around big industries everywhere proves this argument.

To capitalize on this indispensable nature of tiny industries, innovative entrepreneurial initiatives are necessary. Through that, opportunity utilization could be achieved and sustained. That could contribute substantially to the fulfillment of the nation's industrial and social aspirations. In this context, the role of entrepreneurship assumes greater significance. Opportunity utilization is a creative process involving progressive dimensions wherein human initiatives alone could do wonders. Promotion of entrepreneurship will not only create the ambience for realization of socio-economic objectives and contribute to nation building, but also offer a wider range of solutions to some of the ills of the nation. Thus a study of entrepreneurship in the tiny sector becomes highly relevant in the present day context.

The Government is also in a position where it has to compulsorily promote the tiny sector not only as a means to generate employment but also to bridge the gap in existing industrialization and aspiring industrialization. By vigorously pursuing a policy of concentrated promotion, it can achieve the twin objectives mentioned above. In this direction a new act to provide for facilitating the promotion, development and enhancing the competitiveness of micro, small and medium enterprises and for matters connected therewith or incidental thereto, titled as Micro, Small and Medium Enterprises Development Act, 2006 was enacted by Parliament in the Fifty-seventh Year of the Republic of India. It came into force on 2nd October 2006. A Board known as the National Board for Micro, Small and Medium Enterprises was established to implement the new act. Under the new act, the industries engaged in the manufacture or production of goods, specified in the first schedule to the Industries (Development and Regulation) Act, 1951are treated as micro enterprises, where the investment in plant and machinery does not exceed twenty five lakh rupees.

The results of the present study would serve as a guidepost for the development of the tiny industries in the area where the study has been undertaken. The measures suggested for overcoming the problems faced by the tiny industries in Tamil Nadu state might eventually lead to a better utilization of their existing capacity and be found useful by the planners in preparing effective action plans.

OBJECTIVES

The main objectives of the study are:

1. To study the socio-economic background and to assess the personality traits and entrepreneurial competencies of the respondents.
2. To examine the association between the socio-economic variables and the entrepreneurship index.
3. To identify the factors which influence the tiny entrepreneurs to start or manage the enterprise.
4. To study the level of growth of the tiny sector industries and to examine the extent of variation in their growth level.
5. To examine the relationship between the level of growth and the socio-economic factors of the respondents and to identify the factors which influence the growth of the tiny industries.
6. To analyse the problems faced by tiny entrepreneurs and to examine the relationship between the level of growth and the problems faced by tiny entrepreneurs.
7. To offer suitable suggestions based on the findings to foster entrepreneurship and to facilitate rapid growth in the tiny sector industries.

HYPOTHESES

The following is the list of hypotheses formulated for the study.

- The respondent's age and the level of growth of the industry are two independent attributes.
- The level of growth is independent of the educational status of the respondent.

- There is no relationship between the sex of the respondent and the level of growth.
- The marital status of the respondent and the level of growth are independent attributes.
- There exists no relationship between the technical knowledge of the respondent and the level of growth.
- The family size of the respondent and the level of growth are two independent attributes.
- The nature of the family of the respondent and the level of growth are two independent attributes.
- The occupational background of the respondent and the level of growth are two independent attributes.
- The unutilized capacity of the industry and the level of growth are two independent attributes.
- There is no relationship between marketing problems and the level of growth.
- There is no relationship between financial problems and the level of growth.
- There is no relationship between the problems in the supply of raw materials and the level of growth.
- Labour problems and the level of growth are two independent attributes.
- There is no relationship between the problem of inadequate power supply and the level of growth.
- The level of growth is independent of utilization of technical and managerial guidance by the respondent.

METHODOLOGY

This section describes the methodology adopted in the present study which includes the choice of the study area, the sampling technique adopted, the collection of data, the period of study and the tools of analysis.

Choice of the Study Area

Tamil Nadu is one of the state blessed with good basic infrastructural facilities and resources which could contribute to the development of industries in particular to the development of small and tiny industries. But the pace of development in Tamil Nadu was found to be relatively slow. The majority of the working population in most of the districts of Tamil Nadu depends on agriculture. This was found to be the main reason for the stagnation in the industrial development of Tamil Nadu. The Government of India declared most of the districts as an industrially backward area. Hence, incentives have been provided for starting industries in those districts. One would conclude that the policy initiatives were sufficient enough to accelerate the pace of industrial development in the state. There is a scope for promoting the industries based on tourism, since there are a number of tourist spots in Tamil Nadu. These are the main reasons for selecting Tamil Nadu as the study area to evaluate the performance of tiny industries.

Sampling Technique

In order to study the quality of entrepreneurship in tiny sector industries in Tamil Nadu, 250 tiny industrial units which were registered as on 31.03.2005 were selected by adopting the simple random sampling method. These units were classified into five categories, namely agro and food-based industries, textile-based industries, chemical-based industries, forest-based industries and miscellaneous industries which include all other industrial ventures. The proportionate random sampling technique was adopted to select the 250 sample units from the list of tiny industrial units registered in Tamil Nadu. The number of selected sample units classified into five categories is shown in Table 1.7.

Collection of Data

The present study was based on primary as well as secondary data. The personal interview method was adopted to collect the primary data from the sample units. For this, a well-designed and pre-tested interview schedule was prepared to collect the information required for the study. With a view to identifying the growth components of the tiny industrial units, the researcher made an in-depth review of the previous studies related to the topic of the present study. Further, the researcher had preliminary discussions with the officials of the District Industries Centre and a few well informed entrepreneurs of the tiny sector industrial units registered in the District Industries Centre. In the light of the information gathered, the researcher prepared the interview schedule and also identified the ten factors which influence the growth of the tiny sector industries.

Table 1.7: Sample Tiny Industries Selected for the Study

Sl. No.	*Category*	*Sample Units*
1.	Agro-based and food products	25
2.	Textiles and garments	154
3.	Forest-based	26
4.	Chemical based	18
5.	Miscellaneous	27
	Total	**250**

The secondary data were collected from the published as well as the unpublished reports, handbooks, action plans and pamphlets of the office of the Directorate of Industries and Commerce, Chennai.

Period of Study

The study was conducted in the year 2005-06. The primary data were collected from the tiny sector industries during the period from October 2005 to March 2006. The data related to the growth components of tiny industries were obtained for a period of five years from 2000-01 to 2004-05.

Tools of Analysis

The personality traits of the tiny entrepreneurs were assessed using scaling techniques and the personality index created for this purpose. The personality index of the respondents was prepared by the following formula.

$$\text{Personality Index (PI)} = \frac{\sum_{i=1}^{n} PSi}{\sum_{i=1}^{n} MSPi} \times 100$$

where,

PI = Personality Index

PS = Personality factors score

MSP = Maximum score of the personality factor

i ... n = Number of personality factors

In order to examine the entrepreneurship among the respondents, the entrepreneurship components are rated at a four point scale and the scale values of each entrepreneurship variable are used to form the entrepreneurship index.

The formula used for the calculation of the entrepreneurship index is given below.

$$\text{En Index} = \frac{\sum_{i=1}^{n} ESi}{\sum_{i=1}^{n} EMSi} \times 100$$

where, En Index = Entrepreneurship Index

ES = Entrepreneurship variables score

EMS = Entrepreneurship variables maximum score

i...n = Number of entrepreneurship variables.

The chi-square test is an important non-parametric test and as such no rigid assumptions are necessary in respect of the type of population. The chi-square in the present study is used as a test of independence.

$$\chi^2 = \Sigma \frac{(O-E)^2}{E}$$

where,

χ^2 = Chi-square value

O = Observed frequency

E = Expected frequency

The chi-square value is compared with the table value to find out the association between the nominal variables in the present study.

Pearson's product moment correlation co-efficient was used to find the degree of relationship between the personality traits of the respondents and the entrepreneurship index using the following formula:

$$r_{xy} = \frac{\Sigma XY}{\sqrt{\Sigma x^2 \times \Sigma y^2}}$$

where,

x = $X - \overline{X}$

y = $Y - \overline{Y}$

X = Mean of X variable

Y = Mean of Y variable

Calculated 'r' values were tested for 5 per cent level of significance. The correlation co-efficient between the variables was calculated according to the need of the study.

The Orthogonal Varimax Rotation technique was adopted to identify the significant set of factors which influence the tiny entrepreneurs in starting and managing the enterprises.

In order to study the growth of the tiny sector industries, a growth scale was prepared by adopting the scoring technique for ten identified growth factors. The total scores for the construction of the growth scale was taken as 100. The ten components were allotted 10 scores each. Ten scores were distributed among the 10 components on the basis of the percentage growth of each of the components. The growth percentage was calculated on the basis of the data collected for the period 2000-2001 to 2004-05 by using the following formula.

$$\text{Growth} = \frac{\text{Current year - Base year value}}{\text{Base year value}} \times 100$$

In order to classify the levels of growth into high, medium and low, the arithmetic mean ($\overline{X}$) of the total score and the standard deviation (S.D) obtained were used as follows:

$\overline{X}$ + SD ≥ were classified as high level growth units.

$\overline{X}$ – SD ≤ were classified as low level growth units; and

Units which were between $\overline{X}$ + SD and $\overline{X}$ – SD were classified as medium level growth units. The co-efficient of variation was used to study the extent of the variations in growth.

Multiple log linear regression was estimated to identify the factors influencing the growth of entrepreneurship in the tiny sector industries. A multiple regression of the following model was estimated:

$$\text{Log } Y = \beta_0 + \beta_1 \log X_1 + \beta_2 \log X_2 + \ldots\ldots\ldots\ \beta_7 \log X_7 + U$$

where,

Y = Total growth scale value for ten components (in numbers)

X_1 = Age of the units in years

X_2 = Capacity utilization in percentage

X_3 = Fixed investment (Rs. in lakhs)

X_4 = Working capital (Rs. in lakhs)

X_5 = Borrowed capital (Rs. in lakhs)
X_6 = Value of production (Rs. in lakhs)
X_7 = Sales turnover (Rs. in lakhs)
U = Disturbance term.
$\beta_1, \beta_1, ...\beta_7$ are the parameters to be estimated.

LIMITATIONS OF THE STUDY

The present study was based mainly on annual reports and balance sheets of the selected tiny industrial units. Hence, the extent of the reliability of the financial data provided by the tiny sector industrial units through their balance sheets may be a serious limitation of the present study. Further, the present study was confined to the period 2000-01 to 2004-05. In view of this, the study might disclose a limited picture of the group of units instead of providing an insight into the problems of individual units.

CHAPTERISATION

The report of the present study, "Entrepreneurship in Tiny Sector Industries- an Indian Scenario" is presented in six chapters.

The first chapter introduces the subject and deals with small and tiny sector industries in India and their achievement during the Five Year Plan periods. This chapter includes details related to small-scale industries particularly the tiny sector industries in Tamil Nadu State. Besides, the statements of the problem, objectives, methodology, limitations and chapterization have also been presented.

The second chapter deals with the theoretical concepts and review of earlier literature related to entrepreneurship and small and tiny sector industries. Further, it discusses the concepts used in the present study.

The third chapter deals with the socio-economic profile of the selected respondents, personality traits of the tiny entrepreneurs, the association between the socio-economic profile variables and entrepreneurship index, the correlation between personality traits and entrepreneurship and the factors influencing the entrepreneurs in starting or managing the enterprises.

The fourth chapter analyses the growth of tiny sector industries and an attempt has been made to identify the factors which are responsible for the growth of tiny enterprises. Further, it examines the relationship between the level of growth and the socio-economic background of the respondents.

The fifth chapter discusses the problems faced by the tiny sector industries and examines the relationship between the level of growth and the problems encountered by the tiny entrepreneurs.

The sixth chapter presents the summary of the findings along with the conclusions and suggestions based on the study.

REFERENCES

1. http://www.tn.gov.in/policynotes/sind2004-05
2. Development commissioner (SSI), Ministry of SSI Government of India.

2

Theoretical Concepts and Review of Literature

INTRODUCTION

This chapter presents the review of literature of the past research studies on the subject and the concepts used in the present study. Though a large volume of literature is available on the subject of small-scale industries, only a few important studies have been reviewed here. Such a review would facilitate the researcher to have a comprehensive knowledge of the concepts used in the earlier studies and would enable the researcher to adopt, modify and formulate an improved conceptual framework for the use of the present study with a view to drawing meaningful and useful conclusions. For a better exposition, the chapter has been presented under three broad heads namely:

(i) Theoretical concepts relating to entrepreneurship Review of Literature; and

(ii) The Concepts used.

Most of the definitions on entrepreneur throw light on the role played by him. They also state the various functions which a person as an entrepreneur will have to perform. An entrepreneur is a person who initiates and establishes an enterprise. Entrepreneurs refer to the decisions one takes in setting up and running a new enterprise. The individual constitutes the most important element in entrepreneurship. It is an individual who takes a decision to start of not to start an enterprise. It is 'HE' or 'SHE' who strives, to make it a success. Entrepreneurship involves a few major decisions. They are:

- Decision to become an entrepreneur
- Identification and selection of an opportuniy
- Business plan formulation and its implementation
- Entrepreneurial continnum.

1. **Becoming an Entrepreneur:** Decision to be one's own master is the first major step. The motivational factor, hence, should be, considered crucial to entrepreneurship. The inner urge of the individual to do something new, to be on one's own has been found to be and is an important factor. This may be reinforced by one or more of the following:
   (a) to prove oneself
   (b) to be independent
   (c) to do something unique
   (d) to utilize skills
   (e) to acquire greater economic reward
   (f) to excel.
2. **Finding an Opportunity:** For effective coping with inner desire, to be an entrepreneur the individual starts searching for an 'opportunity', the focus of his entrepreneurial desires. He looks around for different possibilities of business, reads about them, meets people who could give ideas and inspires and collects information and data on various/several possibilities.
3. **Business Plan Formulation and Implementation:** This function refers to making of a project report and subsequent implementation of it. The efforts of the entrepreneur are

directed towards visualizing the establishment of the enterprise. He studies the feasibility and profitability of the project. He has to take crucial decisions, which have a far reaching effect, at this juncture.

ENTREPRENEURIAL CONTINUUM

Once the entrepreneur establishes the enterprise, he has to manage it well by translating problems into opportunities and must endure to mobilize relevant production factors such as capital and human resources. Entrepreneurial Continuum can be achieved through a series of decisions, actions and functions directed towards the following factors:

- Response to change and in addition or deletion of activities and modification in working and in strategy
- Fund generation and allocation towards growth and expansion
- Perception of expanding or contracting opportunities
- Research and development
- Product diversification or expansion
- New product development

ENTREPRENEURIAL ROLES

Entrepreneurship is different from management, as Paul H. Wilken states:

Management refers to the ongoing co-ordination of the production process, which can be visualised as a continual combining of the factors of production. But entrepreneurship is a discontinuous phenomenon, appearing to initiate changes in the production process and then disappearing until it reappears to initiate another change.

Entrepreneurs often play roles especially those of capitalists and managers, while people who primarily act as capitalists or managers may at times become entrepreneurs. Many people who want above all to be entrepreneurs, find that they must eventually leave the new ventures, they create because they do not have the proper state of mind to run an established business. Entrepreneurship is above all about change. In the chart given below Wilken's categorisation of types of changes' initiated by entrepreneurs is given.

Types of Changes

1. Initial Expansion-original production of goods.
2. Subsequent Expansion - subsequent change in the amount of goods produced.
3. Factor Innovation -increase of supply or productivity of factors:
   - *(a)* Financial - procurement of capital from new source or in new form.
   - *(b)* Labour - procurement of labour from new source or of new type; or upgrading of existing labour.
   - *(c)* Material - procurement of old material from news source or use of new material.
4. Product innovations - changes in the production process:
   - *(a)* Technological - use of new production techniques.
   - *(b)* Organisational- change of form of structure of relationships.
5. Market Innovations - changes in the size or composition of market:
   - *(a)* Product - production of new goods or change inequality or cost of existing goods.
   - *(b)* Market - discovery of a new market.

Entrepreneurs see change as the norm and as healthy. Usually, they do not bring about the changes themselves *(i.e.,* they are usually not inventors) and this defines, entrepreneur and entrepreneurship, the entrepreneur always searches for change, responds to it and exploits It is an opportunity.' These words were written by Peter Drucker, a well known contemporary management writer. But they might just as easily have come from the pen of Joseph Schumpeter, the **Austrian** economist who assigned the term "Entrepreneurship". For Schumpeter, indeed, the whole process of economic change hung ultimately on the person who makes it happen, the entrepreneur.

A successful entrepreneur recognises the commercial potential of a product or service and designs operating policies in marketing, production, product development and the organisational structure. He carries out the whole set of activities of the business. He has a high capacity of taking calculated risk and has faith in his own capabilities.

FUNCTIONS OF AN ENTREPRENEUR (ROLES)

According to some writers the functions of an entrepreneur are co-ordination of the business management of the enterprise, risk taking, controlling the enterprise, innovation for change, motivation and other related activities.

In reality, an entrepreneur has to carry out a combination of these, keeping in tune with time and environment. Truly entrepreneurship calls for the ability to react to new ideas, demands and exploit the opportunities and thereby contribute to progress. An entrepreneur is expected to perform the following functions/role:

1. Assumption of risk
2. Business decisions
3. Managerial function
4. Function of innovation.

1. **Assumption of Risk:** The entrepreneur assumes all possible risk of business. A business risk also involves risk due to the possibility of changes in the taste of consumers, techniques of production and new inventions. Such risks are not insurable. If, they materialize, the entrepreneur has to bear the loss himself. Thus, risk bearing or uncertainty still remains the most important function of an entrepreneur. An entrepreneur tries to reduce the uncertainties by his initiative, skill and good judgment.

2. **Business Decisions:** The entrepreneur has to decide the nature and type of goods to be produced. An entry into a particular industry is due to his judgment as it offers him the best prospect and whatever commodities produced would pay him well and would employ those methods of production which seem to him the most profitable. He effects suitable changes in the size of business, its location, techniques of production and does everything that is needed for the development of business.
3. **Managerial Functions:** The entrepreneur also has to perform the managerial functions, though the managerial functions are different from entrepreneurial functions. Formulation of production plan, arranging finance, purchasing raw materials," providing production facilities, organising sales, and assuming the task of personnel management are all managerial functions performed by the entrepreneur in case of small enterprises. Otherwise in a large establishment, these management functions would be delegated to pay managerial personnel.
4. **Function of Innovation:** An important function of an entrepreneur is 'INNOVATION'. An entrepreneur conceives the idea for the improvement in the quality of production line or considers the economic viability or technological feasibility in bringing about improved quality. The introduction of different kinds of electronic gadgets is an example of such an innovation of new products. Innovation is an ongoing function, rather than once and for all or possibly intermittent activity. Thus, the functions of entrepreneur can be performed by different kinds of people under different economic systems.

Arther H. Cole described an entrepreneur as a decision maker and attributed the following functions:

1. Determination of the objectives of the enterprise and the change in those objectives as conditions require.
2. Development of an organisation, including efficient relation with subordinates and employees.

3. Securing adequate financial resources and maintaining good relations with the existing and potential promoters.
4. Requisition of efficient technological equipment and the revision of it.
5. Development of a market for the products and the devising of new products to meet or anticipate consumer's demand.
6. Maintenance of good relations with public authorities and with the society at large.

Modern writers have outlined the following three broad functions of an entrepreneur, namely:

1. Innovation - "Doing new things or doing of things that are already being done in a new way."

   Example: E-mail vs. Postal Correspondence.
2. Risk taking.
3. Organisation and management of business.

ENTREPRENEURSHIP

Entrepreneurship refers to a process of action an entrepreneur (person) undertakes establish his/her enterprise. It is a creative and innovative response to the environment. Entrepreneurship is a cycle of actions to further the interest of the entrepreneur. Entrepreneurship is the composite skill, the resultant mix of many qualities and traits. It involves taking of risk, making I the necessary investments and the ability to put other factors of production (land, labour, capital) into productive use through scientific and technological methods for creating wealth for an individual and economy. Entrepreneurship perhaps lies more in the ability to maximize resources.

Entrepreneurship is "the propensity of mind to take calculated risk with confidence to achieve a pre-determined business/industrial objective." Entrepreneurship, equals ability to take risk and take correct decisions. Hence,

Entrepreneurship = R+D+O+E where,

'R' stands for Risk taking

'D' stands for Decision making

'0' stands for Opportunities

'E' stands for Environment

CHARACTERISTICS OF ENTREPRENEURSHIP

Entrepreneurship means the function of creating something new, organising and coordinating and undertaking risk and handling economic uncertainty.

DEFINITIONS

Higgins: By "Entrepreneurship is meant the function of seeing investment and production opportunity, organising an enterprise to undertake a new production process, raising capital, hiring labour, arranging for the supply of raw materials and selecting top managers for the day-to-day operation of the enterprise."

A.H. Cole: "Entrepreneurship is the purposeful activity of an individual or a group of associated individuals, undertaken to initiate, maintain or organise, a profit oriented business unit for the production or distribution of economic goods and services."

McClelland: "Entrepreneurship involves doing things in a new and better way. It calls for decision-making under uncertainty. If there is no significant uncertainty and the action involves applying known and predictable results, then entrepreneurship in not at all involved."

Peter Drucker: "Entrepreneurship is neither science nor art, it is a practice. It has a knowledge base. Knowledge in entrepreneurship is a means to an end. Indeed, what constitutes knowledge in practice is largely defined by the ends that are by the practice."

From the above definitions, following are the characteristics of entrepreneurship emerging.

- Innovation.
- Risk taking.
- Decision making.

- Accepting challenges.
- Organisation and management.
- Ensuring the success of enterprise.

Reasons for increase in entrepreneurship are:

1. An increasing focus on capital formation. Availability of capital is one of the reasons why individuals get ideas to start new firms/enterprises.
2. Ability to transform scientific and technical developments.
3. Supportive government programmes.
4. Availability of required training and inputs.
5. Collaborative relationship between business and research and their direct attempts to transfer technology to market.

   Example: Tata Institute of Fundamental Research
6. Environment conducive to innovation and entrepreneurial activities.

CAUSES OF SLOW GROWTH OF ENTREPRENEURSHIP IN INDIA

In spite of all the policies, government support, change in the attitude of the society, the growth of entrepreneurship in India is slow. The three main factors to cause slow growth o l entrepreneurship are:

1. Discouraging social factors, namely unfavourable family background, family burden, lack of education, dual role of women, influence of sex, caste, custom, lack of attitudes, spirits, urge, etc.
2. Discouraging economic factors, which consist of inadequate infrastructural facilities, shortage of capital, shortage of technical labour, lack of transportation and communication facilities, absence of regular and cheaper supply of power and raw materials, etc.
3. Discouraging environmental factors, which include unstable government, lack of security, absence of ideal market conditions, redtapism in administration, complicated statutes etc.

Entrepreneurship is thus an attitude of mind which can take risk but calculated ones; a true entrepreneur is one who can see possibilities in a given situation, where others see none and has the patience, perseverance and optimism to work out the idea into a scheme for which financial support can be provided. The stimulation of entrepreneurship is a function of both internal and external variables.

India has a proud record of entrepreneurship. Its present status among the ten industrialized countries in the world is its proof. However, it has to prepare itself for entrepreneurship of a different order. Tremendous advancement of Science and technology will have to be harnessed since industrial growth in the country can only be achieved through a mix of science, technology, large and small industry. In fact, the SSI sector is considered as an ideal nursery for testing out new technologies and for enhancing the industrial growth and development of entrepreneurship. Entrepreneurship is thus the cornerstone of emerging economic scene in the world.

David McClelland was not far from truth when he stated, "What accounts for the rise in civilization is not the external resources such as markets, minerals or factories but the entrepreneurial spirit which exploits the resources - a spirit found most often among businessmen."

ENTREPRENEURSHIP STIMULANTS

A variety of factors have, helped to stimulate entrepreneurial activity and generate economic development. These stimulants are the following:

1. Increasing focus on capital formation, making capital available to the entrepreneur to start a new enterprise.
2. The environment to transform scientific and technical developments into economically viable projects.
3. Supportive government programmes.
4. Availability of sufficient training facilities.
5. A collaborative relationship between business and research and the easy transferability of technology to the market place.

6. Finally the endeavour to create the ideal climate for innovation and the entrepreneurial activities.

ENTREPRENEURSHIP AND ECONOMIC DEVELOPMENT

Only purposeful human activity can bring about economic development. Man stands at the centre of the whole process of economic development. Schumpeter feels that economic development will be a reality if new combinations of the means of production are undertaken. This is the work of the entrepreneur, he locates ideas and puts them into effect in the process of economic development. Thus, the entrepreneur occupies a crucial place in the process of economic development. Schumpeter further states that economic progress depends on the rate of applied technical progress or innovation: The rate of applied technical progress in turn depends on the supply of entrepreneurs in the society. Therefore, entrepreneurial activity or entrepreneurship is the agency which brings about change in the society.

David McClelland has introduced a new dimension to the importance of entrepreneurship in economic development. He says that the development of entrepreneurship depends on human motivation to achieve or need for achievement. McClelland's hypothesis is that a society with a generally high level of achievement will produce more energetic entrepreneurs who in turn would accelerate the process of economic development. That is why there is a steady stream of entrepreneurs in developed countries where the motivation to achieve is very high. Similarly, in the underdeveloped regions this motivation is either lacking or low, causing short supply of entrepreneurs.

Here it will be worth looking into this aspect in the context of India. The typical Indian entrepreneur is not an "innovator" but an "imitator". He copies the organisation, technology and the products of innovation from other developed regions. But as an imitator the Indian entrepreneur is able to adapt the innovative technology in the conditions prevailing in the country. This type of imitative entrepreneurship is playing a crucial role in India's progress specially in the industrial and service sectors.

This analysis goes to establish that entrepreneurial activity or entrepreneurship is an important source of economic development. It is a must that motivational training programmes are conducted to stimulate entrepreneurship in developing countries. Innovative entrepreneurship can alter the production function of nations and bring about rapid development. Entrepreneurship appears to be the best medicine for underdeveloped countries to overcome their ills and bring about substantial economic development.

ENTREPRENEURSHIP AND ECONOMIC SYSTEMS

Entrepreneurship can be analysed with reference to different types of economic systems. In fact, entrepreneurship and the economic system complement each other. An economic system determines the nature and scope of entrepreneurship. Entrepreneurship gives a fillip to new organisational forms and the economy has to adjust to these demands. Entrepreneurship can bring about changes in the very structure of the economy thus strengthening the economic system.

ENTREPRENEURSHIP IN DIFFERENT ECONOMIC SYSTEMS

Capitalism: Capitalism has freedom as its hallmark. A capitalist economy is characterised! by free enterprise, freedom to save, invest competition, consumer sovereignty and minimum interference from the government. The price mechanism solves the problem of "What to produce"?! The forces of demand and supply determine the price with reference to the cost of production. The entrepreneur controls the process of production and distribution and entrepreneurship has a place' I of prominence. Entrepreneurship in the domestic market is characterized by the entrepreneur I assuming the role of a competitor or a monopolist or a monopolistic competitor. In the overseas] market, he is a cut-throat competitor where the price of his product is determined by his capacity to[unload goods, a special case of discriminating monopoly.

Socialism: Private, entrepreneurship is absent in a socialist economic system. Entrepreneurship is provided by a central authority consisting of economic and financial experts who perform the role of the entrepreneur not for profit but for social good. This central authority is appointed by the government to frame plans for the proper mobilization of resources and the allocation of resources into these industries of national importance. Thus, entrepreneurship plays a crucial role under socialism also, the only distinction is that the private entrepreneur has neither a role nor responsibility in this economic system.

Mixed Economy: Entrepreneurship has a vital role in the mixed economy. The mixed economy is characterized by the co-existence of both the private and public sectors in the same line of production. However, we find that in this economic system the government undertakes the production of capital goods while the production of consumer goods is left in the hands of private enterprises. Like in a capitalist economy basic problems are solved with the help of price mechanism. When the price mechanism is not able to solve basic problems the State intervenes in order to find a better solution to the various problems. Similarly, when the problem of production is not solved satisfactorily through private entrepreneurship, the State tries to increase the production of essential goods and discourage the production of non-essential goods.

In a mixed economy restrictions are placed by the government to remove the evil of monopolistic capitalism. The mixed economy gives equal importance to both the public and private sectors and entrepreneurship is given due significance. In the private sector, profit motive acts as an incentive to the entrepreneur and the market mechanism plays its own role and this enhances the role of entrepreneurship in the mixed economy.

Thus, entrepreneurship has a great importance in all major economic systems. It has a special role under capitalism and mixed economy, where its responsibilities in production and distribution are recognised. Therefore, its importance stands beyond challenge in every economic system where it appears in different forms. Yet entrepreneurship continues to exist in one form or the other in all economic systems.

OBSTACLES INHIBITING ENTREPRENEURSHIP

Entrepreneurship development is greatly hindered in the less developed countries due to the presence of several obstacles. Though these obstacles are present in almost all countries they hardly have any strength in the developed countries. In the developed countries the environment is most ideal for entrepreneurship. Similarly, the presence of aggressive entrepreneurs has made the society in these countries realise their vital importance in economic advancement. Unfortunately, in most less developed nations, the role of entrepreneurship in the progress of the country has not been fully realised. The result is the presence of a number of obstacles which inhibit the development of entrepreneurship. These obstacles can be summarised as follows:

1. An unwillingness to devote organisational abilities to business purposes.
2. Restrictive effects of customs and traditions.
3. Lack of adequate response to monetary incentives.
4. Low status of businessmen in the eyes of the public.
5. High risk involved in new enterprises.
6. Lack of sufficient infrastructure and high cost of production.
7. Market imperfections which deny potential entrepreneurs the resources they need for organising new enterprises.
8. Arbitrary changes in the administration of law by the Government which spread the element of uncertainty among entrepreneurs.

India provides us with a good example, where the environment has been highly hostile to promote entrepreneurship. The stimulation of entrepreneurial abilities is a complicated long run sociological problem. Social institutions like caste, joint family system, schools can actually motivate entrepreneurship. But in India they are not conducive to the development of entrepreneurship. The policy of the government had been more to promote "imitative" entrepreneurs rather than the "innovative" ones. The result is the country is facing the problem of "brain-drain". All enterprising individuals finding the going tough in this country started migrating, no wonder this country has such a large number of Non-Resident Indians having immense financial power.

The recent trend towards liberalisation is aimed at removing the economic obstacles that are standing in the way of aggressive entrepreneurship. Non-Resident Indians are being accorded special status for investing their large financial resources in this country. The drastic changes in government's economic policy clearly shows the realisation in this country that the future of this nation is in the hands of vigorous entrepreneurship and all efforts must be made to remove the obstacles which are hindering the full play of this vital factor of production.

FACTORS AFFECTING ENTREPRENEURSHIP GROWTH

The countries of the world are experiencing an unprecedented burst of inventions. Even the least developed of nations is making conscious efforts in encouraging research and development. While the developed countries have the record of commercialising these inventions to their fullest advantage, the less developed ones find their inventions either lying idle or flowing out to the more prosperous nations. The proverbial "brain-drain" that is affecting countries like India, is due to the absence of the necessary infrastructure to capitalise on the numerous inventions that are taking place. This essential is provided by the entrepreneur of the country. The secret of the success of most developed countries is the presence of a large number of dynamic entrepreneurs who provide the fillip for newer and better inventions. The less developed countries, on the other hand are confronted by a situation where the entrepreneurs just do not seem to come; those present tend to leave their countries in search of better opportunities. The economically backward nations are characterised by the scarcity of entrepreneurship. Several inimical factors are affecting the growth of this important factor of production.

Some societies, notably in the United States, South Korea and many South East Asian countries like Thailand and Singapore abound with entrepreneurs. Others like China and India have fewer entrepreneurs although these countries recently changed their laws to encourage entrepreneurship. Countries like England where many companies such as airlines and automobile manufactures have been operated by the government, have in recent times turned these firms on to the private sector encouraging entrepreneurship through new opportunities in private ownership. Other nations such as Japan, though are bound by strong traditions have in recent times started favouring entrepreneurship. Both economic and non-economic factors can affect the level of entrepreneurship within any society.

A careful analysis of the factors that affect entrepreneurial growth will reveal that these factors can be classified under four major heads. They are economic factors, social factors, and cultural factor and personality factors. Economists agree that the lack of entrepreneurs is caused not by economic conditions alone, as was the earlier feeling, it is also due to the whole set of socio-cultural and institutional environments prevailing in the less developed countries.

The factors affecting growth of entrepreneurship are:

1. Economic factors
2. Social factors
3. Cultural factors
4. Personality factors
5. Psychological and Sociological factors.

Economic Factors

- The economic factors that are affecting the growth of entrepreneurship in the less developed countries are:
- Lack of adequate overhead facilities
- Non-availability of capital
- Great risks
- Non-availability of sufficient labour and skills.

(a) **Lack of adequate overhead facilities:** Profitable innovations require certain basic facilities and services like transportation, communication, technical and economic information, supply of power, irrigation facilities, etc. They provide external economies and improve the efficiency of investments by entrepreneurs. They reduce the cost of production and increase output. These facilities are scarce in the less developed countries. Entrepreneurs have therefore to obtain them at their own expenses. They have either to provide these facilities themselves or obtain them at exorbitant costs. This greatly affects their profit margin and discourages the entrepreneur. One cannot expect an entrepreneur to construct his own railway network or set up his own power project and then indulge in innovational activity.

(b) **Non-availability of capital:** Reduction of cost and maximising of output are the twin objectives of all inventions. Therefore, inventions have a tendency to be capital oriented. The requirements of capital for innovation are specially large in less developed countries where most capital equipment have to be imported. Imports involve large shipping and insurance expenses. Even the basic expertise has to be imported. Such imports also involve the use of considerable amount of foreign exchange, which would raise difficult problems especially if there are foreign exchange controls. The inadequacy of basic facilities makes initial expenses of investment extremely high. Very often the entrepreneur may have to obtain them at very high costs or provide for his own overhead facilities.

Another problem associated with this aspect is the necessity for the entrepreneur to store large stocks of inventories because a network to provide adequate industrial supplies is lacking in a less developed country. This raises the amount of working capital needed for the entrepreneur. These capital requirements cannot be easily met. Due to the low rate of domestic savings and the deficiencies in the channelisation of savings, capital does not flow into productive enterprises. Moreover, an entrepreneur is confronted by banking systems who charge very high interest rates for borrowed capital. Thus, the non-availability of capital hampers entrepreneurial growth in the poor nations.

(c) **Great risks:** Risks in business are greater in a less developed country than in a developed nation. Three reasons are given for this situation.

1. There is the lack of reliable information on cost size of the market conditions of demand, overhead facilities etc. An entrepreneur cannot make correct estimates under these circumstances.

2. The market for goods and services is small. Ragnar Nurkse has pointed out that the lack of a strong domestic market inhibits new investments.

3. Less developed countries are characterised by instability in both domestic and foreign economic policy. This discourages entrepreneurs. Several less developed nations are highly export oriented nations depending on a few primary products. These products are subject to violent swings of prosperity and depression that originate abroad.

The entrepreneurs are thus faced with situations where the capacity of their plant and the size of their investments are placed at the mercy of unforeseeable events. Moreover, the entrepreneurs face instability caused by seasonal fluctuations. In these circumstances of uncertainty and risks, entrepreneurs have a tendency to prefer short-term investments to long-term industrial ventures.

(d) **Non-availability of labour and skills:** less developed countries are labour rich nations owing to a dense and ever increasing population. But entrepreneurship in economic and emotional security inhibits labour's mobility. Entrepreneurs, therefore often find difficulty to secure sufficient labour. They are forced to make elaborate and costly arrangements to recruit the necessary labour.

Apart from the non-availability of labour, there is also general scarcity of skills at all levels. This acts a strong deterrent, to entrepreneurship. Labour is not trained and lacks industrial skills. The traditional skills of the workmen are highly insufficient for modern industrial jobs. The lack of labour skills is the characteristic feature of the less developed nations, which are having primarily an agrarian character. There is also extreme scarcity of specialised skills. An entrepreneur finds difficulty to get in sufficient numbers skilled foremen, supervisory personnel, technicians, accountants and industrial managers.

Social Factors

Social factors can go a long way in encouraging entrepreneurship. In fact, it was a highly helpful society that made the industrial revolution a glorious success in Europe. It will not be wrong if one says that favourable social factors that prevailed in Europe during the 17th and 18th centuries following the "Renaissance" led to the very emergence of the "entrepreneur" as a factor of production.

A society that is rational in decision-making would be favourable to entrepreneurial growth. We call a society rational when decisions regarding resource uses are based on empirical facts and critical scientific standards. It would be non-rational if decisions regarding the use of capital, hiring of labour, designing of the products etc., are based on custom, tradition, and transcendental powers. While rational behaviour is the order of the day in the developed nations, most of the less developed nations are characterised by a non-rational society which is unsuitable to entrepreneurship.

When important production decisions are taken not on the basis of a critical assessment of facts and on the basis of custom and belief entrepreneurs are, discouraged. Society is also functionally, diffused. This means that the rights and duties of relationship of an individual are ill-defined and unlimited. This also discourages individual initiative. For example, in a society where the joint family system is in vogue, those members of the joint family who gain wealth by their hard work are denied the opportunity to enjoy the fruits of their labour because they have to share their wealth with the other members of the family. In these circumstances, very few people would dare to be venturesome.

Several less developed countries are also characterised by the presence of a social set-up, which is generally hostile to entrepreneurship. Education, research and training are given very little importance. Appointments to responsible positions are guided by narrow parochial and caste considerations "who a person is" is given more importance than "what a person can do." Therefore, there is very little vertical mobility of labour. The process of division of labour comes to be decided upon by the hereditary principle rather than by aptitudes, skills and attainments of individuals.

Cultural Factors

Motives impel men to action. Entrepreneurial growth requires proper motives like profit making, acquisition of prestige and attainment of social status. Ambitious and talented men would take risks and innovate if these motives are strong. The strength of these motives depends upon the culture of the society. If the culture is economical or monetarily oriented, entrepreneurship would be applauded and praised. Wealth accumulation as a way of life would be appreciated. In the less developed countries people are not economically motivated, monetary incentives have relatively less attraction. People have ample opportunities of attaining social distinction by non-economic pursuits; men with organisational abilities are therefore not dragged into business. They use their talents for non-economic ends. The absence of proper economic motives is a general characteristic of agrarian societies in which people do not attach great value to business talents, industrial leadership etc.

Personality Factors

According to Schumpeter, the social atmosphere in advanced capitalist societies is becoming inimical to entrepreneurship. In the less developed countries the entrepreneur is looked upon with suspicion. The result is the personality of the entrepreneur has got greatly affected. Public opinion in the less developed nations sees the entrepreneur only as profit maker and an exploiter. Further, many of the less developed nations had the mortification of being exploited by foreigners for centuries.

The people and their leaders therefore tend to see in the entrepreneur a suspect personality. As one writer puts it, "the figure of the entrepreneur has become odious."

If public opinion has become hostile to private entrepreneurship it has tended to favour direct state activity in the economy. It is argued that as the private entrepreneur has failed to promote economic development, the state must take steps in this direction. This has led to the emergence of planning, as means of achieving economic progress - in which the state shall play a pivotal role. It is difficult for an entrepreneur to work in a planned economy. Planning imposes controls and this goes against the very personality of the entrepreneur. In a planned economy, the entrepreneur should not only have initiative but also have the ability and willingness to adjust his attitudes and activities within the socio-economic framework set by the state. These qualities are contradictory and an entrepreneur cannot easily combine them.

Psychological and Sociological Factors

Psychological and sociological factors are not always easy to distinguish. So in this analysis they are considered together.

The Theory of Need Achievement: This theory was put forward in the early 1960s by David McClelland and is regarded as the most important psychological theories of entrepreneurship. According to McClelland "need achievement" is a social motive to excel that tends to characterise successful entrepreneurs especially when reinforced by cultural factors. He found that certain kinds of people especially those who became entrepreneurs had this characteristics. Moreover, some societies tend to produce a larger percentage of people With high 'need achievement" than other societies McClelland attributed this to sociological factors. Differences among societies and individuals accounted for "need achievement" being greater in some societies and less in certain others. Analysing this phenomenon Paul Wilken has said "entrepreneurship becomes the link between need achievement and economic growth," the latter being a specifically social factor.

The theory states that people with high need achievement are distinctive in several ways. They like to take risks and these risks stimulate them to greater effort. The theory identifies the factors that produce such people. Initially, McClelland attributed the role of parents specially the mother in mustering her son or daughter to be masterful and self-reliant. Later, he put less emphasis on the parent-child relationship and gave more importance to social and cultural factors. He concluded that the need achievement is conditioned more by social and cultural reinforcement, rather than by parental influence and such related factors.

Psychosocial Theories: There are several other researchers who have tried to understand the psychological and sociological roots of entrepreneurship. One such individual is Everett Hazen, who stresses the psychological consequences of social change. Hazen says at some point many social groups experience a radical loss of status. He gives the example of Catholic France where Protestants were tolerated in the 17th century, but were subjected to legal and social persecution. There are many ways of responding to such a loss of status. Hazen categories them into retreatism, situationlism, innovation, reformisms and rebellion.

Retreatism is most important in promoting entrepreneurship. At first, there is confusion in the ranks of those persons who have lost their status. But soon the women of such groups starts holding high expectations about their sons. These sons would grow up with high need achievement. Since the law on social attitudes prevents them from seeking the usual forms of achievement like political office or owning land, they seek other outlets for their abilities. Business happens to be the only outlet available and consequently a group of highly motivated and achievement oriented individuals are created.

Other psychological theories of entrepreneurship stress, the motives on goals of the entrepreneur. Cole is of the opinion that besides wealth, entrepreneurs seek power, prestige, security and service to society. Stepanek points particularly to non-monetary aspects such as independence, personal self-esteem/power and regard of the society.

On the same subject Evens distinguishes by motive, three kinds of entrepreneurs, *viz.*

(a) managing entrepreneurs whose chief motive is security.

(b) innovating entrepreneurs who are interested only in excitement.

(c) controlling entrepreneurs who above all other motives want power and authority.

Finally, Rostow has examined inter-generational changes in the families of entrepreneurs. He believes that the first generation, seeks wealth, the second prestige and the third art and beauty.

Thomas Begley and David P. Boyd studied in detail the psychological roots of entrepreneurship in the mid-1980s. They came to the conclusion that entrepreneurial attitudes based on psychological considerations have five dimensions.

1. First came "need achievement" as described by McClelland. In all studies of successful entrepreneurs a high achievement orientation is invariably present.

2. The second dimension is what Begley and Boyd call "Locus of Control". This means that the entrepreneur follows the idea that he can control his own life and is not influenced by factors like luck, fate and so on. Need achievement logically implies that people can control their own lives and are not influenced by external forces.

3. The third dimension is the willingness to take risk. These two researchers have come to the conclusion that entrepreneurs who take moderate risk earn higher returns on their assets, than those who take no risk at all or who take extravagant risk.

4. Tolerance is the next dimension of this study. Very few decisions are made with complete information. So all business executives must have a certain amount of tolerance for ambiguity.

5. Finally, here is what psychologists call "Type A" behaviour. This is nothing but "a chronic incessant struggle to achieve more and more in less and less." Entrepreneurs are characterised by the presence of "Type A" behaviour in all their endeavours.

ENTREPRENEURSHIP DEVELOPMENT

The importance of entrepreneurial resource as a critical input in economic development has been well recognised, but a consensus about the definition of an entrepreneur is yet to emerge. However, personality characteristics of entrepreneur and entrepreneurial competencies are briefly indicated below:

Personality Characteristics of Entrepreneurs

Need for achievement

Average intelligence

Sense of efficacy

Moderate risk-taker

Open to feedback and learns from experience

Drive and energy

Need for independence

Hope of success

Procreative

Action oriented

Need for influencing others

Problem solving rather than problem avoiding attitude

Initiative taking rather than confronting attitude

Concern for society

Money, an important measure

Creative and innovative

Take personal responsibility

Opportunity seeker

Time oriented

Realistic

Not too discouraged by failures

Sensitive and perceptive

Good communicator

Assertive

High tolerance of ambiguity

Goal oriented

Wants to make money

Persistent

Family and friends, second to business

Good problem solver

Resourceful, makes good use of resources

Knowledge of the business.

Entrepreneurial Competencies

Initiative

Sees and acts on opportunities

Persistence

Information seeking

Concern for high quality of work

Commitment to work contract

Efficiency orientation

Systematic planning

Problem solving

Self-confidence

Assertiveness

Persuasion

Use of influence strategies

Monitoring

Concern for employees' welfare.

Larger the number of these attributes a person possesses, greater could be the chance of his or her entrepreneurial success.

ENTREPRENEURS IN INDIA

It is generally believed that people coming from certain business, castes/communities and religious groups have been more enterprising than the rest. However, the findings of several research studies conducted in different parts of the country indicate contrary to such beliefs.

A study of manufacturing units in and around Chennai and Coimbatore cities in Tamil Nadu revealed that initial entry into industry was open to persons of diverse social standing and economic position (Berna, 1960). A study of small entrepreneurs in Andhra Pradesh revealed that all the entrepreneurs were persons having initiatives, drive and hard work, though a majority of them had neither technical knowledge nor strong economic base and political connections (Gaikwad and Tripathi, 1970). A study of small entrepreneurs in Gujarat revealed that entry into industry and success need not be the privilege of a few traditionally dominant groups (Patel, 1981). Further study on small entrepreneurs in Uttar Pradesh revealed that the entrepreneurs coming from non-business families had higher degree of entrepreneurial orientation and commitment than the entrepreneurs coming from business families, business castes and business regions (Sharma, 1975).

PHASES OF ENTREPRENEURSHIP DEVELOPMENT

Broadly, entrepreneurship development consists of the three following phases:

Initial phase - Creation of awareness about the entrepreneurial opportunities based on service and research.

Development phase - Implementation of training programmes to develop motivation and management skills.

Support Phase - Infrastructural support of counselling, assisting to establish new enterprises and to develop existing units.

Entrepreneurship itself is a complex phenomenon, some thinking of it as job of innovators, some as managers of enterprise, some as bearers of risks and others as mobilizers and allocaters of capital. In the Indian context, however entrepreneurship may best be considered as creators of economic wealth for self and society at large, through commercial and productive activities.

Hence, entrepreneurship development would mean all those activities aiming at development of individuals in such a way that an urge is ignited for becoming an entrepreneur. Phases could be three or more, all occurring one after another or simultaneously or concurrently.

ENTREPRENEURSHIP DEVELOPMENT IN INDIA

It is true a person must have certain entrepreneurial attributes and need not necessarily belong to a particular caste, community or group to become an entrepreneur. But mere personality traits of an individual would not be sufficient condition for him/her becoming an entrepreneur. Other social, cultural and economic factors as well as support-system also influence to a considerable extent, promotion and development of entrepreneurship, however it has been found that the entrepreneurial attributes of an individual can be improved to a certain extent through stimulation and training, provided he or she has latent potential for entrepreneurship. The entrepreneurial potential of an individual thus developed can lead to the promotion of an enterprise with the help of counselling, infrastructural support and financial assistance from institutional sources. In this way, the constraints in development of entrepreneurship due to unfavourable personality traits, social conditioning, cultural ethos and economic factors could be reduced to a great extent.

Though India has had a long tradition of institutional support for the promotion and development of industries, the first step towards developing entrepreneurs was taken in the early 1960s. The first programme on motivation training for developing entrepreneurship in India was organised by the National Institute of Small Industries Extension Training (NISIET), Hyderabad in 1964, under the leadership of David C.McClelland. In the first programme fifty-two persons were trained in four batches in Kakinada District of Andhra Pradesh. This was followed by another programme in which twenty-six persons from Vellore in Tamil Nadu were trained in two batches in 1965. Later on, NISIET evolved an integrated model for entrepreneurship, development based on its previous experience. This model was first of all tried in Assam and similar programmes were conducted later on in the states of Andhra Pradesh, Bihar and Jammu and Kashmir. During the period of April 1970 to September 1973, 1,240 potential entrepreneurs were trained at different centres in Gujarat through a series of Entrepreneurship Development Programmes (EDPs) sponsored by the state level financial institutions.

Following the success of these initial EDPs, entrepreneurship development through training came to be viewed as a useful instrument for widening and diversifying the entrepreneurial base of the country.

Several national and state level institutions have been set up exclusively for entrepreneurship development. Also a variety of agencies in a large number have come forward to conduct EDPs, all over the country. In addition, a great deal of sophistication has also been achieved over the years in planning EDPs, selecting potential entrepreneurs, motivation, training, business opportunity, guidance and business management inputs.

EFFECTIVENESS OF ENTREPRENEURSHIP DEVELOPMENT PROGRAMMES IN INDIA

Though a systematic documentation of entrepreneurship development and their effectiveness in India is yet to be done, some limited facts available provide an insight into the spread and effectiveness of EDPs.

During the period of April 1970 to March 1980, 376 EDPs had been conducted in Gujarat and the effectiveness of these EDPs was reported to be about 63%. In the state of Maharashtra and Goa, 88 potential entrepreneurs were trained during the year 1974, through several EDPs conducted in other 5 districts of Maharashtra during the years 1976 and 1977 was reported to be 31%. The State Bank of India had conducted 10 EDPs in its 13 circles till 1985 and the effectiveness of these EDPs was reported to be about. 28%. In Pondicherry, the effectiveness of 32 EDPs conducted during the period 1985-87 ranged between 22% in 1985 and 51% in 1987.

From this limited information, it is obvious the EDPs have become popular throughout the country and their effectiveness has been varying from one region to another. With the growing awareness of the need for entrepreneurship development and increasing availability of trained manpower, the effectiveness of EDPs is bound to increase in future. However, it must be clear to all concerned that mere improvement in the quality of men and material for conducting EDPs would not make much difference. Equally or even more important are the quality and adequacy of institutional support provided by financial institutions and promotional, agencies to the EDPs trained candidates for setting up and running of their enterprises.

Not much information is at present available on the reasons for not setting up of enterprises by a good proportion of the candidates trained through a variety of EDPs. Collection and analysis of such information would be very useful for identifying weakness in the process of entrepreneurship development and for evolving the strategy to overcome them in future. This becomes all the more important, keeping in view the rapid growth of population causing acute unemployment problem.

RESEARCH FINDINGS

Apart from a broad review of the progress of Entrepreneurship Development in the country as presented above it may be appropriate to highlight some of the factors that have influenced the existing entrepreneurs to choose entrepreneurial careers. A study of small entrepreneurs conducted in Kamataka, (Tewari Philip and Pandey, 1991) revealed that the better performing, entrepreneurs were relatively young and the desire to be self-employed, was the greatest motivating factor for becoming an entrepreneur. Entrepreneurs were motivated by their own ambitions rather than the ambitions of their parents and other relatives. Also dissatisfaction with previous job or occupation was found to be the most compelling factor for motivating them to become entrepreneurs. While the greatest source of encouragement was entrepreneur's previous experience. Entrepreneurs developed greater confidence from their own abilities and skills rather than from financial and other material resources available to them.

Previous employment in industries or trade was found to be the most important consideration for the selection of products. Accommodation in an industrial estate and the availability of financial support from the institutional sources were the two greatest expectations of entrepreneurs. The entrepreneurs belonging to the sick group had received greater financial support in the initial stage than those belonging to the very successful group.

Manufacturing as a sole activity was more prominent in the successful group than in the sick group and smaller size of an enterprise in the initial stage was not a limiting factor for the growth and outstanding performance in future. Besides, utilisation of capital was more efficient and the repayment behaviour of the entrepreneurs was better in the better performing groups.

While ability and immediate environment of the entrepreneurs were considered to be the main factor responsible for outstanding performance, rather unsatisfactory performance of average group was attributed to their greater dependence on market situations than on their own entrepreneurial ability. Poor performance of the units belonging to the sick group was largely due to the unsatisfactory entrepreneurial efforts entailing a variety of problems.

ENVIRONMENT FOR ENTREPRENEURSHIP

Entrepreneurs do not come into existence spontaneously on their own. While the other factors of production in principle can be hired, enterprise cannot be done so. Even, the educational system in most of the developing countries is designed in such a way as to create more of job seekers. In many countries to sum up, entrepreneurs appear to have been motivated by a continuation and interaction of the following factors of environment:

- Socio-economic Environment
- Family Background
- Standard of Education and Technical knowledge
- Financial Stability
- Political Stability and Government's Policy
- Caste and Religious Affiliation
- Availability of Supporting Facilities
- Achievement Motivation
- Personality and Personal Skills.

The environmental factors may be summarized as follows:

1. Entrepreneurship is not influenced by a single factor but is the outcome of the interaction and continuation of various environmental factors.
2. By changing the environment, society can be recreated.
3. It is the "desire to make money" that drives one to start an industry rather than the amount of money one owns.
4. Encouraging government policy and social recognition influence a person to become an entrepreneur.

BARRIERS

Entry barriers are defined as those factors limiting access to identified business opportunities and capitalisation on those opportunities. Survival barriers are defined as constraints on the conditions essential for the continuity of the small business entity. Exit barriers are defined as those constraints limiting the termination of those small industrial ventures that have outlived their business viability or the growth of such ventures to a different size category.

The existing entry barriers are:

1. A cultural bias in identifying and managing the entrepreneurial development process.
2. Limited industry - specific data and insufficient market information.
3. Limited effectiveness of the infrastructural base.
4. Existence of visible and invisible obstacles to entry of a specific societal group (e.g., women) into business.
5. Unorganised capital market and traditional feasibility assessment processes.
6. Unsympathetic and cumbersome government attitude.
7. Hostile environment.
8. Limited access to technology.

Observed survival barriers include the following:

1. A behavioural pattern that could impair basic managerial practices.
2. Constraining practices within the capital market.
3. The threatening shadow of changing technology.
4. Limited learning.
5. The cultural management of resources.
6. Failure of guidance agencies to guide.
7. Scarce information and limited dissemination of that information.

Identified exit barriers include:

1. The emotional commitment of the entrepreneur to his venture.

2. Specialised assets, sunk funds.
3. The increasing demand for managerial skills.
4. Fear of failure.

POSITION OF ENTREPRENEURSHIP IN INDIA

India does not possess a very good record of entrepreneurship. However, its image is definitely improving, concerted efforts at liberalisation have made the countries of the world sit back and look at india develop its own brand of entrepreneurship. In the recent past India's status, in the industrial world has grown. From humble surroundings, India is now the tenth largest industrialized nation of the world.

However, India has essentially been an "adoptive" entrepreneur. It has now to prepare it self with an entrepreneurship of a different order, that of the innovative type. This will require harnessing of India's true potential through tremendous advances of science and technology. It is essential that the government and the people must have a more mature and finer approach towards the concept of entrepreneurship. Then only would it be possible for this nation to match the level reached by advanced countries. A good beginning in this direction has been made and one hope the adage "Well begun is half done," will hold good in case of India.

GOVERNMENT POLICIES-SMALL SCALE INDUSTRIES

Policies constitute the framework or guidelines for appropriate decisions at varied levels. They generally consist of statements that affect the working of a sector of the economy. The working of small scale industries, too, is moulded by a number of policies which are the base for effective plan development.

The living standards of the people in the world vary considerably. Generally speaking, industrialised countries are known as developed countries in which industrial development is based on modern technology and research. The countries in which agriculture predominates are referred to as underdeveloped/developing countries. Under-developed countries are those where even agriculture is quite traditional. Developing countries have accepted mechanisation as a way of life all along and have concentrated on developing large industries.

For a developing country like India, the growth of small scale industries is of great significance. Apart from increased production, the growth of small scale industries helps to serve as an important milestone in the country's march towards industrial democracy. This movement has to be fostered by all-round efforts, so that a new class of talented entrepreneurs, endowed with initiative and enterprise, come to the forefront, in this country.

OBJECTIVES

The basic objectives of these industries are to create immediate and permanent employment on a large scale at a relatively small cost to meet a substantial part of the increased demand for consumer goods, and simple producer's goods, to facilitate the mobilisation of resources of capital and skill, which might otherwise remain inadequately utilised, and to bring about an integration of the development of these industries with the rural economy on the one hand and large scale industry on the other. Further, these industries are said to offer a method of ensuring a more equitable distribution of the national income and of avoiding some of the problems that unplanned urbanisation tends to create.

Basically, small industries are important for national development programmes because they can make a definite contribution to the realisation of the central purpose of such a problem *i.e.,* to bring about an efficient utilisation of natural, human and capital resources of the country and for the achievement of predetermined ends.

TRACING THE SMALL SCALE INDUSTRIAL POLICY SINCE INDEPENDENCE

The need for the development of small scale, village and cottage industries has been the objective of the government since independence. Before we discuss the New Industrial Policy

Resolution, it would be proper to recapitulate the important features of the earlier Industrial Policy Resolutions, since 1948.

INDUSTRIAL POLICY RESOLUTION, 1948

The importance of small scale industries was specifically defined in the Industrial Policy Resolution dated 6th April 1948. It was stated:

"Cottage and Small Industries have a very important role in the national economy, offers as they do scope for individual, village or co-operative enterprises and means for rehabilitation displaced persons. These industries are particularly suited for the better utilisation of local resource and for the achievement of local self-sufficiency in respect of certain types of essential consumer goods."

The Resolution added:

'The healthy expansion of cottage and small scale industries depends on a number of facto such as the provision of raw materials, cheap power, technical advice, organised marketing of th products and, where necessary, safeguards against intensive competition by large sc* manufacturers; it also depends on the education of the workers in the use of the best avail techniques."

INDUSTRIAL POLICY RESOLUTION, 1956

The Second Industrial Policy Resolution, enunciated in 1956, reiterated the desirable features of small industry. In this resolution, an attempt was made to rephrase industrial policy in the light the changes that had taken place in the intermediate period of eight years. The objective of economic policy now was to establish a socialistic pattern of society.

The role of village and small scale industries in the development of the national economic was stressed once again. "The State has been following a policy of supporting cottage as well village and small scale industries by restricting the volume of production in the large scale sector differential taxation, or by direct subsidies. While such measures will continue to be taken when" necessary, the aim of State Policy will be to ensure that the decentralized sector acquires sufficient vitality to be self-supporting, for its development is integrated with that of large scale industry. State will; therefore, concentrate on measures designed to improve the competitive strength of small scale producer. For this purpose, it is essential that the techniques of production should be constantly improved and modernised and the pace of transformation should be so regulated as to avoid, as far as possible, technological unemployment. Lack of technical and financial assistance, of suitable working accommodation and inadequacy of facilities for repair and maintenance are among the serious handicaps of small scale producers. A start has been made with the establishment of industrial estates and rural community workshops to make good these deficiencies. The extension of rural electrification and the availability of power at prices which the workers can afford will also be of considerable help. Many of the activities relating to small scale production will be helped by the organisation of industrial co-operatives."

The basic objectives of all these measures were to ensure that the decentralised sector acquires sufficient vitality to be self-supporting and its development is integrated with that of large scale industries."

"This programme of industrial development will make large demands on the country's resources, of technical and managerial personnel. To meet these rapidly, growing needs for the expansion of the public sector and for the development of village and small scale industries, proper managerial and technical cadres in the public services are being established, steps are also being taken to meet shortages of supervisory levels, to organise apprenticeship schemes of training on a large-scale both in public and in private enterprises and to extend, training facilities in business management in universities and other institutions."

The Resolution recognised the importance of locational factors like the availability of raw materials, cheap water supply, transport facilities etc. It reiterates very clearly that these facilities will be provided in those regions where they are not available at present, so that the unbalanced growth in the various regions may be corrected and the country as a whole may achieve higher standards of living.

INDUSTRIAL POLICY, 1977

Industrial Policy presented to Parliament on 23rd December, 1977 was primarily directed towards removing the distortions of the past, so that the goals of faster economic development can be achieved within a time-bound programme.

The essence of the Industrial Policy 1977 was that the prosperity and distribution of income arising from a broad based growth of agriculture and related activities in rural areas can be achieved only when the "basic demand" for a wide range of industries producing articles of mass consumption is adequately met. The policy objective was to achieve through a process of reinforcing the interaction of agricultural and industrial sectors, employment for larger number of the rural population who cannot be absorbed in the agricultural sector. Considering, the vast rural manpower and the reservoir of highly technical personnel, the new industrial policy aims at placing man at the centre of planning and implementation of projects and schemes.

The salient features of the policy were:

Small Scale Industries: The main thrust of the. Industrial Policy, 1977 was on an effective promotion of cottage and small industries widely dispersed in rural areas and small towns. It is the policy of the Government that whatever can be produced by small and cottage industries must only be so produced. For this purpose, the list of industries which would be exclusively reserved, for the small scale sector had been significantly expanded, and included more than five hundred and four items against about one hundred and eight items, reserved for this sector in the past.

Tiny Sector: While the existing definition of small scale industries will remain, within the] small scale sector itself, special attention will be given to units in the tiny sector, namely those investment in machinery and equipment up to Rupees one lakh and situated in towns and village with a population of less than fifty thousand according to the 1971 census. Schemes will be drawn up with a view to making available margin money assistance to tiny units in the small scale sector as well as cottage and household industries.

Arrangements for Provisions of Credit: The financial assistance given to small and cottage credits under the rural industries programme will be extended to all the districts in the country within the next four years. In order to provide effective financial support for the promotion of small village and cottage industries, the Industrial Development Bank of India has taken steps to set up a separate wing to deal exclusively with the credit requirements of this sector. It will co-ordinate, guide and monitor the entire range of credit facilities offered by other institutions for the small and the cottage industrial sector for which separate wings will be set up in these institutions, particularly in nationalised banks. Banks will also be expected to earmark a specific proportion of their total advances for promotion of small, village and cottage industries. It was the policy of the government to see toil] that no worthwhile scheme of small or village industry is given up for want of credit.

Arrangements for Marketing: The marketing of the production of the small scale and cottage industries, with its concomitants of product standardisation, quality control, market survey etc., would receive special attention. The government would provide maximum support for these activities on a priority basis. It would encourage the purchase of the products of the small-scale by government departments and public sector undertakings with a view to supporting the marketing of these products.

Promotion of Khadi and Village Industries: The Khadi and Village Industries Commission presently have twenty two, village industries within its purview, but the promotional work in this area has been haphazard and the progress has been slow. It will henceforth, have to work out details' plans for the development of these village industries by adopting modern management technique In this context, special programmes would be drawn up to increase the share of village Industries the total production of footwear and soaps in the country. The list of items currently under the purview of the Commission will be expanded and the organisational structure of the Commission will be revamped to make it more effective.

The Khadi and Village Industries Act, has been amended to permit the implementation of a large scale programme for the manufacture of 'Nai Khadi'. The government would provide maximum financial and marketing support needed for the promotion of the khadi programme.

Along with khadi , the clothing need of the masses would be progressively met by development of the handloom sector, which provides employment to a large number of people. To effect this, government will not permit any expansion in the weaving capacity in the organized mill and power loom sectors. It will give priority to handloom sector in the allocation of yarn spun in the organized sector. Further, in order to provide a market for handloom products, it would be ensured that the organized mill sector does not provide unfair competition to the handloom sector. The government will enforce the existing reservation of certain items of textiles for the handloom sector and further expand it to other items.

Appropriate Technology: It will be an integral part of the government policy to ensure that the development and application of technology-appropriate to the country's social-economic conditions receives adequate attention. Special arrangements will be made to ensure an effective and co-ordinated approach for the development and widespread application of suitable small and simple machines and devices for improving the productivity of the village industries. It will further, be the government's endeavour to fully integrate such appropriate techniques of production with the broader programme of all round rural development.

Role of Large Scale Industries: The role of. large scale industry will be essentially related, to the programme for meeting the basic minimum needs of the population by effecting a wider dispersal of small scale and village industries and strengthening of the agricultural sector. These will be:

1. **Basic industries**, which are essential for providing infrastructure facilities as well as for the development of small and village industries, such as steel, non-ferrous metals, cement and refineries;

2. **Capital goods industries** required for meeting the machinery requirements of basic industries and small scale industries;
3. **High technology industries** requiring large scale production and which are related to agriculture and small scale industrial development such as fertilisers, pesticides and petro- chemicals; and
4. **Other industries** which are outside the list of items reserved for the development of the economy like, machine tools, organic and inorganic chemicals.

Indigenous and Foreign Technology: The government's policy is that the future development of industries in India must as far as possible, be based on indigenous industries. Full scope will be given to the development of indigenous technology, which would subserve the objective of efficient production of increasing quantities of the goods, which society urgently needs. The government also recognises the necessity of continued inflow of technology in sophisticated and high priority areas, where Indian skills and technology are not adequately developed. In such areas, government's preference would be for outright purchase of the best available technology and then adopting it to the country's needs.

Foreign Investment: The provision of the Foreign Exchange Regulation Act, will be strictly enforced as far as the existing foreign companies are concerned. After the dilution of equity, companies with direct non-resident investment not exceeding forty percent will be treated on par with Indian companies, except in cases, specifically notified, and their future expansion will be guided by the same principles as those applicable to Indian companies. Foreign investment and acquisition of foreign technology as necessary for India's industrial development will be allowed only on such terms as determined by the Government of India, to be in the national interest. In areas, in which foreign technological know-how is not needed, existing collaborations will not be renewed. The government will issue a revised illustrative list of industries for which no foreign collaboration, financial or technical is considered necessary, if indigenous technology has fully developed in this field. For all approved foreign investments, there will be complete freedom for remittance of profits, royalties, dividends as well as remittance of capital, subject to rules and regulations. While, as a rule, the majority interest in ownership and effective control will be in Indian hands, the government will make exceptions in highly export oriented cases. It may even consider, permitting a fully owned foreign company to operate in India.

Indian Joint Ventures Abroad: The government's policy is that, at the present stage of industrial development of the country, the contribution of Indian entrepreneur to joint ventures abroad will be mainly in the form of machinery and equipment, structurals, technical know-how and management expertise. If such investment is found necessary, the government will be willing to consider such investment up to a maximum limit to be prescribed for this purpose.

Location of Industries: No licences will be issued to new industrial units within certain limits of large metropolitan cities having a population of more than one million and urban areas with population with more than five lakhs as per the 1971 census. Further the State Governments and financial institutions will be requested to deny support to such new industries in these areas which do not require an industrial licence. The Government of India would also consider providing assistance to large existing industries which want to shift from congested metropolitan cities approved locations in backward areas

INDUSTRIAL POLICY RESOLUTION, 1980

The Industrial Policy statement made, on 23rd July, 1980 primarily seeks to harmonise the growth in the small scale sector with that in the large and medium sectors. The emphasis in the new policy is on fostering the complementarity between the small and large sectors so that the dichotomies, (which are more apparent than real) between the two sectors do not distort the economic pattern. In the words of the latest policy statement: "It will be government's endeavour to reverse the trends of the last three years towards creating artificial divisions between the large and the small industry under the misconception that these interests are essentially conflicting."

The broad socio-economic objectives of the new policy have been set out as follows:

- Optimum utilisation of installed capacity;
- Maximising production and achieving higher productivity;
- Higher employment generation;
- Correction of regional imbalances through a preferential, development of industrially backward areas;
- Strengthening of the agricultural base by according a preferential treatment to agro based industries and promoting optimum inter-sectoral relationship;
- Faster promotion of export oriented and import substitution industries;
- Promoting economic federalism with an equitable spread of investment and! dispersal of returns amongst widely spread small but growing units in rural as well urban areas;
- Consumer protection against high prices and bad quality.

An important element of the new policy is the raising of the investment limits of the tiny and small scale sectors. These limits have been redefined in terms of investment in plant and machinery and have been fixed at Rupees two lakhs for tiny sector instead of Rupees one lakh, Rupees lakhs for the small scale sector instead of Rupees ten lakhs and Rupees twenty five lakhs ins of Rupees fifteen lakhs for ancillaries. This step is essentially a pragmatic one and takes account the significant price rise that has occurred in the last five years, following the fixation ofj investment limits for the small scale sector.

However, this decision would bring into the fold of the small scale sector a number of technology oriented units whose growth will have to be backed by a suitable system of incentives. The new industrial policy spells out some of these incentives which are proposed to be pr that the small scale sector may grow in a significant measure and contribute to the national economy.

Financial Support to Small Units: One of the major constraints on the growth decentralised sector has been the difficulty of finance which has been experienced particular industrial entrepreneurs in small, cottage and rural sectors. Although, there is an adequate network of institutional finance, it is nevertheless essential to co-ordinate the flow of capital both short term and long term. The Government should evolve a system of co-ordination to ensure the flow of credit to the growing units in the decentralised sector at the right time and on appropriate terms, It should strengthen the existing arrangements and make such changes as may be necessary to facilitate the availability of credit to the growing units in the small scale sector.

Buffer Stock for Critical Inputs: In order to assist in the growth of small scale industries, it has been proposed to introduce a scheme for the building up of buffer stocks of essential materials which are often difficult to obtain. For this purpose, the existing set up of Small Industries Development Corporations in the States and the National Small Industries Corporation (NSIC) at the centre will also be utilised. The special needs of the states which rely heavily on a few essential raw materials will receive priority.

Marketing Support and Reservation Items for Small Industries: Policies related to marketing support of the decentralised sectors and the reservation of items for small scale industries shall continue to be in force, in the interests and growth of small industries.

Village Industries: Government is determined to promote such a form of industrialisation in the country as would generate economic viability in the villages. The promotion suitable to industries in rural areas will be accelerated to generate higher employment and higher per capita income for the villagers without disturbing the ecological balance. Handlooms, handicrafts, khadi and other village industries will receive greater attention to achieve a faster rate of growth in the villages.

District Industries Centres: The Government has reviewed the scheme of District Industries Centres, which has not produced benefits commensurate with the expenditure incurred on them. It therefore proposes to initiate more effective alternatives.

The Policy Statement of 1980, makes it clear that the existing support programme for marketing as well as for the reservation of items in the small scale sector will continue. These form an important I underpinning of the small industry development programme. It is, therefore proposed, that the I exisiting policies will continue to operate to strengthen the small scale sector.

The basic thrust of the new policy is to ensure a continuous growth of the small scale sector without, at the same time, inhibiting the growth of other sectors. In this context, automatic growth for a large number of industries in the medium and large sector has been ensured so that they can grow without hindrance.

A special emphasis has been laid on the establishment of "nucleus plants" in backward districts around which a programme of ancillarisation would be developed. To quote from the statement:

"The proposed nucleus plants in industrially backward districts would generate a network of small-scale units, on the existing network of small scale units in an area which would acquire a faster growth by the coming up of a nucleus plant in the area. In between, the nucleus, large plants and the satellite ancillaries, the Government would permit a system of linkages for an integrated industrial development."

1991, POLICY MEASURE

Over the last few decades small enterprises emerged as leaders in industrial sector. They [also played a more significant role in creating balances for economic and social development in the country. In recognition of their significance and stature, the new government announced Policy Measure on August 6th, 1991 for promoting and strengthening of small, tiny and village enterprises.

Objectives:

- To impart more vitality and growth impetus to the small scale sector.
- To decentralise and delicense the sector.

- To deregulate and debureaucratise the sector.
- To review all statutes, regulations and procedures and effect suitable modifications where necessary.
- To promote small enterprises especially industries in tiny sector.
- To motivate small and sound entrepreneurs to set up new green enterprises in country.
- To involve traditional and reputed voluntary organisations in the intensive development of KVI through area approach.
- To maintain sustained growth in productivity and attain competitiveness in the ma economy, especially in the international markets.
- To industrialise backward areas of the country.
- Accelerate the process of development of modern small enterprises, tiny enterprises and village industries through appropriate incentives, institutional support and infrastructure investments.

Salient features:

- Legislation to limit financial liability of new and non-active partners/entrepreneurs the capital invested.
- Hike in investment limit for tiny sector up from Rupees two lakhs to Rupees five lakhs.
- Service sector to be recognised as tiny sector.
- Support from National Equity Fund for projects up to Rupees ten lakhs.
- Single window loans to cover projects up to Rupees twenty lakhs. Banks also involved.
- Relaxation of certain provisions of labour laws.
- Sub-contracting Exchanges to be set up by industry association.
- Easier access to institutional finance.

- Factoring services through SIDBI to overcome the problem of delayed payment legislation to ensure payment of bills.
- Women enterprises redefined.
- Marketing of mass consumption items by National Small Industries Corporation under common brand name.
- Composite loans under the single window scheme also to be given by banks. Tiny sector to be accorded priority in government purchase programme.
- Priority to SSIs and tiny units in allocation of indigenous raw materials.
- Promise to deregulate and debureaucratise small and tiny sector.
- PSUs and NSIC to help market products through consortia approach, both domed and internationally.
- Janata Cloth Scheme to be replaced by a new scheme which will provide funds for loans and modernisation.
- Compulsory quality control for products that pose risk to health and life.
- Legislation to ensure payment of small scale industries bills.
- A special monetary agency to be set up for the small-scale sector's credit needs.
- A new scheme of integrated infrastructural development to be implemented.
- A technology development cell to be set up.
- Incentives and services package to be delivered at the district level.
- An expert development centre to be set up.
- Khadi and Village Industries Commission (KVIC) and Boards to be expanded.
- Investment limit of ancillary units and export-oriented units raised to seventy five lakhs.
- Traditional village industries would be given greater thrust.

OTHER IMPORTANT ASPECTS OF GOVERNMENT POLICIES

Tiny Sector

The Policy Statement gives a new thrust for the development of tiny enterprises which accounts for nearly ninety percent of all small scale units. The investment ceiling has been raised from Rupees two lakhs to Rupees five lakhs. A significant feature of the policy is the due recognition. In order to strengthen the tiny sector it has been decided to recognise all industry related service and business enterprises irrespective of their location, as small scale industries. Their investment ceiling would correspond to those of tiny enterprises.

While the small scale sector (other than tiny enterprises) would be, mainly entitled to one time benefits (like preference in land allocation/power connection access to facilities for skills, technology upgradation) the tiny enterprises would also be eligible for additional support on a continuing basis, including easier access to institutional finance, priority in the Government Purchase Programme and relaxation from certain provisions of labour laws.

Handloom Sector

Schemes for the handloom sector will be redesigned keeping in mind the local and regional needs. Substantial funds will be provided for modernisation of looms, training, provision of better designs, provision of better dyes and chemicals and marketing assistance. Spinning capacity, in the co-operative sector will be increased, National Co-operative Development Corporation, will provide more assistance for this in the form of seed money, both for cotton growers, spinning mills and weavers' spinning mills.

The Janata Cloth Scheme which sustains weavers often on a minimum level of livelihood will be phased out by the terminal year of the Eighth Plan and replaced by the "omnibus project package scheme" under which substantial funds will be provided for modernisation of looms, training, provision for better designs, provision of better dyes and chemicals and marketing assistance.

The role of the National Handloom Development Centres (NHDCs) is also being enhanced it would now be a 'nodal agency' for increasing supply of hand yarn, dyes and chemicals.

For the handicraft sector, "craft development centres" are proposed to be set up which would[1], ensure raw materials, design and technical guidance, market support, training and procuring ofj related inputs in an integrated and area based manner. Measures are also proposed to be initiated to increase exports from this sector through new marketing channels like trading companies, departmental stores, etc.

Village Industries

Intensive development of KVl through area approach with tie-up with DRDA, TRYSEM and ongoing developmental programmes relating to weaker sections like scheduled castes, scheduled! tribes and women would be extended throughout the country. The traditional village industries would be given greater thrust.

Involvement of traditional and reputed voluntary organisations will be encouraged for this purpose. The new policy's success depends substantially on the quality of the service provided by bodies like Small Scale Industries Development Organisation, Prototype Development Centres NS1C, *etc.*, whose services in the past have not inspired much success.

Rural Industries

Rural industry embraces different kinds of village and small industries. The cottage industries are an important component of rural industries. By the term "rural industry" is meant industry appropriate for the rural areas as demarcated by the census records. The concept here has a special demographic undertone. The rural industry serves the requirements of rural people as w« as other markets. By and large, the financial needs of rural industry are small. More importantly they function in the absence of infrastructure facilities and are environmentally friendly.

Types of Rural Industry: By and large rural industries are interlinked with agricultural activities rural development and service sector. They may also be grouped into small scale industry, tiny industry and rural artisans (self-employed). The scope for process industry is vast and unexplored The need of the hour is the proper organisation of rural industries and integrate them into the rural ethos and development.

Importance of Rural Industrialisation: Rural industrialisation is important not only as a means of generating employment opportunities in the rural areas with low capital cost and rail the real income of the people, but because it contributes to the development of agriculture urban industries. Without rural industrialisation it would be considerably more difficult to solve problem of agricultural unemployment and widespread underemployment. Rural industrialisation promotes rural industry. The development of rural industries, increases the level of income in the rural areas, and tends to break down the old self-sufficiency of the family and to lessen its cohesiveness, creating opportunities for youth, women and the able bodied as well in changing the pattern of leisure and work. Rural industrialisation should be looked upon not merely as a way of contain the rural workers and stopping them from migrating to urban areas by providing them some kind of remunerative employment in the villages, but as a dynamic element in the process of raising productivity and income levels of the workers in rural areas.

The main characteristics of these industries are to develop local initiative, co-operation a spirit of self reliance in the economy and at the same time help in utilisation of the available manpower for processing locally available raw materials by adopting simple techniques.

These are capable of offering employment opportunities at the place of residence to a large section of population. The village industries are an antidote to the widespread problems of disguised unemployment or underemployment.

These decentralised industries require loss gestation period on the one hand and produce goods of common necessities on the other.

These industries have the capacity to correct regional imbalances by initiating industrial activities on dispersed basis in the most neglected, backward, inaccessible areas where perhaps large scale sector is unable to penetrate.

Being small, these activities can ensure maximum participation of workers in management thus ensuring a feeling of involvement which is so uncommon with the large scale sector.

These industries possess an additional advantage wherein the maximum participation of women-folk can be ensured.

Rural industrialisation has taken roots in the rural economy in India. This is so because simple forms of manufacture, typical of consumer goods industries and varied service industries are everywhere developed before the more complex process involved in the production of capital goods and because the size of the home market at the time of industrialisation, prohibits the establishment of optimum sized plants in the production of certain capital goods.

Khadi and Village Industries

The development of village and khadi industries provides opportunities for work albeit part time work in certain cases and thereby helps to mitigate the severity of rural unemployment and underemployment. With this end in view, the Khadi and Village Industries Commission (KVIC) were established in April 1957, under the Khadi and Village Commission Act, 1956.

Under the guidance of Mahatma Gandhi, provisional activities of khadi were started in 1922, when they were symbolic of the "Fight for Freedom". The khadi programme was thus closely linked with the struggle for freedom. The All-India Congress Committee, then known as the All-India Spinner's 'Association (AISA) was established in 1952, to organise hand-spinning and hand-weaving. This was followed by the establishment of another organisation in 1935, called the All India Village Industries Association (AIVA), to look after other village industries, such as hand pounding of paddy, ghana oil, palm gur, bee keeping, hand made paper, etc. The establishment of Khadi Commission was the culmination of the efforts to organise cottage/village industries during the freedom movement. In 1951, the Sarva Seva Sangha took over the work of AISA and AIVA, as a part of an integrated plan for rural industrialisation.

The Government of India evolved a general policy framework for the development of these industries. In the First Plan, these industries were treated as an integral part of agriculture and the emphasis was on the local consumption. In the Second Plan on the advice of the Village and Small Scale Industries Committee (Karve) 1955, was in consonance with the Industrial Policy Resolution of the whole plan for the country's industrialisation. The Third Plan retained the emphasis on these programmes while highlighting the need for an integrated approach. In the successive plans, the emphasis and policy were shifted from one of protection of such industries to positive forms of assistance, such as improving skills, supplying technical guidance, better equipment and adequate credit with a view to increasing productivity and reducing cost. The government is committed to the encouragement of the production of textiles and textile products in the khadi sector. Considering its large employment potential, it should be the endeavour of the government to make products of these sectors, more competitive and of better quality.

The infrastructure for the distribution of controlled cloth, particularly in rural areas, will be strengthened and stream-lined. State governments will be encouraged to open more rural outlets and exercise stricter control over distribution.

Functions of KVIC: The functions of KVIC, also comprise building up a reserve of raw materials and implements for supply to producers, creation of common service of facilities for processing, marketing and training. Other functions are:

- To promote the sale and marketing of khadi products of village industries or handicrafts. The KVIC may forge times with established marketing agencies wherever necessary and feasible.
- The KVIC is also charged with the responsibility of encouraging and promoting research in the production techniques employed in the khadi and village industries

sector and providing facilities for the study of the problems relating to it, including the use of non- conventional energy and electric power with a view to increasing productivity, eliminating drudgery and otherwise enhancing their competitive capacity and to arrange for dissemination of salient results obtained from such research.

- Further, the KVIC is entrusted with the task of providing financial assistance to institutions or persons engaged in the development and operation of khadi and village industries and guiding them through supply of design, prototypes and other technical information.
- In implementing KVI activities, the KVIC may take such steps to ensure genuineness of the products and to set up standards of quality and ensure that the products! khadi and village industries do conform to the standards, including issue of certificates] or letters of recognition, to the concerned.
- The KVIC may also undertake directly or through other agencies studies concerning the problems of khadi or village industries besides experiments or pilot projects for the development of khadi and village industries.
- The KVIC is authorised to establish and maintain separate organisations for the purpose of carrying out any or all of the above matters incidental to its activities.

Industrial Estates

Industrial estates and ancillary industries were started in India with great hopes in their efficacy as tools of industrial dispersal, rural industrialisation and to sustain growth of the small scale industries. In India, industrial estates and ancillary industries have been utilised as an effective tool for the promotion and growth of small scale industries. They have also been used to decentralise, industrial activity to rural and backward areas.

According to P.C. Alexander, an Industrial Estate is "a group of factories, constructed on an economic scale in suitable sites with facilities of water, transport, electricity, steam, bank, post office, canteen, watch and ward and first-aid; and provided with special arrangements for technical guidance and common service facilities."

The United Nations has defined an Industrial Estate as "a planned clustering of enterprises, offering standard factory buildings, erected in advance of demand and variety of services and facilities to the occupants."

Types of Industrial Estate: The service term, industrial estate covers all the four variants of the concept namely, industrial areas, industrial estates, industrial townships and galas.

An industrial area is one wherein the infrastructure facilities and services are provided but factory accommodation is constructed by entrepreneurs. In an industrial estate, both infrastructural facilities and factory sheds having accommodation and other civic amenities associated with a town are also provided.

In galas, space is provided in a big building to set up small scale industries along with infrastructural facilities.

On the basis of functions, industrial estates are classified into:

(a) Conventional (general) type;

(b) special type.

General type industrial estates provide accommodation to a wide variety and range of industrial concerns, while, special type estates attempt the establishment of industrial units, which are vertically or horizontally dependent. In India, general type estates are very popular.

On the basis of the organisational set up, industrial estates are classified into:

(a) Government;

(b) Private;

(c) Co-operative; and

(d) Municipal estates.

There are a number of other variants of industrial estates such as:

Ancillary Industrial Estate: Only small industries which are ancillary to a particular large industry are housed in this estate, just like the one attached to the HMT Bangalore.

Functional Industrial Estate: This is a small and fully serviced unit which serves as a reception centre for displaced small firms. It also serves as a 'Pilot-cell' for small firms going into production and is a base for expansion into larger factories.

The Workshop Bay: This is designed for very small firms and is usually meant for artisans who does mainly repair works.

The Service Industrial Bay: This is usually located in the shopping centres to provide space for repair shops and enterprises such as job-printing.

Objectives of Industrial Estates: The objectives underlying the establishment of industrial estates in India are as follows:

- to encourage the growth of small-scale industries;
- to shift small scale industries from congested areas to estate premises with a view to increasing their productivity;
- to achieve decentralised development in small towns and large villages;
- to encourage growth of ancillary industries in the townships, surrounding major industrial undertakings, both in public and private sector; and
- to faster the development of industry as well as entrepreneurship by providing economies and incentives.

Lessons of Experience: According to the Development Commissioner of Small-Sea Industries, the following lessons of experience could be drawn for future:

1. Industrial estates have to be properly co-ordinated with the broader development programme. They have to be not only an integral part, of the industry development programme but also of the overall economic development programme of the a region.

2. Industrial estates should be planned with a view to developing them into focal points of healthier industrial growth in an area rather than as a cluster of merely inward looking, group of production units. They are to be so designed and managed that may, later be in a position to provide necessary common service facilities, technical advice, guidance etc., to other industrial units in the area.

3. Homogeneity (rather than heterogeneity) is to be the guiding criterion while selecting industrial units. This would lead to better planning and utilisation of common facilities, inter-firm co-operation and inter-linked development.

4. While planning an industrial estate, due consideration is to be given to "secondary growth" effect in order to regulate any haphazard growth around the estates.

5. Location of an industrial estate is to be decided only on techno-economic considerate A techno-economic feasibility study should always precede the setting up of an estates.

6. While planning industrial estates in an area uniform pattern need not be followed, organisational structure in a particular area/region may be adjusted taking into consideration factors such as special requirements of an area, economic developments, availability of skills, talents and enterprise, level of development of the region etc.

7. Instead of building sheds in advance of demand, sheds may be built on the expressed demand as revealed at the time of conducting techno-economic or feasibility studies.

8. Elaborate and costlier construction has to be avoided and instead, functional types of sheds at cheaper rates may be provided.

9. When private initiative is ready, or the success of industrial estates has been demonstrated by one or more examples, government may confine its role to prescribing minimum factory standards, etc., and increasingly associate the entrepreneurs in the work of construction and maintenance of buildings.

10. To keep construction costs to the minimum, adequate attention should be paid to reduce the cost by improving design efficiency, increasing the size coverage reducing to the minimum the area allotted for on-factory purposes. The scope for reducing expenditure and non-development and administrative activities in the estates may also be explored and the consequent implications of cost of construction on may be kept in view.
11. In backward and rural areas greater efforts would have to be made to stimulate local entrepreneurship. The industrial estates in such areas have to play promotional role and act as pace-setters in the process of industrial development besides guiding the entrepreneurs in selecting the right lines of manufacture. It may also be necessary to offer additional incentives for locating industrial units. These incentives may be in the shape of concessional credit, rebates, in various taxes, preferential, allotment of scarce raw materials etc. The industrial estates in backward areas have also to be nursed over longer periods and provided with adequate inducements to counter-balance the inherent disadvantages from which they suffer. The concessions could be given preferably as a 'package deal' on a tapering basis.
12. The selection of products to be manufactured in the industrial estates should be in accordance with other development programme, *viz.* mechanisation of agriculture, utilisation of agriculture produce, electrification, items of mass consumption, etc.
13. While general purpose industrial estates are very useful for backward and rural areas in urban areas functional or special types of industrial estates may be preferred in view of the emphasis on modernisation, ancillary developments etc.

An industrial estate is a method of organising, housing and servicing industry for an orderly development. It is considered as a multipurpose tool supposed to take care of provision of suitable factory premises utilities, facilities and services, economy in the investment on social overheads and the increased scope for inter-servicing and inter-trading development of complementarity in production and creation of the spirit of co-operation, decentralisation of industry for development of backward areas, more industrialisation, achieving a specific locational pattern, town planning, etc. In short, it accelerates the integrated development of small-scale industries in the country.

Ancillary Industries

A balanced industrial development consistent with social justice calls for diffused ownership and control and also decentralised growth of industries. This is possible only if new entrepreneurship is developed. The process ancillarisation is one of the most handy methods of encouraging new entrepreneurs to set up small scale units. This is so because the running of ancillary industry does not give rise to complex problems which the uninitiated new entrepreneur will have to face, if he is to run an independent manufacturing unit. Also, ancillarisation makes it possible for him to establish a coherent relationship with small and large units. It is in these circumstances that ancillaries can provide a strong and widespread base for industrial development.

A major problem faced by ancillary units is their vulnerability to variations in demand. When the large scale manufacturer producing end product face slackness in demand the ancillary unit supplying the components is hit hard and may have to remain practically idle until the demand for the end product revives. Since the production apparatus in the ancillary units is highly specialized and tailored to meet the requirements of a particular assembly, it is not possible to switch over to any other item without incurring losses on account of machinery installed.

An ancillary unit, therefore, is a "Captive unit" with no alternative outlet. Its difficulties are often aggravated by delay in the payment of bills. During times of financial stringency, there is a tendency on the part of the parent firms to squeeze the ancillary units by giving "themselves the credit through non-payment of bills. A survey of industries in Japan revealed that only eight percent of the firms received payment within sixty days and that the remaining ninety two percent received it after the lapse of sixty days to one hundred and fifty days. In this particular respect, therefore ancillary units are in more vulnerable position, than small scale industrial units. A small scale industrial unit producing consumer items or other products will be able to make quick adjustments in its production plan as well as product design in order to minimise the adverse impact of a fall in demand. It may consider diversifying its activity with marginal addition to its machinery and/or equipment. It may even supply its products to other markets if the traditional markets fail but ancillary units are tied to the "apron strings" of one or two specific large scale units and often find it extremely difficult to make such adjustments. As a result they get adversely affected. While ancillary units suffer from these disabilities, they are free from the usual worries about the marketing of their products. An ancillary unit produces for a pre-determined market because production is effected against advance orders. It may be provided with scarce raw materials or even finance by the parent firm depending upon the type of relationship between the two and during periods of rising demand and plentiful orders, the ancillary unit can continue to operate with hardly a problem.

In India, unlike other countries, the ancillaries sponsored by large units, suffer from a major handicap. They lean too heavily on the large units. This dependence may be, unavoidable in the initial stage of development, but the ancillary should be able to stand on its own legs after a time, which would be possible only if the accent is placed on product improvement, cost reduction and the development of export outlets, especially when the ancillary product is able to meet the requirements of the replacement market abroad.

Factors Affecting Ancillarisation

Recently, there has been a growing trend toward ancillarisation, due to the series of the rapid developments that have taken place in the industrial structure in the country. The various factors affecting ancillarisation are:

1. The size of the operations of several industrial units has increased enormously, with the result that they are compelled to sub-contract some of the items of production ancillaries. During the 1950s, these industrial units were set up, so that the production of all the components against the stipulated targets might be met in terms of the licenses granted to them. In those days, there were few ancillary units adequately equipped to produce the components according to specifications. But during 1960s, a large number of small scale units, which were capable of producing a variety of items emerged with the result that large scale manufacturers developed enough confidence in them to assign the production of specific items to these units.
2. It was more convenient for large scale manufacturers to get the ancillary units to produce certain items for them with the growing complexity of management, the large scale manufacturer can now concentrate on the problems of organization, marketing, finance etc., rather than fritter away his energies on finding raw materials and framing production plans for the manufacture of the several minor items which go in the final assembly. For example, a bicycle manufacturer does not have to bother about buying and stocking of rubber used in the production of pedals; he prefers to get this items supplied to him by an ancillary units.
3. Large scale manufacturers can economies on transport cost, storage space etc. by sub contracting rather than by producing the same components by themselves.
4. It is economic to have some items manufactured by ancillary units because the cost of these items is higher when they are fabricated by large scale manufacturers.
5. By sub-contracting a large scale manufacturer is able to insulate himself against fluctuations in the prices of raw materials over a period of time by entering in to contracts for the supply of these items. A more accurate assessment of the input cost as well as the returns on manufacture is possible is if the components are available at fixed price.

All these facts underscore the points that the development of ancillaries and their growing popularity have been well supported by economic and management considerations.

REVIEW OF LITERATURE

In this section, an attempt has been made to review the previous studies carried out in relation to the Small and Tiny industries sector.

McConnel and Peter[1] (1963) conducted an empirical study among 248 small manufacturing concerns in Nebraska to establish the relationship between growth and technological research, product diversification and product differentiation. The study revealed that over two-thirds of the respondent firms had made some provision for formal or informal research for keeping pace with technological advancement. Twenty eight per cent of the respondents were found to have engaged themselves in formal research. Formal internal research activity was more frequently confined to certain industries such as industries engaged in electrical machinery, paper and allied products and transportation equipment. It was found that there was no correlation between the volume of sales and the expenditure on research.

The survey conducted by the Central Small Industries Organization (1969), which was set up by the Administrative Reforms Commission revealed that on an average only 20 per cent of the credit needs of the small industries were met through institutional sources[2].

Kopardekar[3] (1974) attributed the unutilized excess capacity in small firms to lack of finance. The lack of finance, especially, the shortage in the working capital led to the inefficient utilization of the installed capacity. Inadequate funds usually led to inconsistent operations among the small-scale units. Many units were not in a position to apportion funds to provide sufficient amounts for the fixed and working capital.

Nag[4] (1978) in his study, reviewed the functioning of the small-scale sector, and brought to light the growing mortality of the small-scale industries. He urged the public sector to rescue the small-scale sector in the larger interests of the many skilled and unskilled people employed in these various small enterprises. A great responsibility for the public sector in the form of direct participation in entrepreneurial activities was found to be very essential for ensuring the balanced growth of the industry in the future.

G.K. Moorthy[5], (1980) focused his attention on the financing of the small-scale industries in the Rayalaseema region of Andhra Pradesh. His emphasis was on the role of the Government agencies, financial institutions and commercial banks in augmenting adequate finance for the small-scale sector.

V.S. Mahajan[6] (1980) focused his attention on the critical evaluation of the government assistance and the policy measures adopted by the Government to protect the small-scale industries. He conducted a survey at Moga to assess the impact of the Government's assistance on the growth of the small-scale industries. The units which produced agricultural implements were taken up for investigation and it was concluded that the small-scale units were not dependent on Government assistance only. They flourished mainly because of a sudden spurt in demand for their products and through the initial investments made by them from out of their own funds or through their borrowed funds.

A.H. Advani[7] (1981) analysed the growth of the small-scale industries during the period 1972-1979 with reference to the growth in the number of units, fixed capital, employment, output and the total value added. The study covered all the states as well as the union territories. Based on his macro analysis, he concluded that for the economy as a whole, the figures were highly impressive. According to the report of the Reserve Bank of India, the total number of sick units in 1979 was found to be 20,700. In Kerala, 66 per cent of the units were reported sick, in Bihar it was 55 per cent, in West Bengal it was 50 per cent, in Andhra Pradesh it was 30 per cent and in Uttar Pradesh it was 27 per cent. These states exhibited a very high level of incidence of sickness among the small industries. Madras entrepreneurs found faulty planning and omnibus assistance as the major reasons for the growing sickness among the small industries. They blamed the Government agencies for their lack of response.

J.C. Sandesara[8] (1982) analysed the incentives offered and their impact on the small-scale industries. The Government of India, the State Government and the agencies sponsored by them for the development of the small-scale sector initiated a number of special programmes over a long period. The objective of the study was to evaluate one of such assistance progammes namely, long-term finance provided by the State Finance Corporation in Bombay, Thane, Jaipur, Hyderabad and the Secunderabad areas. The evaluation was conducted in terms of the impact of finance on the assisted units, as judged by their financial and economic performance as against some other units, which had not received such assistance. Ten product groups, namely, metal products, machine tools, paper, industrial fasteners, printing press, chemicals, agricultural implements, casting, electronics and plastics were included for the study. The major hypothesis of the study was that the sample units might show a better performance compared to the control units at a given point of time.

It was found that profitability, productivity, value added to fixed assets and the surplus to the total assets of the control units disclosed better results in a majority of the units of the different product groups. In the case of surplus per worker, wages per worker and total assets per worker, the sample units indicated a better level of performance. As regards the overall position, it was found that the performance of sample units was not superior to that of the control units in all the categories of industries.

Shambo Prasad[9] (1981-83) undertook a macro level study related to particular regions. The regional studies focused their attention on the problems which were faced by the small-scale sector units of the concerned regions. An examination by the researcher revealed that the problems faced by the small industries located in the different regions were different because of certain basic differences in the different geographical regions. The small-scale units of the underdeveloped regions had more problems than the small-scale sector units of the developed regions. Moreover, the nature of the problem in the undeveloped regions differed from those of the developed regions.

S.K. Goyal[10] (1984) in his study, "Small-scale sector and Big Business", pointed out that the number of areas reserved for the small-scale sector have no significance. He estimated the changes in the share of the output and briefly commented on the structure of the exports of the assisted SSI sector units. Further, as there were reportedly an equal number of industrial units which had not registered themselves with the State Directorate of Industries (SDI's), the size of the assisted SSI sector units were to be assessed only in relation to the total manufacturing capacity, according to the researcher.

Edapen[11] (1984) in his study found that, between 1961 and 1981, the share of employment in the household industries had declined. He recognized the fact that the non-household sector could not be treated equally with the factory or the modern sector, as it represented a higher form of industrial organization. A sub-sector of the non-factory non-household segment, which was generally referred to as the small unregistered workshop was found by him to be different. A rising trend in the non-factory non-household segment was observed by him in his study.

Sinha[12] (1985) in a study of about 100 small scale enterprises in Patna, highlighted the problems and bottlenecks faced by the small enterprises in their path of growth. He reported that the major problems faced by them were the procurement of adequate financial resources and the non-availability of raw materials at reasonable prices. He attempted to explain the patterns of growth of the different categories of industries in terms of the utilization of their installed capacity, the expansion of the markets, and finally through their margin of profits. Ninety three per cent of the sample units studied by him expressed their unwillingness to expand the size of their units and were not generally satisfied with the prospects for their growth.

N. Thanulingam Nadar[13] (1985) made a study of the small-scale industry and its inter-relationship with the large scale industry in 1980. The study proved to be a worth while experiment as it became evident from the study that:

(i) the mean inter-relationship score for the small-scale engineering units in Coimbatore lay between 32.37 and 44.79. This revealed that the inter-relationship of the small-scale units with large- scale ones in the Coimbatore region was not much encouraging;

(ii) the technical qualifications of the small-scale entrepreneurs, their nearness to the large-scale units, the training facilities made available in the large-scale units, the amounts due from the large-scale units to the smaller units and issue of orders by the large-scale units to the small-scale units were the major factors which influenced the degree of inter-relationship;

(iii) the goodwill of the business and the quick disposal of the finished products were the two benefits which were enjoyed by the units having a low degree of inter-relationship.

Goldan[14] (1986) in his study found that the growth rate in labour productivity in the small-scale sector was lower than that of the large-scale sector but it was found that the small-scale industries did not experience a fall in capital productivity as was the case with the units in the large scale sector. It was also found that there was no marked upward or downward trend in the capital intensity of the units in the small-scale sector.

A study of the small-scale enterprises carried out by Ian D. Little[15] (1987) examined the relative factor intensity, productivity and economic efficiency in five industries engaged in producing shoes, printing, soap, machine tools and metal carting. This study revealed that the technical efficiency differentials among the firms were positively associated with the Total Factor Productivity. The other variables contributing to productive efficiency in one or more of the industries indicated that the age of the enterprise, the advantage of capital stock, the level of experience, the level of managerial education and their training were the other factors which contributed to productive efficiency.

N.Durairaj and M.Soundara Nageswaran[16], (1988) in their study "Entrepreneurship in small-scale industries in Paramakudi

Taluk", attempted to examine the role of the entrepreneurs in the small-scale industries. Though it was a micro level study, it threw much light on the social profile of the entrepreneurs in the small-scale industries units and disclosed the problems faced by them.

Kalchetty Eresi[17] (1989) in his study pointed out that the lack of self finance for the additional capital requirements of the productive units was more common among the smaller units. The reason was that they lack the capacity to offer sufficient security for their loans and their external references were suspected, when they desired to borrow.

S. Gangadharan[18] (1989) stated that the root cause of the sickness in small-scale industries was the outdated technology adopted by them and the misuse of the soft loans obtained for modernization. The findings were confirmed by B.G. Patel (1988), Tiwari (1987), M.A. Khan (1990) and R.N. Krishnan (1993). The inability to modernize and the overall stagnation in per capita demand have also added to the intensity of the sickness among the small-scale units.

Neelamegam[19] (1990) in his article on "Small Business Financing", emphasized the fact that the small firms had suffered much for want of capital. Inadequate capital had resulted in lesser investments on labour saving devices, resulting in lesser productivity and low levels of profit. The inadequacy of capital had also contributed to the short life span of the small-scale firms.

Vaidyanathan[20] (1991) treated the small-scale industry as an equivalent of the non-factory sector industries and found that nearly three fourths of the addition in the manufacturing non-factory industry was contributed by such types of industries. He stated that this was a reflection of the shift of the industries from the household to the non-household sector. He also stated that it was perhaps better to approximate the small-scale sector to the non-household non-factory segment of the manufacturing sector.

Bhagwan Prasad[21] (1992) in his study stated that the SSI sector had witnessed a rapid expansion in production as well as in employment, in the past 15 years. The rise of the food products industry was found to be the most dramatic feature in the structure of the SSIs as recorded by the census. The total number of units in the food products industry had increased from 6,600 in 1972 to 96, 100 in 1987-88.

Sandesara[22] (1993) treated the enterprises which were eligible for Government assistance under the purview of the Small Industries Development Organisation (SIDO) as the small-scale sector. Based on the data pertaining to such units collected from the two censuses, he argued that during the period 1972-73 to 1987-88 productivities of both labour and capital had increased. Structural changes had taken place in the form of increased employment, value additions and increased shares of fixed capital in the industrial groups of food, textiles and services. He also noted the poor performance of the units producing exclusively reserved products and he attributed this feature to the possibility that reservation might have attracted more units, compared to the other small-scale industries and also to the continuation of the productive activity by the inefficient producers.

Chandra, *et al.*, (1993)[23] in their study, found that the importance of the small-scale sector could be positively emphasized in view of its potential for creating employment on the assumption of a low capital output ratio. The employment generating capacity of the small-scale and the village industries was observed to be higher by eight times than that of the large-scale industries. With the increasing mechanization of the SSI units this potential might get lowered.

Reddy[24] (1994) pointed out that the small-scale sector which registered high rates of growth since the 1970s was affected by the new economic reforms which harmed the small-scale units in more ways than one. Despite its impressive records of production, the growth of employment was a mere three per cent increase. It was widely believed that a shift in favour of the growth of the small-scale industry would result in the generation of more employment and also bring about a more equitable distribution of income and wealth.

Nanjundan[25] (1994) emphasized the fact that the use of the micro processors brought about a technological revolution and affected the manufacturing methods in the enterprises in the developed countries in a significant way which tended to favour small-scale production. This technological revolution known as the Flexible Manufacturing System (FMS) would become the most important factor affecting the small-scale industries in the developing countries in the next one or two decades. It might be too early to judge the efficacy of the strategy to bring about the desired outcome. But rapid technological changes taking place in all the countries of the world were expected to revitalize the small-scale sector. It could be perceived that the future prospects of the small-scale industry would be based on competition, productivity and efficiency.

S.P. Kashyap[26] (1995) pointed out that the small-scale sector has helped in generating large scale employment, production of wage goods and increase in levels of income in a fairly dispersed manner and has succeeded in mobilising dormant skills and resources. It has also enhanced the entrepreneurship skills, developed village economies and aided the process of backward area development. It also has played an important role in the overall process of industrialization and economic development.

T.L.N. Swamy[27], (1995) in his study "Eighth Five Year Plan – Role of Small Industry", concluded that the small-scale industry has exhibited a high growth of productivity and a low growth of employment during 1980-90 compared to the period 1973-1980 in India. It might be due to the fact that the small-scale industry became more and more capital intensive during the eighties, since use of capital has grown at a higher rate compared to the growth in employment. Moreover, the growth in capital was also closely associated with technological advancement which reduced the employment of labour.

M. Prasad Kumar and S. K. Narayanan[28] (1995) made an attempt to identify the causes of sickness in the industries in Coimbatore. According to them the shortage of power, the inadequacy of raw materials, and the lack of finance were the major causes for the sickness of the small industries. Further the diversion of funds and the lack of qualified and competent skills had also contributed to the ill-health of the small-scale industries.

M. Srinivasalu Bayineni[29] in his article on the "Development of Small Scale Industries", said that the economic prosperity of a developing economy like India depended much upon the integration of its agricultural activities with those of the industries. The dynamic features of the development of the agro-based industries were of paramount importance in all rural reconstruction programmes. The strengthening of the agro-industries would help the economy in its attempt to bring about Rural Industrialization.

Nanjundan[30] (1996) in his article on "Economic Reforms and SSI Units" published in the Economic and Political Weekly said that the composition and terms of reference of the expert committee to review the policies and programmes for the SSI sector were a clear indication of what was expected of the committee in respect of finance, technology, regulation and entrepreneurship.

Sidharthan[31] (1998) in his article on "The Budget and Industrial Development" published in the Economic and Political Weekly said that the Budget of 1997-98 had failed to focus on the institutions that were capable of promoting the growth of the most dynamic sector in terms of employment and technology. The focus of the Budget was on large corporate firms whose role in employment and manufacturing was diminishing in most of the countries.

Rajendran[32] (1998) in his article on "Small-scale Industrial Policies" published in the Southern Economist said that the most significant aspect of the small-scale industry was the stimulation of the economic activity through a large number of far reaching and able entrepreneurs. He was considering the Small Scale Industrial Policies and the growth of the SSI units, after the year 1991. According to him small industries have grown because of their significant position in attaining the major objective of self-reliance, creating wide employment opportunities and raising the levels of output, income and also the standard of living.

Vikram Chadha[33] (1999) in his article pointed out that the small industry which was predominant in the Indian industrial scene needed urgently an up gradation of its production technologies and methods in order to survive in the environment of the emerging competitive pressure from large-scale industries. The problems encountered by the SSIs ranged from shortage of credit and finance, underutilization of capacities, lack of competitiveness in input and product markets, to the inadequacy in respect of infrastructural facilities such as power and transport.

The Economic Unit of the Indian Institute of Public Opinion[34] (1999) suggested that indigenous as well as imported raw materials should be made available to the small- scale sector at reasonable prices. Organizations such as the State Trading Corporation and the State Export Corporation should take the entire responsibility for providing raw materials and also for the marketing of the products of the small sectors. It was necessary to incorporate special export promotion cells in organizations created for the development of the small-scale sector in trade fairs and exhibitions in overseas markets. It was necessary to encourage the SSI units to participate in the overseas exhibitions free of cost and the expenses of their personnel at these exhibitions should be heavily subsidized by the Government.

M.G. Basavaraja[35] (1999) in his study on "Role of SSI: A study of Karnataka", stated that the SSI entrepreneurs should unite and fight for a swadeshi movement and try to create a public opinion in favour of the indigenous goods. In Karnataka, there were about 2,35,000 registered SSI units with a capital investment of about Rs. 3000 crores. They manufactured more than 8000 items. The total output was estimated at about Rs. 20,000 crores per annum. About 39 per cent of the total exports from Karnataka were being made by the SSI units. The SSI sector received much emphasis in the 1999-2000 budget of the State Government, on account of the fact that this sector was labour-intensive, and contributed a lot towards the development of the traditional and non-traditional exports. In the newly emerging business scenario, the Government which in former times, used to come to the rescue of the SSI would find it very difficult to continue and extend such policies for helping the SSIs. Taking into consideration all these factors, the SSI sector should seriously look into issues like quality improvement, cost reduction, appropriate technology, and large scale marketing for their very survival.

Robin Mukherjee, *et al.*, (1999)[36] in their study attempted to examine the growth performance of the small-scale industries in West Bengal over the past 25 years. For this purpose, alternative growth rates were calculated by them for the SSI units as well as for their employment potential for each district. Broadly speaking, the alternative measures of growth rates presented more or less the same situation. However, there exists much scope for increasing the number of units as well as employment. On the other hand, the year-to-year growth rate did not increase much over a period of time for any of the districts.

Sunday L. Owualah[37], (1999), presents the evidence that promoting entrepreneurship consciously among youths can be an effective way of tackling unemployment within this group. This conclusion was drawn from the analysis of survey data collected from a stratified sample of loan beneficiaries of the Small Scale Industries and Graduate Employment Programme in Nigeria. This programme is one of four programmes of the National Directorate of Employment (NDE) set up in Nigeria in 1987 to encourage and assist unemployed youths to establish and operate their own small scale firms. The analysis shows that an average of four new jobs was created by each of the respondent firms in the first four years of the programme. It further reveals that the firms achieved an appreciable growth in their assets, while previous training, experience and personal inclinations of their owners largely influenced the choice of types of small-scale firms that were established.

M.H.Balasubrahmany[38] (1999-2000) in his study, "India's Small Industry Policy in the 90's: Waning Protectionism", attempted to probe into the redefined India's small industries policy of the 90's. He reviewed the strategy evolved for the development of the small-scale industry and proposed a few policy measures. He concluded that the characteristics of the small-scale enterprises were favourable for the achievement of the desirable socio-economic objectives which made the Indian Policy makers to bring the small-scale sector into the central focus in their economic development strategy. The subsequent thrust on strengthening the institutional framework for the promotion of small-scale industries and incentives provided for the protection of small industries became the distinctive feature of India's small industries policy.

John B.Miner[39] (2000) follows upon previous research among established entrepreneurs indicating that a four-way psychological typology (i.e. personal achievers, real managers, expert idea generators, and empathic super sales people) predicts firm growth. It extends support for the typology to the venture initiation phase and to a student population. The results confirm that those students who are characterized by one or more of the types are more likely to be entrepreneurs after graduation. Measures of entrepreneurial propensities and skill in business plan preparation both obtained prior to graduation are also predicted by the typology. As a test of the basic theory, this research provides substantial support. It also extends the domain of that theory to incorporate the enterprise start-up phase.

Sue Marlow[40], (2001) says, there is little information regarding how, or whether, small-firm owners use their own and their management team's skills and experiences as part of a strategic approach for achieving business goals, durability and, if desired, growth. It would appear that firms which do utilize a strategic approach, however informal, are more likely to endure. Design school strategic management techniques have traditionally been sited in, and associated with, corporate enterprises and, as such, would not be readily accessible to most small firms. Recent critics of this design school approach argue that strategic activity, in the majority of firms, is far more intuitive and flexible than previously believed and describe this emergent approach to strategy.

Tomas M.Hult, *et al.*, (2003)[41], examined the role of entrepreneurship in building cultural competitiveness in organizations. Cultural competitiveness is defined as the degree to which organizations are predisposed to detect and fill gaps between what the market desires and what is currently offered. It is examined in this study as the collective result of interactions among four variables: entrepreneurships, innovativeness, market orientation, and organizational learning. Among these variables entrepreneurship represents the most influential and proactive means of developing a market-based culture. However, the role of entrepreneurship differs depending on organizational type. Based on data from a sample of 764 organizations, superior performance occurs when certain aspects of cultural competitiveness fit each of four organizational types. Specially, large and young organizations achieve strong performance by focusing directly on entrepreneurship. In the other organizational types, entrepreneurship has an indirect effect on performance.

Duane Ireland, *et al.*, (2003)[42] say that Strategic Entrepreneurship (SE) involves simultaneous opportunity-seeking and advantage-seeking behaviours and results in superior firm performance. On a relative basis, small entrepreneurial ventures are effective in identifying opportunities but are less successful in developing competitive advantage needed to appropriate value from those opportunities. In contrast, large, established firms often are relatively more effective in establishing competitive advantages but are less able to identify new opportunities.

Rolland LeBrasseur, *et al.*, (2003)[43] utilized an empirical study of 145 new venture start-ups to explore a model of growth momentum as measured by sales. The primary interests are the relationship among pre-startup activities, intended and actual business expansion activities, and early stage performance. Results indicated that the sales level achieved in the second year had a positive correlation with *(i)* the breadth of pre-startup activities; and *(ii)* the range of expansion activities. Business performance had a negative correlation with the firm's relative dependence on the technical skills of the owner-manager. In addition, the study revealed a consistent gap between owner-managers' expansion intentions and actual expansion.

Cantner, *et al.*, (2004)[44] says that the competition driven innovation central to technical progress and responsible for keeping large enterprises vibrant, however, creates peculiar difficulties for the new firm. As technical progress accelerates, innovation becomes even more focused and competitive. New products spring up and disappear before people have a chance to look at them and the inventors have time to exploit the gains of their creation.

Ayda Eraydin, Bilge Armatli-Koroglu[45] (2005), Elaborating on the literature on industrial districts, this paper suggests that innovation and networking are the two key issues, which provide the new generation industrial clusters' competitive capacity in the globalization process. The paper presents the findings on the innovative and networking capabilities of the three important industrial clusters of Turkey based on the data collected from the sample firms in each of these industrial clusters through in-depth interviews. The findings clearly show the importance of local and national networking as well as global linkages and confirm the positive relation between intensity of local networking and innovativeness. Moreover, the paper provides evidence that firms within global networks have higher numbers of innovations than firms with higher intensity of locally embedded linkages.

Vijay Vayas[46] (2005) outlined the essence of the strategies for the survival and growth of new ventures. According to him the productivity, profit and growth of an enterprise are closely linked to its ability to innovate successfully. The accelerating technological change, however, has made innovation increasingly difficult for the small business. Notwithstanding the high profile success of a few start-ups, innovative confrontations with mature business [sic] a large number of ordinary entrepreneurs are losing in this battle of the unequals. The very spirit of entrepreneurship embodied in ever sprouting small enterprises is endangered by this trend. To counter it, a strategy of imitation facilitated entry and subsequent consolidation through incremental innovation should be targeted at the lower part of the value chain.

Joseph Andrew Kuzilwa[47] (2005) in his study had combined qualitative case studies and sample survey to assess the extent to which credit determined successful entrepreneurial activities. Credit has been instrumental to the success of the enterprise at different stages of the life of a business. Start-ups seemed to have been funded from own sources. Use of credit was made mainly for business expansion. Going by the indicators of survival, growth, output and employment creation for family members, finance has a positive impact on entrepreneurial activities. The study also showed that many of the problems faced by entrepreneurs were not related to credit, but rather the result of macro and institutional constraints, including demand and supply problems, tax regimes and energy problems [sic]. The study also suggested the need for credit level to be provided on the basis of business viability and the absorptive capacity of the firm rather than predetermined ceilings that do not address the real needs of the enterprise.

K.R.G. Nair[48] (2006), in his study "Characteristics of Entrepreneurs: An Empirical Analysis" examines the socio-economic and attitudinal characteristics of entrepreneurs on the basis of primary data for the state of Kerala. It does not appear that business acumen runs in families nor is there evidence that religion has an impact on entrepreneurship. The economic status of the family, age, technical education, training and work experience in a similar or related field seem to favour entrepreneurship. In comparison to the rest of the population, entrepreneurs tend to be more innovative in their attitude, but do not seem to have greater faith in the internal locus of control.

T.J.Kamalanabhan, *et al.*, 2006[49] in their study "Evaluation of Entrepreneurial Risk–Taking using Magnitude of Loss Scale" attempts to distinguish entrepreneurs on their risk taking propensity. Data on two measures of risk-taking propensity were collected from entrepreneurs and non-entrepreneurs. While the groups did not differ significantly on risk–taking propensity as measured by the Choice Dilemma Questionnaire, entrepreneurs and non-entrepreneurs differed significantly on the Magnitude of Loss Questionnaire. Similarly, entrepreneurial aspirants differed significantly from the non-entrepreneurial group. These results highlight the significance of loss, an important aspect in risk-taking, which is often ignored in entrepreneurial and managerial studies. The risk in business ventures which has been the main stumbling block for many is not the low probability of success but the high stakes involved in entrepreneurship.

REFERENCES

1. Campbell Mac Connel and W.C. Peter, 1963. *Research Activity, Product Diversification and Product Differentiation by Small Manufactures in Nebraska,* University of Nebraska.
2. Administrative Reforms Commission, 1969. *Report of the Working Group on Small Scale Sector,* Simla: The Government of India Press, p. 68.
3. Kopardekar, D.1974. *Small Scale Industries,* Pune: G.Y. Rane Prakasham.
4. Nag, A. 1978 "Growth of the Small-scale Sector: An Assessment", *Yojana,* pp. 27-30.
5. Moorthy, G.K. 1980. *Financing of Small Scale Industries in Rayalaseema Region,* Ph.D., Thesis, Andhra Pradesh, Waltair.
6. Mahajan, V.S. 1980. "Small and Tiny Units", *Economic Times,* October 2.
7. Advani, A.H. 1981. "Small Scale Sector Cracking Up", *Business India,* March 2-15, No. 78.
8. Sandesara, J.C. 1982. "Incentives and Their Impact on Small Industries", *Economic and Political Weekly,* Vol. 17, No. 48.
9. Shamboo Prasad, 1981-83. *Role of Small Scale Industries in a Developing Region with Special Reference to Bihar,* Magadh University, Bihar.
10. Goyal, S.K. 1984. *Small Scale Sector and Big Business,* New Delhi: Indian Institute of Public Administration.
11. Edapen, Mridul, 1984."Structure of Manufacturing Workforce, A Preliminary Analysis of Emerging Tendencies", *Economic and Political Weekly,* Vol. 19.
12. Ramesh P. Sinha, 1985. *Problems of Small Scale Industries,* New Delhi: Janak Prakashan.
13. Thanulingam Nadar, N. 1985. *Small Scale Industry Inter-Relationship with Large-scale Industry-Coimbatore,* Rainbow Publications.
14. Goldan, B.N. 1986. *Productivity Growth in Indian Industry,* New Delhi: Allied Publishers.

15. Ian D. Little, 1987. *Small Manufacturing Enterprises, A Comparative Study of India and other Countries*, New York: Oxford University Press.

16. Durariraj N. and Soundara Nageswaran, M. 1988. *Entrepreneurship in Small-scale Industries in Paramakudi Taluk*, Tirunelveli: Doss Printers.

17. Kalchetty Eresi, 1989. *Management of Finance in Small Scale Industries*, Allahabad: Vohra Publishers and Distributors.

18. Gangadharan, S. 1989. "Textile Industry – Modernisation Pace and Crisis Deepening", *The Economic Times*, Research Bureau, pp.1-12.

19. Neelamegam, R. 1990. "Small Business Financing", *The Economic Times*, January 3.

20. Vaidyanthan, A. 1991. "Cottage and Small Industries: Policy and Performance", *Fortune India*, June 16.

21. Bhagwan Prasad, 1992. "Organization Structure of Small-scale Sector", *Financial Express*, November.

22. Sandesara, J.C. 1993."Modern Small Industry 1972 and 1987-88: Aspects of Growth and Structural Change", *Economic and Political Weekly*, Vol. XXVIII. No. 5.

23. Chandra, J. Narayana Rao, V. and Visweswara Rao, K. 1993. "Small Scale Sector- Prospects and Problems", *Business Spectrum*, November.

24. Reddy, P.N. 1997. "Small Scale Industry: Moving Towards Viability", *Business Line*, July.

25. Nanjundan, S. 1980. *Changing Role of Small-Scale Sector in India's Economic Policies, (1947-77)*, ed. by J.N. Mongia, New Delhi: Allied Publishers Pvt. Limited.

26. Kashyap, S.P. 1995. Emerging Industrial Policy Reforms: Implication for Small Size Enterprises", *Productivity*, Vol. 36, No. 1.

27. Swamy, T.L.N. 1995. "Eighth Five Year Plan – Role of Small Industry", *Productivity*, Vol. 36, No. 1.

28. Prasad Kumar, M. and Narayanan, S.K. 1995. "Industrial Sickness: A Case Study of Small Scale Engineering Units in Coimbatore", *Journal of Accounting and Finance*, Vol. 9, No. 1, pp. 62-67.

29. Srinivasalu Bayineni, M. 1996. "Development of Small Scale Industries", *Third Concept*, Vol. 1, No. 7, p. 43.

30. Nanjundan, 1996. "Economic Reforms and SSI Units", *Economic and Political Weekly*, Vol. XXXI, No. 5. p. 191.

31. Sidharthan, N. 1998. The Budget and Industrial Development, *Economic and Political Weekly*, Vol. XXXIII, No. 18, p. 36.

32. Rajendran, 1998. "Small Scale Industrial Policies", *Southern Economist*, Vol. 37, No. 17, p. 13.

33. Vikram Chadha, 1999."Financing the Modernisation of Small Industries in India: Opportunities and Constraints", *Southern Economist*, Vol. XXXVIII, No. 2.

34. Indian Institute of Public Opinion Economic Unit, 1999. "Export Potentiality and Small Scale Industries", *Monthly Public Opinion Surveys*, Vol. XLV, No. 3.

35. Basavaraja, M.G. 1999. "Role of SSIs: Study of Karnataka", *Southern Economist*, Vol. 38, No. 4.

36. Robin Mukherjee, Pranab Kumar Das and Uttam Kumar Bhattacharya, 1999. "Small Scale Industries in West Bengal 1971-97: Data Analysis for Study of Growth", *Economic and Political Weekly*, Vol. 36, No. 48, pp. M.157-M.161.

37. Sunday L.Owualah, 1999. "Tackling Youth Unemployment through Entrepreneurship", *International Small Business Journal*, Vol. 17, No. 3, pp. 49-59.

38. Balasubrahmany, M.H. 1999-2000. "India's Small Industry Policy in the 90's: Waning Protectionism", *The Indian Economic Journal*, Vol. 47, No. 2.

39. John B.Miner, 2000. "Testing a Psychological Typology of Entrepreneurship Using Business Founders", *The Journal of Applied Behavioral Science*, Vol. 36, No. 1, pp. 43-69.

40. Sue Marlow, 2001. "Investigating the Use of Emergent Strategic Human Resource Management Activity in the Small Firm", *Journal of Vocation Marketing*, Vol. 7, No. 2, pp. 135-148.

41. Thomas M.Hult, G. Charles C.Snow, Destan Kandemir, 2003. "The Role of Entrepreneurship in Building Cultural Competitiveness in Different Organisational Types", *Journal of Management*, Vol. 29, No. 3, pp. 401-426.

42. Duane Ireland, R. Michael A.Hitt, David G.Sirmon, 2003. "A Model of Strategic Entrepreneurship: The Construct and its Dimensions", *Journal of Management*, Vol. 29, No. 6, pp. 963-989.

43. Rolland LeBrasseur, Louis Zanibbi, Terrence J.Zinger, 2003. "Growth Momentum in the Early Stages of Small Business Start-Ups", *International Small Business Journal*, Vol. 21, No. 3, pp. 315-330.

44. Cantner, U. Guth, W. Nicklishc, A. and Weiland, T. "Competition in Innovation and Imitation: A Theoretical and Experimental Study," *www.mplew-jena.mpg.de/esi/disscussion*

45. Ayda Eradyin, Bilge Armatli-Koroglu, 2005. "Innovation, Networking and the New Industrial Clusters: The Characteristics of Networks and Local Innovation Capabilities in the Turkish Industrial Clusters", *Entrepreneurship & Regional Development*, Vol. 17, No. 4, pp. 237-266.

46. Vijay Vayas, 2005. "Imitation Incremental Innovation and Climb Down: A Strategy for Survival and Growth of New Ventures", *The Journal of Entrepreneurship*, Vol. 14, No. 2, pp. 103-116.

47. Joseph Andrew Kuzilwa, 2005. "The Role of Credit for Small Business Success: A Study of the National Entrepreneurship Development Fund in Tanzania", *The Journal of Entrepreneurship*, Vol. 14, No. 2, pp. 131-161.

48. Nair, K.R.G. 2006. "Characteristics of Entrepreneurs: An Empirical Analysis", *Journal of Entrepreneurship*, Vol. 15, No. 1, pp. 47-61.

49. Kamalanabhan, T.J. 2006. "Evaluation of Entrepreneurial Risk–Taking using Magnitude of Loss Scale" *Journal of Entrepreneurship*, Vol. 15, No. 1, pp. 37-46.

3

Forces Behind Entrepreneurial Development in Tiny Sector Industries

INTRODUCTION

The socio-economic and psychological profile of the respondent acts as a base for the personal factor leading to entrepreneurial development[1]. The social factors related to the family and the community has a bearing on entrepreneurship. The economic factors act as a base for financial support to develop entrepreneurship[2]. The psychological factors include the aspects of the personality of an individual to develop entrepreneurship[3]. In this chapter, an attempt has been made to analyse the socio-economic profile of the selected respondents such as age, education, sex, caste, nature of family, marital status, family size, earning members in the family, occupational background, personal income, family income, family expenditure and savings. Further, the personality traits include confidence, optimism, independence and the like have also been discussed. For better exposition the analysis has been divided into three heads as under:

(i) Socio-economic profile of the selected respondents;

(ii) Personality traits of the respondents; and

(iii) Factors influencing the development of the enterprise.

MEASUREMENT OF VARIABLES

The procedure for measuring the dependent and independent variables used in the study are given below.

Profile Variables

1. Age

The respondent completed years of age at the time of enquiry was considered for the study. The completed years of the respondents were classified into less than 30, 30-40, 41-50, and above 50. The scale developed by Venkatesan (2001)[4] with suitable modifications was used to measure the variable. The scoring procedure is given in Table 3.1

Table 3.1: Age of the Respondents

Sl. No.	*Age*	*Score*
1.	Less than 30	1
2.	30 – 40	2
3.	41 – 50	3
4.	Above 50	4

2. Educational Status

This refers to the educational status of the respondents. The sub-items are school level, college level and technical level. School level refers to schooling up to the higher secondary class (i.e. up to +2). College level includes under graduate and post graduate level education. Technical level includes formal and non formal technical education. The scoring procedure in the present study is given in Table 3.2

Table 3.2: Educational Status

Sl. No.	*Level of Education*	*Score*
1.	School Level	1
2.	College Level	2
3.	Technical	3

3. Sex

The sex of the respondents is classified as male and female. The score assigned to male and female are 1 and 2 respectively.

4. Social Class

The caste classification of the Tamil Nadu Government namely forward community, backward community, most backward community and schedule caste/tribe was followed in the present study and it is presented in Table 3.3.

Table 3.3: Caster Classification

Sl. No.	Caste	Score
1.	Forward Community (FC)	1
2.	Backward/Most Backward Community (BC/MBC)	2
3.	Scheduled Caste/Tribe (SC/ST)	3

5. Nature of Family

Nature of family indicates the family system. The family system is categorised into two namely nuclear and joint families. These two family systems are treated as dummy variables as done by Trivedi (1962)[5]. The score values for nuclear family and joint families are 1 and 2 respectively.

6. Marital Status

The marital status of the respondents indicates their status in the family at present. The marital status is classified into unmarried, married and widow/widower. The scoring procedure developed by Paulraj (1990)[6] was applied and it is presented in Table 3.4.

Table 3.4: Marital Status

Sl. No.	Marital Status	Score
1.	Unmarried	1
2.	Married	2
3.	Widow/Widower	3

7. Family Size

The size of the family refers to the number of individuals who are living together in a household. The scoring procedure developed by Trivedi (1962)[7] was adopted with suitable modifications.

Table 3.5: Family Size

Sl. No.	*Family Size*	*Score*
1.	Below 3	1
2.	3-5	2
3.	Above 5	3

8. Earning Members in the Family

The earning members are the family members who earn on daily, weekly or monthly basis. The number of earning members in the family is classified into one, two, three, four and more than four. The scale developed by Venkatesan (2001)[8] is followed in the present study.

Table 3.6: Earning Members in the Family

Sl. No.	*Earning Members Per Family*	*Score*
1.	One	1
2.	Two	2
3.	Three	3
4.	Four	4
5.	More than four	5

9. Occupational Background

Occupational background in the present study means the profession in which the father/husband of the respondent spends much of their time for a livelihood to maintain their family. The scoring procedure followed by Venkatesan (2001)[9] was adopted with suitable modifications.

Table 3.7: Occupational Background

Sl. No.	*Occupational Background*	*Score*
1.	Agricultural Labourer	1
2.	Farmer	2
3.	Non-agricultural labourer	3
4.	Government employee	4
5.	Private employee	5
6.	Micro entrepreneur	6

10. Material Possession

Material possession in this study means the total value of movable and immovable property belonging to the respondents excluding the value of lands. The schedule followed by Venkatesan (2001) was used with slight modifications. The scoring procedure is presented in Table 3.8.

Table 3.8: Marital Prosession

Sl. No.	*Material Possession*	*Score*
1.	Nil	1
2.	Below Rs. 50,000	2
3.	Rs. 50,000-1,00,000	3
4.	Rs. 1,00,000-2,00,000	4
5.	Above Rs. 2,00,000	5

11. Monthly Income

Monthly income means the income earned by the respondents from all possible sources in a month. The scoring procedure applied for monthly income among the respondents is given in Table 3.9.

12. Family Income

Family income means the income from all earning members living in a household from all possible resources in a month. The scoring procedure followed to measure family income in the present study is given in Table 3.10.

Table 3.9: Monthly Income

Sl. No.	Monthly Income (in Rs.)	Score
1.	Less than 1,000	1
2.	1,001-2,000	2
3.	2,001-3,000	3
4.	3,001-4,000	4
5.	Above 4,000	5

Table 3.10: Family Income

Sl. No.	Monthly Family Income (Rs.)	Score
1.	Below 3,000	1
2.	3,001-5,000	2
3.	Above 5,000	3

13. Family Expenditure

Family expenditure indicates the total amount spent on consumption and household necessities by the respondents. The scoring procedure followed to measure family expenditure is shown in Table 3.11.

Table 3.11: Monthly Family Expenditure

Sl. No.	Monthly Family Expenditure (Rs.)	Score
1.	Less than 2,000	1
2.	2,000-3,000	2
3.	3,001-4,000	3
4.	4,001-5,000	4
5.	Above 5,000	5

14. Monthly Savings

Savings is the difference between income and expenditure. Surplus income is the major source for potential savings. The monthly savings of the respondents are computed by taking the difference between the monthly income and the expenditure of the respondents. The scoring procedure followed to measure family savings is shown in Table 3.12

Table 3.12: Monthly Savings

Sl. No.	*Monthly Savings (Rs.)*	*Score*
1.	No Savings	1
2.	Less than 1,000	2
3.	1,000-2,000	3
4.	Above 2,000	4

Personality Traits

The personality traits of the respondents represent the psychological frame work of the respondents to know the business opportunities and to start and manage the business. Personality consists of so many psychological aspects. In the present study, fourteen personality variables namely, information seeking, mass media exposure, social participation, level of aspiration, attitude towards self-employment, scientific orientation, decision making ability, economic motivation, managerial ability, problem recognition, risk taking willingness, urban pull and extension contact were considered. Summated rating scale was used for measuring the variables (Edwards,1969).[10]

1. Information Seeking

Information seeking represents the mindset of the respondents to know about the business environment in the world which consists of so many aspects such as, entrepreneurship, entrepreneur development programmes and business opportunities in the locality. The following scoring procedure was used in the study.

2. Mass Media Exposure

Mass media exposure means that the respondents read newspapers, leaflets, bulletins, listen to programmes in radio, view television or educational films, attend exhibitions, field trips and witness demonstrations. The scoring system developed by Knight (1973)[11] was used in the study.

Table 3.13: Information Seeking

Sl. No.	*Information Seeking*	*Score*
1.	Knowing all aspects about the business and interested to know further	4
2.	Knowing all the aspects about the business	3
3.	Knowing something about the business	2
4.	Knowing very little about the business	1

Table 3.14: Mass Media Exposure

Sl. No.	*Frequency*	*Score*
1.	Regularly	4
2.	Occasionally	3
3.	Rarely	2
4.	Never	1

3. Social Participation

Social participation is the degree of involvement of the respondents in formal organizations. The following scoring procedure followed by Noor Jahan (1999)[12] was used in the study with slight modifications.

Table 3.15: Social Participation

Sl. No.	*Category*	*Score*
1.	Office bearer in many organisations	4
2.	Office bearer in any one organisation	3
3.	Member in many organisations	2
4.	Member in any one organisation	1
5.	None of the above	0
4.	Level of Aspiration	

The level of aspiration indicates the degree of inner urge to attain some special goal in one's life. The level of aspiration in the present study is measured by the following scoring procedure.

Table 3.16: Level of Aspiration

Sl. No.	*Category*	*Score*
1.	Knowing the specific goal and trying to achieve it	4
2.	Knowing the goal and trying to achieve it	3
3.	No goal but trying to do something	2
4.	No idea of goals and achievement	1

5. Attitude towards Self-employment

The respondents' attitude towards self-employment indicates their mind status to do any business. The scoring procedure adopted in this study is as follows:

Table 3.17: Attitude towards Self-employment

Sl. No.	*View on Self-employment*	*Score*
1.	Challenging	4
2.	Interesting	3
3.	Risky	2
4.	No other alternative	1

6. Scientific Orientation

Supe (1969)[13] defines scientific orientation as the degree to which a person was oriented towards the use of scientific methods. The scale developed by the same author was used in this study. The scoring procedure adopted is as follows.

7. Decision-making Ability

The decision making ability of the respondent is the art to decide on some solution when a problems arises in their life. The scoring procedure adopted in this study is as follows.

Table 3.18: Scientific Orientation

Sl. No.	Responses	Score
1.	Frequent changes according to the environment	4
2.	Moderate changes according to the environment	3
3.	Copied changes from others	2
4.	Rigidity	1

Table 3.19: Decision Making Ability

Sl. No.	Nature of decision taken	Score
1.	Consulting others who are related to the problem and justly decide on a solution	4
2.	Consult a few in the relevant field and decide	3
3.	Consult any family members or friends and decide	2
4.	Take own decision	1

8. Economic Motivation

Economic motivation means the relative value placed by the respondents to maximize the profit. It was measured with the help of the scale developed by Supe (1969) and followed by Meera (2001)[14]. The following scoring procedure was used.

Table 3.20: Economic Motivation

Sl. No.	Responses	Score
1.	Profit maximization through social orientation	4
2.	Profit maximization through customer satisfaction	3
3.	Profit maximization through increased sales	2
4.	Profit maximization through any thing possible	1

9. Managerial Ability

Managerial ability among the respondents is measured with the help of the activities which are required to manage others. The scale developed to measure managerial ability in the present study is the way in which the respondent manages an enterprise.

Table 3.21: Managerial Ability

Sl. No.	*Managerial Ability*	*Score*
1.	Co-ordination	4
2.	Controlling others	3
3.	Ask others to do it	2
4.	Personally do all the work	1

10. Problem Recognition

Problem recognition indicates the power of respondents to understand the problems in their business or life and take decisions according to the intensity of the problem. The scale developed to measure problem recognition in the present study is stated below.

Table 3.22: Problem Recognition

Sl. No.	*Opinion*	*Score*
1.	Analyse the problem and find the solution	4
2.	Ask others to solve it	3
3.	Worry about the problem	2
4.	Think it is fatal	1

11. Risk-taking Willingness

This refers to the degree to which an individual was oriented towards encountering risks and uncertainties in adopting new ideas in business. The risk orientation scale developed by Supe (1969)[15] was used in this study with necessary modifications.

Table 3.23: Risk-taking Willingness

Sl. No.	*View on profit*	*Score*
1.	Windfall	4
2.	Managerial functions	3
3.	Normally occurs in business	2
4.	No idea	1

12. Urban Pull

Urban pull indicates the proximity and attractions of the urban environment to the respondents. The urban setting attracts for several reasons independent life, self motivation, courage and opportunities. If the urban pull experienced by the respondents is high rationally, their personality traits may be improved. In the present study, the scale developed to measure urban pull is presented in Table 3.24

Table 3.24: Urban Pull

Sl. No.	*Access and Frequency of Visit*	*Score*
1.	Near and very frequent	4
2.	Near but less frequent	3
3.	Distant and very frequent	2
4.	Distant and less frequent	1

13. Extension Contact

This refers to the frequency of the respondents contact related to tiny entrepreneurship. The measurement was done on the frequency of contact. The scoring procedure adopted by Seema (1999)[16] was followed.

Table 3.25: Extension Contact

Sl. No.	*Frequency of Contact*	*Score*
1.	Very frequent	4
2.	Frequent	3
3.	Occasional	2
4.	Rare	1

Personality Index

The personality index of the respondent is prepared by the following formula.

$$\text{Personality Index (PI)} = \frac{\sum_{i=1}^{n} PSi}{\sum_{i=1}^{n} MSPi} \times 100 \qquad \ldots (3.1)$$

where,

PI = Personality Index

PS = Personality factors score

MSP = Maximum score of the personality factor

i...n = Number of personality factors

The scoring procedure adopted to rate the personality traits of the respondents in the present study is given below

Table 3.26: Personality Index

Sl. No.	*Personality Index*	*Score*
1.	Less than 20	1
2.	20 - 40	2
3.	41 - 60	3
4.	61 - 80	4
5.	Above 80	5

Entrepreneurship

Entrepreneurship among the respondents reflects their self-confidence, task orientation, risk bearing, leadership and originality. The above said aspects consist of their own components. All components are rated by a four point scale of score values 4, 3, 2 and 1. The scale value of each entrepreneurship variable is used to form the entrepreneurship index as followed by Puhazhenthi and Satyasai (2002)[17].

$$\text{En Index} = \frac{\sum_{i=1}^{n} ESi}{\sum_{i=1}^{n} EMSi} \times 100 \qquad \ldots (3.2)$$

where,

En Index = Entrepreneurship Index

ES = Entrepreneurship variables score

EMS = Entrepreneurship variables maximum score

i...n = Number of entrepreneurship variables.

Entrepreneurship index among the respondents is classified into five categories. The scoring procedure adopted to rate the entrepreneurship of the respondents in the present study is given in Table 3.27.

Table 3.27: Entrepreneurship Index

Sl. No.	*Entrepreneurship Index*	*Score*
1.	Less than 20	1
2.	20 - 40	2
3.	41 - 60	3
4.	61 - 80	4
5.	Above 80	5

SOCIO-ECONOMIC PROFILE OF THE SELECTED RESPONDENTS

This section discusses the socio-economic background of the selected respondents from among the tiny sector entrepreneurs in Tirunelveli district.

Age of the Respondents

Age is one of important aspects of self development since the resistance to change is relatively less at the young age compared to the old age. Youngsters are generally interested in learning things and they take risks in their lives, which are highly essential for entrepreneurship. At the same time, the aged have more knowledge and experience in their own field. Since the age of the respondents influences entrepreneurship, it is included in the present study.

Table 3.28: Age-wise Distribution of the Respondents

Sl. No.	*Age*	*Number of Respondents*	*Percentage*
1.	Less than 30	37	14.80
2.	30-40	76	30.40
3.	41-50	91	36.40
4.	Above 50	46	18.40
	Total	**250**	**100.00**

Source: Survey data.

It is inferred from Table 4.28 that the dominant age groups among the respondents are 30-40 and 41-50 which constitute 30.40 and 36.40 per cent respectively. The respondents who are above 50 years constitute 18.40 per cent. The respondents who are less than 30 years old constitute 14.80 per cent.

Educational Status of the Respondents

Education enlarges one's thinking and understanding horizons. It enables one to comprehend conditions more easily and clearly and in a better manner. An educated person can also easily adjust with the changed environment, hold better discussion and communicate in a more convincing manner.[18] Education is one of the important factors to run an enterprise and it is one of the prime necessities to become entrepreneurs.[19] The level of education may facilitate the enrichment of the personality of the respondents in all aspects. By education, the respondents may widen their scope of operation and become aware of the economic opportunities etc. In the present study, the level of education of the respondents is classified into three broad categories namely, school level, college level and technical. School level education covers primary, middle and higher secondary school education. College level education covers under graduate and post graduate education. Respondents having technical education are covered under technical education. The respondents under different levels of education are represented in Table 3.29.

Table 3.29: Education of the Respondents

Sl. No.	Level of Education	Number of Respondents	Percentage
1.	School Level	61	24.40
2.	College Level	143	57.20
3.	Technical	46	18.40
	Total	**250**	**100.00**

Source: Survey data.

The level of education is categorised into school level, college level and technical for the purpose of analysis. Table 4.29 reveals that 57.20 per cent of the respondents have college level education, 24.40 per cent have school level education and 18.40 per cent respondents have technical education.

Respondents' Gender

Women entrepreneurs are key players in any developing country particularly in terms of their contribution to economic development[20]. The eighth five year plan gave greater emphasis on women as equal partners and participants in the development process and thereby the conceptual thinking shifted from development to empowerment of women[21]. The sex of the entrepreneur may play a dominant role in determining the success of the enterprise, so the gender of the respondents is included in the present study. The percentage of business started and operated by women in India is less than that of business started by men. According to the Third All India Census of Small Scale Industries 2001-02, only 10 per cent of registered SSI units are operated by women.

Table 3.30: Sex-wise Distribution of the Respondents

Sl. No.	Sex	Number of Respondents	Percentage
1.	Male	221	88.40
2.	Female	29	11.60
	Total	**250**	**100.00**

Source: Survey data.

It is inferred from Table 3.30 that 88.40 per cent of the respondents are male entrepreneurs. Only 11.60 per cent of the respondents are women entrepreneurs. The above figures indicate the dominance of male entrepreneurs in the study area.

Social Class Among the Respondents

Social class represents the caste of the respondents. The caste system was introduced in ancient India on the basis of occupation. Even now to some extent people of a particular caste or community stick on to a particular trade. Hence, the caste system prevailing in the study area is also taken up for this study. Even though the caste behaviour can be altered with the help of education and exposure to technological development, still it plays its own role in entrepreneurship. Table 3.31 depicts the caste classification of the sample respondents.

Table 3.31: Caste-wise Distribution of the Respondents

Sl. No.	*Caste*	*Number of Respondents*	*Percentage*
1.	Forward Community (FC)	78	31.20
2.	Backward/Most Backward Community (BC/MBC)	138	55.20
3.	Scheduled Caste/Tribe (SC/ST)	34	13.60
	Total	**250**	**100.00**

Source: Survey data.

Table 3.31 reveals that 138 (55.20 per cent) out of 250 respondents interviewed belong to backward/most backward class communities. 78 (31.20 per cent) respondents belong to forward communities. Only 34 (13.60 per cent) respondents belong to scheduled castes/tribes. It is evident from the above table that backward/most backward class communities constitute a dominant class among the tiny sector entrepreneurs.

Nature of Family

Nature of family indicates the family system nuclear or joint family. Both the systems have their own merits and demerits in developing entrepreneurial behaviour. The nuclear family system creates an urge among the people to stand on their own legs whereas the joint family system provides some moral and financial support to promote entrepreneurial behaviour. The family system of the respondents is presented in Table 3.32.

Table 3.32: Nature of the Families of the Respondents

Sl. No.	*Nature of Family*	*Number of Respondents*	*Percentage*
1.	Nuclear Family	171	68.40
2.	Joint Family	79	31.60
	Total	**250**	**100.00**

Source: Survey data.

The above table shows that out of the 250 respondents 171 (68.40 per cent) belong to the nuclear family system and the remaining 79 (31.60 per cent) belong to the joint family system. It is evident from the above table that the joint family system which was followed in the earlier days is changing significantly giving way to the nuclear family system.

Martial Status of the Respondents

The martial status of the respondents may influence the need of finance and the mode of earning. It may also determine the ability to start an enterprise and the selection of the enterprise. The psychological framework of a person changes according to the marital status. In the present study the marital status of the respondents is classified into unmarried, married and widow/widower.

Table 3.33: Marital Status of the Repondents

Sl. No.	*Marital Status*	*Number of Respondents*	*Percentage*
1.	Unmarried	46	18.40
2.	Married	178	71.20
3.	Widow/Widower	26	10.40
	Total	**250**	**100.00**

Source: Survey data.

It is understood from Table 3.33 that out of the 250 respondents a maximum 178 (71.20 per cent) are married and 46 (18.40 per cent) are unmarried, whereas a minimum 26 (10.40 per cent) of the respondents are widows/widowers.

Family Size of the Respondents

The most important social character of the respondent is the family size. The family size indicates the number of family members who are living together with the respondents. The family size may be an asset or liability which depends upon the earning capacity of the population. In general, the increase in family size leads to the financial and social commitments of the respondents with a few exceptions. This commitment may hinder the growth of entrepreneurship among the respondents. The family size is classified as below 3, 3 to 5 and 5 and above. Table 3.34 depicts the family size of the respondents.

Table 3.34: Family Size of the Respondents

Sl. No.	*Family Size*	*Number of Respondents*	*Percentage*
1.	Below 3	47	18.80
2.	3-5	126	50.40
3.	Above 5	77	30.80
	Total	**250**	**100.00**

Source: Survey data.

The family size of 126 (50.40 per cent) out of the 250 respondents interviewed is 3-5 members. 77 (30.80 per cent) respondents have more than 5 members in their families. Only 47 (18.80 per cent) respondents have less than 3 members in their families. It is revealed from Table 3.34 that a majority of the respondents have 3 to 5 members in their families.

Earning Members in the Family

The earning members are the family members who are earning on a daily, weekly or monthly basis. The earnings of the family members increase the per capita income of the respondent's family. It provides financial and moral support to the respondents in all aspects. The higher the earning members in a family, the higher will be the financial support to the respondent. Apart from that, the standard of living of the respondent will also increase by the earnings of the members in the family which is highly essential for entrepreneurship. Table 3.35 represents the earning members in the families of the respondents.

Table 3.35: Earning Members per Family in the Households

Sl. No.	*Earning Members Per Family*	*Number of Respondents*	*Percentage*
1.	One	141	56.40
2.	Two	66	26.40
3.	Three	30	12.00
4.	Four	11	4.40
5.	More than four	2	0.80
	Total	**250**	**100.00**

Source: Survey data.

It is inferred from Table 3.35 that a majority of 141 (56.40 per cent) respondents have only one earning member per family and 66 (26.40 per cent) respondents have two earning members per family. 30 (12.00 per cent) respondents have three earning members per family and 11 (4.40 per cent) respondents have four earning members per family. Only 2 (0.80 per cent) respondents have more than four earning members in their families.

Occupational Background of the Respondents

Occupational background represents the occupation of the father or husband of the respondent in the present study. Occupational background provides a lot of ideas to start and manage an enterprise. It also moulds the psychological behaviour of the respondents which is essential for the enterprise. Sometimes occupational background provides some training to the respondents in the enterprises. In the present study, occupational background is classified as agricultural labourer, farmer, non agricultural labourer, Government employee, private employee and micro-entrepreneur.

Table 3.36: Occupational Background of the Respondents

Sl. No.	*Occupation*	*Number of Respondents*	*Percentage*
1.	Agricultural Labourer	26	10.40
2.	Farmer	90	36.00
3.	Non-agricultural labourer	32	12.80
4.	Government employee	15	6.00
5.	Private employee	37	14.80
6.	Micro entrepreneur	50	20.00
	Total	**250**	**100.00**

Source: Survey data.

Table 3.36 represents the occupational background of the 250 respondents. Farming is the occupation of the majority (36 per cent) of the respondents. Next to farming occupation, 50 (20 per cent) respondents have a micro entrepreneurship background. 37 (14.80 per cent) respondents' family members are employed in private sector organizations. Respondents from non agricultural and agricultural labourers' families occupy 12.80 and 10.40 per cent respectively. The least (6 per cent) number of respondents are from the families of Government employees.

Material Possessions

Material possessions mean the total value of the movable and immovable property belonging to the respondents at a particular point of time. Material possessions exclude the value of the lands owned by the respondents. Material possessions provide a financial base to the respondents to start or manage any enterprise. This may provide some liquidity and better standard of living to the respondents which are highly essential for entrepreneurship. The material possessions of the respondents in the present study are classified into four categories namely below Rs. 50,000, Rs. 50,000 to 1 lakh, Rs. 1 lakh to 2 lakhs and above Rs. 2 lakhs.

Table 3.37: Material Possessions of the Respondents

Sl. No.	*Material Possession*	*Number of Respondents*	*Percentage*
1.	Below Rs. 50,000	35	14.00
2.	Rs. 50,000 – 1,00,000	50	20.00
3.	Rs. 1,00,000 – 2,00,000	87	34.80
4.	Above Rs. 2,00,000	78	31.20
	Total	**250**	**100.00**

Source: Survey data.

Table 3.37 shows that out of 250 respondents 87 (34.80 per cent) have property worth Rs. 1 lakh to 2 lakhs. 78 (31.20 per cent) respondents have more than Rs. 2 lakhs worth of property. Only 35 (14per cent) respondents possess less than Rs. 50,000 worth of property. It is observed from Table 3.37 that 165 (66 per cent) out of the 250 respondents possess movable and non movable assets worth more than Rs. 1 lakh.

Monthly Income of the Respondents

Monthly income means the income of the respondents from all possible sources. Monthly income includes the income form the enterprise, employment, service, agriculture and other activities in which the respondents are engaged. Since the monthly income of the respondents indicates their standard of living and the earning capacity, it is included in the present study. Monthly income in the present study is classified into five categories namely less than Rs. 1,000, Rs. 1,001-2,000, Rs. 2001-3000, Rs. 3001-4000 and above Rs. 4000.

It is revealed from Table 4.38 that out of 250 respondents a majority of 79 (31.60 per cent) have a monthly income of Rs. 2,001 to 3,000 and 52 (20.80 per cent) respondents have earnings between Rs. 1,001 and 2,000. 43 (17.20 per cent) respondents have a monthly income of above Rs. 4,000. 40 (16.00 per cent) respondents have earnings less than Rs. 1,000 per month. Only 36 (14.40 per cent) respondents have a monthly income of Rs. 3,001-4,000.

Table 3.38: Monthly Income of the Respondents

Sl. No.	*Monthly Personal Income (in Rs.)*	*Number of Respondents*	*Percentage*
1.	Less than 1,000	40	16.00
2.	1,001-2,000	52	20.80
3.	2,001-3,000	79	31.60
4.	3,001-4,000	36	14.40
5.	4,000 and above	43	17.20
	Total	**250**	**100.00**

Source: Survey data.

Family Income

Family income represents the income earned by all the earning members in the family from all the sources in a month. The higher the family income the better the standard of living and the better the education to the children of the members. The personalities of the family members are shaped by education and the standard of living. Moreover, a high family income provides a base for finance to start an enterprise.

The respondents with a better financial base may utilize their income for the development of enterprises. In the present study, the family income of the respondents is grouped into three categories namely, below Rs. 3,000, Rs. 3,001 to 5,000 and above Rs. 5,000. The distribution of respondents according to their family income is shown in Table 3.39.

It is clearly seen from Table 3.39 that out of 250 respondents a maximum of 99 (39.60 per cent) respondents have a monthly family income of Rs. 3,001-5,000 and 91 (36.40 per cent) respondents have a family income of more than Rs. 5,000. Only 60 (24 per cent) respondents have a family income below Rs. 3,000.

Table 3.39: Family Income of the Respondents

Sl. No.	*Monthly Family Income (in Rs.)*	*Number of Respondents*	*Percentage*
1.	Below 3,000	60	24.00
2.	3,001 – 5,000	99	39.60
3.	Above 5,000	91	36.40
	Total	**250**	**100.00**

Source: Survey data.

Family Expenditure

Family expenditure indicates the total amount spent on consumption and household necessities by the respondents during a month. Family expenditure may influence the nature of savings by the respondents or their indebtedness.

The habit of savings or being in a state of indebtedness directly affects the entrepreneurial activities of the respondents and also the growth of their enterprises. The higher family expenditure may affect the saving potential of the respondents. In the present study family expenditure is classified into five categories, namely less than Rs. 2,000, Rs. 2,000 to 3,000, Rs. 3,001 to 4,000, Rs. 4,001 to 5,000 and above Rs. 5,000.

Table 3.40: Monthly Family Expenditure of the Respondents

Sl. No.	*Monthly Family Expenditure (in Rs.)*	*Number of Respondents*	*Percentage*
1.	Less than 2,000	17	6.80
2.	2,000-3,000	43	17.20
3.	3,001-4,000	101	40.40
4.	4,001-5,000	62	24.80
5.	Above 5,000	27	10.80
	Total	**250**	**100.00**

Source: Survey data.

Table 3.40 shows that out of the 250 respondents 101 (40.40 per cent) spend Rs. 3,001-4,000 per month on family expenditure and 62 (24.80) respondents spend Rs. 4,001-5,000 on family expenditure. The family expenditure of 43 (17.20 per cent) respondents is between Rs. 2,000 and Rs. 3,000. 27 (10.80 per cent) respondents spend more than Rs. 5,000 towards family expenditure. Only 17 out of the 250 respondents spend less than Rs. 2,000 for their families.

Monthly Savings

Savings is the difference between income and expenditure. The surplus income is the major source for potential savings. The monthly savings of the respondents are computed by taking the difference between the monthly income and the expenditure of the respondents. The savings of the respondents may directly or indirectly influence their entrepreneurial activity and also the growth of enterprises. In the present study the monthly savings of the respondents are classified into four categories namely, no savings, less than Rs. 1,000, Rs. 1,000-2,000 and above Rs. 2,000. The distribution of respondents according to their monthly savings is shown in Table 3.41.

Table 3.41: Monthly Savings of the Respondents

Sl. No.	*Monthly Savings (in Rs.)*	*Number of Respondents*	*Percentage*
1.	No Savings	91	36.40
2.	Less than 1,000	78	31.20
3.	1,000-2,000	52	20.80
4.	Above 2,000	29	11.60
	Total	**250**	**100.00**

Source: Survey data.

It is observed from Table 3.41 that out of the 250 respondents, a maximum 91 (36.40 per cent) have no savings. Only 11.60 per cent of respondents have savings above Rs. 2,000 per month. Among the entrepreneurs, the number of respondents who save less than Rs. 1,000 constitute 31.20 per cent. 20.80 per cent of the respondents have savings ranging from Rs. 1,000 to Rs. 2,000 per month.

PERSONALITY TRAITS OF THE SELECTED TINY ENTREPRENEURS

Personality Traits

It is likely that there are some social and psychological factors which might hinder the responsiveness and growth of poor sections of the people due to their continued deprivation over a long period of time for want of economic opportunities.

Some psychologists such as Albert Ellis (1962)[22] suggest that it is important to understand the way a person views or thinks about life. Others like B.F. Skinner (1973)[23] and William Glasser (1975)[24] take the position that the most appropriate means of understanding a person is to observe that person's behaviour and actions. Rogers (1961)[25] suggests becoming aware of the emotions or feelings of a person. It is evident from the above mentioned studies that most of them were of a general nature in investigating the psychological factors affecting entrepreneurial behaviour and performance.

In the present study an attempt was made to assess the personality traits of the entrepreneurs in order to identify whether they have the requisite personality dispositions to undertake activities which are independent and self sustaining. Such personality factors are too many, and so the present study is confined to only fourteen factors, namely information seeking, mass media exposure, social participation, cosmopoliteness, aspiration, attitude towards self employment, scientific orientation, decision making ability, economic motivation, managerial ability, problem recognition, risk taking willingness, urban pull and extension contact.

The Analytical Frame Work

The above said fourteen personality factors are assessed by a four point scale of 4, 3, 2 and 1 mark. The marks obtained by the respondents were used to find out the personality index of the respondents by using the following formula.

$$PI = \frac{\sum_{i=1}^{n} PSi}{\sum_{i=1}^{n} MSPi} \times 100 \qquad \ldots (3.3)$$

PS = Personality factors score

MSP = Maximum score for the personality factor

i...n = Number of personality factors

Results and Discussion

The average scores for the different personality factors calculated for the entrepreneurs in the study area are presented in Table 3.42.

Table 3.42: Personality Traits of the Respondents

Sl. No.	*Personality Traits*	*Average Score*
1.	Information seeking	2.91
2.	Mass media exposure	3.19
3.	Social participation	2.41
4.	Cosmopoliteness	1.83
5.	Aspiration	2.69
6.	Attitude towards self-employment	3.21
7.	Scientific orientation	1.42
8.	Decision making ability	3.30
9.	Economic motivation	2.81
10.	Managerial ability	3.06
11.	Problem recognition	3.20
12.	Rick taking willingness	3.04
13.	Urban pull	2.12
14.	Extension contact	2.06
	Overall score	2.6607

It is revealed from Table 3.42 that the entrepreneurs are very good in the aspects such as decision making ability, attitude towards self-employment, problem recognition and mass media exposure since the mean values for these personality factors are as high as 3.30, 3.21, 3.20 and 3.19 respectively. The overall score for the personality traits of the entrepreneurs is 2.6607.

Personality Index of the Respondents

The personality index of the respondents is calculated by the personality index formula given in 3.1. Personality Index is classified into five categories in the present study namely, less than 20, 20-40, 41-60, 61-80 and above 80. The distribution of respondents as per their Personality Index is presented in Table 3.43.

Table 3.43: Personality Index of the Respondents

Sl. No.	*Personality Index*	*Number of Respondents*	*Percentage*
1.	Less than 20	12	4.80
2.	20-40	61	24.40
3.	41-60	85	34.00
4.	61-80	69	27.60
5.	Above 80	23	9.20
	Total	**250**	**100.00**

Source: Computed data.

34 per cent of the total respondents have a personality index of 41-60. 69 respondents (27.60 per cent) have a personality index of 61-80. The number of respondents who have a personality index more than 80 constitute only 9.20 per cent of the total. Thus it is inferred that around 70 per cent of the respondents have a personality index more than 40.

ENTREPRENEURSHIP

Joseph Schumpeter regarded an entrepreneur as one who through new combinations of means of production, carried out the introduction of new goods, new methods of production, the opening of new markets, the conquest of a new source of supply of half manufactured goods and effecting the new organization of any industry.[26]

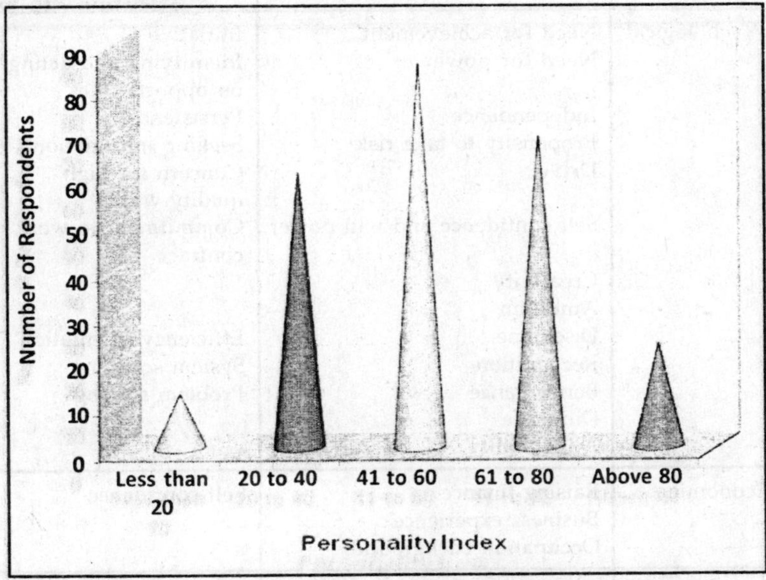

Fig. 3.1: Personality Index of the Respondents

Entrepreneurs always search for change, respond to it and exploit it as an opportunity[27]. Thus entrepreneurship entails the ability to identify available resources, to perceive their economic potential, the ability and willingness to utilize the resources and to invest in their development deferring immediate rewards in favour of future investment[28]. It appears that entrepreneurship is essentially a function, creativity and behaviour manifestation of a person for shifting resources from areas of low productivity to areas of higher productivity. They are traits like willingness to take risk, high economic and achievement motivation, self confidence, problem solving disposition, adequate knowledge and skills, ability to face uncertainty and good managerial ability[29].

The characteristics and competencies of the entrepreneurs are classified under psychological, economic, sociological and general categories by Mansfield *et al.*[30] They are presented in Table 3.44.

Table 3.44: Characteristics and Competencies of Entrepreneurs

Category	*Characteristics*	*Competencies*
Psychological	Need for achievement	Initiative
	Need for power	Identifying and acting on opportunities
	Independence	Persistence
	Propensity to take risk	Seeking information
	Drive	Concern for high quality work
	Self-confidence and will power	Commitment to work contract
	Creativity	
	Ambition	
	Discipline	Efficiency orientation
	Recognition	System scanning
	Benevolence	Problem solving
	Diligence	
	Adaptability	
Economic	Raising finance	Self-confidence
	Business experience	
	Occupation background	
Sociological	Leadership	Assertiveness
	Social mobility	Persuasion
	Family background	
General	Good salesman	Use of influencing Strategies
	Pleasing personality	
	Integrity	

The most frequent characteristics of the entrepreneurs are identified by Madhu Murthy[31] as self-confidence, perseverance, determination, energy, diligence, resourcefulness, ability to take risks, need to achieve, creativity, initiative, flexibility, positive response to challenges, independence, foresight, dynamism, leadership, versatility, knowledge of product technology, responsiveness, profit orientation, perception and optimism.

Measurement of Entrepreneurship

Entrepreneurship is estimated in the present study with the help of five important aspects namely self confidence, task-orientation, risk bearing, leadership and originality. Each aspect is estimated with the help of an index developed. The aspects and the related variables are given in Table 3.45.

Table 3.45: Components of Entrepreneurship Index

	Aspects	*Components*
1.	Self-confidence	Confidence Optimism Independence Individuality
2.	Task-orientation	Need for achievement Profit orientation Future Plan Initiativeness
3.	Risk Bearing	Business selection Challenge orientation Risk learning level Decision making
4.	Leadership	Headship Leading Sociability Time management
5.	Originality	Resourcefulness Versatility Openness of mind Creativity

The components of entrepreneurship are rated at a four point scale by the respondents. The entrepreneurship index was developed by

$$\text{En Index} = \frac{\sum_{i=1}^{n} ESi}{\sum_{i=1}^{n} EMSi} \times 100 \qquad \text{... (3.4)}$$

where,

En Index = Entrepreneurship Index
ES = Entrepreneurship variables score
EMS = Entrepreneurship variables maximum score
i...n = Number of entrepreneurship variables.

Results and Discussion

The average score obtained by the entrepreneurs in each component of entrepreneurship variables is calculated and the resulted average score is shown in Table 3.46.

Table 3.46: Entrepreneurship of the Respondents

Sl. No.	*Entrepreneurship Variables*	*Average Score*
1.	Confidence	2.95
2.	Optimism	3.06
3.	Independence	3.13
4.	Individuality	3.69
5.	Need for achievement	2.96
6.	Profit orientation	3.46
7.	Future plan	3.16
8.	Initiative	2.66
9.	Business selection	1.39
10.	Challenge orientation	2.79
11.	Risk taking	3.53
12.	Decision making	2.96
13.	Headship	1.49
14.	Leading	2.89
15.	Sociability	3.04
16.	Time management	3.45
17.	Resourcefulness	2.84
18.	Versatility	1.96
19.	Openness	2.87
20.	Creativity	3.41
	Overall score	2.8845

It is noticed from Table 3.46 that the average scores are high in the entrepreneurship variables namely individuality, risk taking, profit orientation, time management and creativity. The mean score values of these entrepreneurship variables are 3.69, 3.53, 3.46, 3.45 and 3.41 respectively. The overall score of entrepreneurship variables is 2.8845.

Entrepreneurship Index

Entrepreneurship index was developed for each and every respondent by using the formula given in 3.2. Entrepreneurship index in the present study is classified into five categories namely, less than 20, 20-40, 41-60, 61-80 and above 80. The distribution of the respondents according to the entrepreneurship index is shown in Table 3.47.

Table 3.47: Entrepreneurship Index of the Respondents

Sl. No.	*Entrepreneurship Index*	*Number of Respondents*	*Percentage*
1.	Less than 20	16	6.40
2.	20-40	55	22.00
3.	41-60	86	34.40
4.	61-80	72	28.80
5.	Above 80	21	8.40
	Total	**250**	**100.00**

Source: Computed data.

It is understood from Table 3.47 that out of 250 respondents, 34.40 per cent have an entrepreneurial index of 41 to 60 and 28.80 per cent of them have an index of 61 to 80. The entrepreneurs who exceed an index of 80 are 21, whereas 6.40 per cent of the respondents have an index less than 20.

ASSOCIATION BETWEEN SOCIO-ECONOMIC PROFILE VARIABLES AND ENTREPRENEURSHIP INDEX

An analysis of the association between socio-economic profile variables and entrepreneurship index was done to find

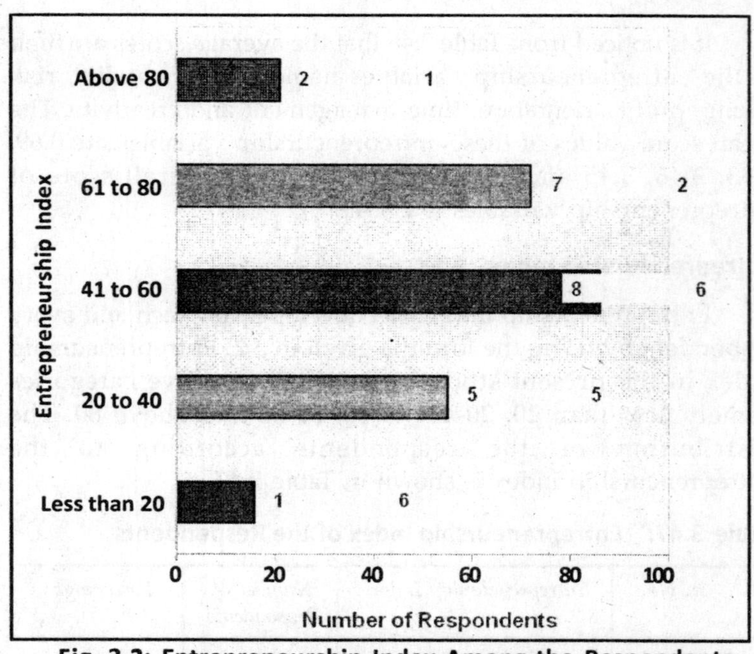

Fig. 3.2: Entrepreneurship Index Among the Respondents

out whether there is any relation between the two. For the purpose of the analysis twelve profile variables were taken into account. The Entrepreneurship Index of the respondents are classified into five groups (vide table 3.20). The analysis was done with the help of the chi-square test using the following formula:

$$\text{Chi-Square } (\chi^2) = \sum \frac{(O - E)^2}{E} \qquad \ldots (3.5)$$

with (c-1) (r-1) degrees of freedom

Where,

O = Observed frequency, E = Expected frequency

$$E = \frac{\text{Row total} \times \text{Column total}}{\text{Grand total}}$$

c = Number of columns, r = Number of rows

The computed results of chi-square values with their degrees of freedom and their table values are shown in Table 3.48.

Table 3.48: Association Between Socio-Economic Profile and Entrepreneurship Among the Respondents

Sl. No.	*Socio Economic Profile Variables*	*Calculated Chi-square Values*	*Table value of Chi-square at 5 per cent level*	*Inference*
1.	Age	36.723	21.026	Significant
2.	Education	38.471	15.507	Significant
3.	Sex	6.741	9.488	Insignificant
4.	Caste	7.194	15.507	Insignificant
5.	Nature of family	6.768	9.488	Insignificant
6.	Marital status	12.673	15.507	Insignificant
7.	Family size	16.723	15.507	Significant
8.	Earning members per family	30.471	26.296	Significant
9.	Occupational background	34.712	31.410	Significant
10.	Material possession	19.962	26.296	Insignificant
11.	Monthly income	28.367	26.296	Significant
12.	Family income per month	24.317	15.507	Significant

It is inferred from Table 3.48 that the association between entrepreneurship and the socio-economic variables namely age, education, family size, earning members, occupational background, monthly income and family income per month are significant at 5 per cent level since the calculated value of chi-square is greater than the table value of these variables. The other variables are not significantly associated with entrepreneurship.

CORRELATION BETWEEN PERSONALITY TRAITS AND ENTREPRENEURSHIP

The personality traits of the respondents were analysed in relation to the entrepreneurship aspects of the respondents to examine the correlation between the two. For this, the correlation coefficient between the score of the personality variables and the entrepreneurship index of the respondents was separately calculated for the entrepreneurs. The computed Karl

Pearson's correlation co-efficient of the personality variables and entrepreneurship index are shown in Table 3.49.

Table 3.49: Correlation Between Personality Traits and Entreperneurship Index

Sl. No.	*Personality Variables*	*Correlation co-efficient*
1.	Information seeking	0.1172
2.	Mass media exposure	-0.1675
3.	Social participation	-0.1567
4.	Cosmospoliteness	-0.0891
5.	Level of aspiration	0.2711
6.	Attitude towards self employment	0.1345
7.	Scientific orientation	0.2125
8.	Decision making ability	0.5115*
9.	Economic motivation	0.5076*
10.	Managerial ability	0.4163*
11.	Problem recognition	0.4561*
12.	Risk taking willingness	0.5261*
13.	Urban pull	0.1972
14.	Extension contact	0.1791

* Significant at 5 per cent level.

It is inferred from Table 3.49 that significant correlation is identified in certain personality variables namely decision making ability, economic motivation, managerial ability, problem recognition and risk taking willingness since the respective correlation co-efficients 0.5115, 0.5076, 0.4163, 0.4561 and 0.5261 are statistically significant at 5 per cent level. The above said personality variables are positively related to entrepreneurship.

FACTORS INFLUENCING TINY ENTREPRENEURS TO START OR TO MANAGE ANY ENTERPRISE

The factors influencing the respondents to start and/or manage an enterprise are economic, social, psychological and environmental. These drives are highly essential to start and/or to manage an enterprise. Even though the variables are too many, the present study confined itself to economic independence, self-prestige, employment opportunities, technical knowledge, urge to achieve, aspiration about children, financial assistance, use of idle funds, self-interest, encouragement of family members, organizational skill, self employment, revival of sick unit, social status, entrepreneurial experience, family background, traditional/hereditary, market potential, earning income, more dependents, unemployment and challenge seeking. The above said 22 variables were rated by the respondents at a five point scale namely highly important, important, moderate, not important and not at all important which has the score value of 5, 4, 3, 2 and 1 respectively. Factor analysis identifies underlying variables or factors that explain correlations within a set of observed variables. This procedure is used in data reduction to identify a small number of factors that explain the variance observed in a much larger number of manifest variables. In this study, the factor analysis technique was used to reduce the long list of motivation variables which influence the entrepreneurs to manage or start the enterprises into meaningful factors.

Analytical Framework

The principal factor analysis method is mathematically satisfying because it yields a mathematically unique solution to a factor problem. Its major solution feature is the extraction of a maximum amount of variation as each factor is calculated. In other words, the first extracts the most variance and so on[32]. Most of the analysis methods produce results in a form that is difficult or impossible to interpret. Thurstone argued that it is necessary to rotate factor matrices to interpret them adequately.[33] He pointed out that original factor matrices are arbitrary in the sense that an infinite number of reference frames (axes) can be found to reproduce any given 'R' matrix.[34] In order to move the axes from the arbitrary location determined by the method of extraction to some position useful for interpretation of the factors for comparison with other studies, the axes are rotated. A major goal of rotation is to obtain meaningful factors that are as consistent as possible from analysis to analysis.[35] There are several methods available for factor analysis. But the principal factor method with Orthogonal Varimax Rotation is mostly used and widely available in factor analysis computer programmes. Further orthogonal rotations maintain the independence of factors, that is, the angles between the axes are kept at 90 degrees. One of the final outcomes of a factor analysis is called Rotated Factor Matrix, a table of co-efficient that express the ratios between the variables and the factors. The sum of the squares of the factor loadings of variables is called communalities (h^2).

The communality of a factor is its common factor variance. The factors with factor loadings of 0.50 or greater are considered as significant factors and the factors with less than 50 per cent common variation with the rotated factor pattern are too weak to report[36]. In the present study, the principal factor analysis method with Orthogonal Varimax Rotation was used to identify the significant set of influencing factors.

Results and Interpretation

The Rotated Factor Matrix for the variables relating to factors influencing the respondents to start and/or manage the tiny sector industries included in the study is given in Table 3.50.

Tabie 3.50 gives the loading received by the factors under $F_{1,}$ $F_{2,}$ $F_{3,}$ and F_4 for tiny enterprises.

The twenty two variables included in the factor analysis resulted in four important factors that influence the respondents to start and/or manage any enterprise. They are: *(i)* achievement and support factor; *(ii)* interest factor; *(iii)* traditional status factor; and (iv) economic necessity factor. The achievement and support factor includes the variables, namely economic independence, self-prestige, employment opportunities, technical knowledge, urge to achieve, aspiration about children, financial assistance and use of idle funds. All these factors have higher factor loadings. The factors namely self interest, encouragement of family members, organization skill, self employment and revival of sick unit are grouped in the interest factor because of their higher factor loading.

Table 3.50: Factors Influencing the Respondents to Manage or Start any Tiny Enterprise

Sl. No.	*Motivation Variables*	*Rotated Factor Loading*				h^2
		F1	*F2*	*F3*	*F4*	
1.	Economic independence	0.7669	0.3321	0.2609	-0.1995	0.8532
2.	Prestige	0.7869	0.2273	-0.06994	-0.1996	0.7156
3.	Employment opportunities	0.7637	0.0644	0.1994	0.2444	0.6869
4.	Technical knowledge	0.6836	0.2826	0.3514	0.2101	0.7148
5.	Urge to achieve	0.6042	0.3994	0.3042	0.1949	0.6551
6.	Aspiration about children	0.5747	0.2871	-0.3119	0.2642	0.5798
7.	Financial assistance	0.5624	0.0945	-0.1406	0.2664	0.4119
8.	Use of idle funds	0.5604	0.1829	0.2097	-0.3042	0.0925
9.	Self interest	-0.2608	0.7624	0.1789	0.3606	0.8113
10.	Encouragement of family members	0.0618	0.7402	0.2243	0.1982	0.6413
11.	Organizational skill	-0.2321	0.5686	0.0985	-0.1245	0.4023

(Contd...)

Sl. No.	*Motivation Variables*	*Rotated Factor Loading*				h^2
		F1	*F2*	*F3*	*F4*	
12.	Self employment	0.0689	0.5571	0.1642	0.2784	0.4196
13.	Revival of sick unit	-0.1126	0.5156	-0.2062	0.2668	0.3922
14.	Social status	0.3241	-0.2246	0.6469	0.3092	0.6695
15.	Entrepreneurial experience	0.0492	0.2943	0.6134	-0.0968	0.4747
16.	Family background	0.1493	0.4914	0.5066	-0.3097	0.6163
17.	Traditional/Hereditary	-0.0967	0.1038	0.5022	0.1048	0.2833
18.	Market potential	0.1229	-0.2969	0.1014	0.5812	0.4513
19.	Earning income	0.2065	-0.1943	0.4118	0.6384	0.6575
20.	More dependents	0.3064	-0.0893	-0.2211	0.5394	0.4417
21.	Unemployment	-0.2871	0.4314	0.2976	0.5196	0.6271
22.	Challenge seeking	0.3016	0.4741	-0.2868	0.5066	0.6546
	Eigen Value	4.2377	3.4929	2.3544	2.5631	

Note: The principal factors method with Orthogonal Varimax Rotation is used to extract factors.

The traditional status factor includes the variables, namely social status, entrepreneurial experience, family background, traditional/hereditary and market potential whereas the economic necessity factor includes market potential, earning income, more dependents, unemployment and challenge seeking.

The communality value indicates the power of a variable to explain the factors altogether. The higher communality represents the degree of variable explaining the factors are higher. By communality values, the important variables which influence the respondents to start and/or manage any enterprise are economic independence, self interest and self prestige since their communality values are 0.8532, 0.8113 and 0.7156 respectively.

The Eigen value of the factor indicates the degree of the factor which explains the variables altogether. The higher Eigen value shows the higher intensity of the factor explaining the variables altogether. By Eigen values, the most important factors that influence the respondents to start and/or manage any enterprise are achievement and support factor and interest factor since their Eigen values are 4,2377 and 3.4929 respectively.

SUMMARY

The socio-economic profiles, personality traits of the respondents and the factors influencing the development of the enterprises were analysed in this chapter. Profile variables were measured by using proper scoring methods. The socio-economic background of the respondents revealed that a majority (66.80 per cent) of the respondents belong to the age group of 30-50 years. 57.30 per cent of the respondents have college level education. Among the respondents, 88.40 per cent are male and the remaining are female. A majority (55 per cent) of the respondents belong to the backward/most backward communities. 68 per cent of the respondents belong to the nuclear family system. Regarding the marital status, 71.20 per cent of the respondents are married. 50.40 per cent of the total respondents have a family size of 3 to 5 members. Among the respondents, those who have only one earning member in the family constitute 56.40 per cent.

The occupational background among the respondents is mainly farming. 34.80 per cent of the respondents have material possessions worth Rs. 1,00,000 to Rs. 2,00,000. 31.60 per cent of respondents have an income ranging between Rs. 2001 and Rs. 3000. It is observed that 39.60 per cent of the respondents have a family income of Rs. 3001 to Rs. 5000 per month. 40.40 per cent of the total respondents spend Rs. 3001- Rs. 4000 on their monthly family expenditure.

The analysis of personality traits revealed that the average personality traits score is 2.66. The number of respondents who have a personality index of above 60 constitute 36.80 per cent. The average scores are high in the entrepreneurship variables namely individuality, risk taking, profit orientation, time management and creativity. The mean score values of these entrepreneurship variables are 3.69, 3.53, 3.46, 3.45 and 3.41 respectively. The overall average of entrepreneurship variables among the entrepreneurs is 2.8845. An analysis of the entrepreneurship indices of the respondents revealed that a maximum of 34.40 per cent have an index of 41-60. 28.80 per cent have an index ranging between 61 and 80.

The analysis revealed that the association between the socio-economic profile and entrepreneurship is significant regarding age, education, family, occupational background, monthly income and family income of the entrepreneur. Correlation between personality traits and entrepreneurship is significant in certain personality variables namely decision making ability, economic motivation, managerial ability, problem recognition and risk taking willingness.

The Rotated Factor Matrix technique was used to reduce the long list of motivation variables into four meaningful factors namely: *(i)* achievement and support factor; *(ii)* interest factor; *(iii)* traditional status factor; and *(iv)* economic necessity factor. The important variables which influence the respondent to start and/or to manage an enterprise are economic independence, self interest and self prestige since its communality values are 0.8532, 0.8113 and 0.7156 respectively. The most important factors that influence the respondents to start or manage an enterprise are the achievement and support factor and the interest factor since their Eigen values are 4.2377 and 3.4929 respectively.

REFERENCES

1. Nasser Ahmed and Kakoly, H.N. 1993. "Determinants of Agricultural Entrepreneurial Success", *Indian Journal of Social Science Research,* 34 (2), p. 252.

2. Patel, M.M. 1995. "Role of Entrepreneurship in Agricultural Development", *Kurukshetra,* Vol. 43, No. 3, p. 43.

3. Venkata Ramaiah, P. 1993. "Entrepreneurial Behaviour of Farmers", *Indian Journal of Extension Education,* Vol. 9, No. 1, p. 90.

4. Venkatesan, S. "Performance of Leadership Roles: Farmer Discussion Group Conveners of Madurai District", Unpublished Thesis, Tamil Nadu Agricultural University, Madurai, p. 29.

5. Trivedi, G. "Measurement and Analysis of Socio-Economic Status of Farm Families", Unpublished Thesis, I.A.R.I., New Delhi, p. 56.

6. Paulraj, L.R. "Profile and Role Performance of FDG Conveners", Unpublished Thesis, Tamil Nadu Agricultural University, Madurai, p. 31.

7. Trivedi, *Op.cit.*

8. Venkatesan, *Op.cit.*

9. Venkatesan, *Op.cit.*

10. Edwards, A.L. 1969. *Techniques of Attitude Scale Constructions,* Bombay: Vilkils, Feffer and Simons Pvt. Limited.

11. Knight, A. John, 1973. "A Study on Relative Effectiveness of Three Modes of Presentation, Preference, Listening and Post Listening Behaviour of Farm Broadcast Listeners", Unpublished Thesis, Division of Agricultural Extension, I.A.R.I, New Delhi, p. 240.

12. Noor Jahan, A.K.A.H. " A Critical Analysis of Technological Gaps in Adoption of Pest Management Practices in Rice", Unpublished Thesis ,Tamil Nadu Agricultural University, Madurai.

13. Supe, S.V. Factors Related to Different Degrees of Rationality in Decision Making among Farmers, Unpublished Thesis, Division of Agriculture, I.A.R.I., New Delhi.

14. Meera, M.J. 2001. "Performance Analysis of Samatha Self-Help Groups in the Empowerment of Rural Women in Panchayats", Unpublished Thesis, KAU, Vellayani, p. 220.

15. Supe, S.V., *Op. cit.,* 1969.

16. Seema, 1999. Marketing Behaviour of Coconut Growers in Andaman and Nicobar Islands, Unpublished Thesis, Tamil Nadu Agricultural University, Madurai, p. 154.

17. Puhazhenthi, V, and Satyasai, K.S.S. 2000. "Micro Finance for Rural People", Department of Economic Analysis and Research, National Bank for Agriculture and Rural Development, Mumbai.

18. Sharma, R.A. 1980. Entrepreneurial Change in Industry, New Delhi: Sterling Publishers, pp. 191-193.

19. Nandi, A. 1973. "Motives, Modernity and Entrepreneurial Competence", *The Journal of Social Psychology,* Vol. 31, No. 2, pp. 127-136.

20. Anita, H.S. and Laxinisha, A.S. 1999. "Women Entrepreneurship in India", *Southern Economist,* Vol. 31, No. 9, p. 28.

21. Tripta and Kaushik, April – June 2002."Impact of Financial Assistance Schemes on the Economic Empowerment of Women", *Indian Journal of Social Research,* Vol. 43, No. 2, p. 93.

22. Ellis Albert, 1962. *Reasons and Emotions in Psychology: Secaus,* New Jersey: Lyle Stuart, p. 18.

23. Skinner, B.F. 1973.*About Behaviourism,* New York: Knopf, p. 46.

24. Glasser William, 1975. *Reality Therapy,* New York: Harper and Row, p. 66.

25. Rogers, Carl, R. 1961. *On Becoming: A Person Loughton,* Miffin.

26. Sharma, R.A. 1980. *Entrepreneurial Change in Indian Industry,* New Delhi: Sterling Publishers Pvt., Limited, p. 29.

27. Drucker, P.F. 1985. *Innovation and Entrepreneurship Practices and Principles,* London: Heinemann, p. 41.

28. Agarwal, V.K. 1975. *Initiative, Enterprise and Economic Choices in India,* New Delhi: Munshiram Manoharlal, p. 82.

29. Nandapurkar, G.G. 1982. *Small Farmers–A Study of their Entrepreneurial Behaviour,* New Delhi: Metropolitan Book Company Pvt Limited, p. 33.

30. Mansfield, Richard, S. McCleveand, D.C. Spenser Lyle and Santiago Jose, 1987. *The Identification and Assessment of Competencies and Other Personal Characteristics of Entrepreneurs in Developing Countries,* Boston: Mc Ber & Co., pp. 136-142.

31. Madhu Murthy, K. December 2003. "Entrepreneurs: Evaluation of the Concept and Characteristics", *SEDME,* Vol.29, No.4, pp.12-17.

32. Harry H. Harman, 1967. *Modern Factor Analysis,* Chicago: The University of Chicago Press, pp. 97-101.

33. Thurstone, L. and Chava, E. 1929. *The Measurement of Attitude,* Chicago: University of Chicago Press, pp. 508-509.

34. *Ibid.*, p. 93.

35. Benjamin, Fructher, 1976. *Introduction of Factor Analysis*, New Delhi: Affiliated East-West Press, p. 106.

36. Fred N. Kerlenger, 1973. *Methods of Factor Analysis, Foundations of Behavioural Research*, Newyork: Holt Rinchart and Winston Inc., p. 470.

4

Growth of Entrepreneurship in Tiny Sector Industries

INTRODUCTION

This chapter deals with the level of growth of entrepreneurship in tiny industrial units in Tirunelveli district. Measurement of growth, extent of growth, variation in growth and the factors influencing the growth of entrepreneurship are highlighted in this chapter. For this purpose, ten growth factors of entrepreneurs have been identified and growth has been measured on the basis of scores awarded to the ten components.

ANALYTICAL FRAMEWORK

This section attempts to describe the measurement of growth of entrepreneurship on the basis of the ten components identified for this purpose.

(i) Measurement of Growth

The researcher has measured the extent of growth of entrepreneurship with the help of a scale constructed by him. In the study, ten components have been identified to measure the growth of entrepreneurs and they form the basis of the measurement. All the ten components are responsible either partly or fully for the growth of entrepreneurship in tiny industrial units.

The scale to measure the growth has been developed on the basis of scores awarded to the select ten components. The growth scale has been constructed with the help of 100 scores as total. This total score is equally distributed among all the ten components namely fixed assets, owned funds, borrowed funds, working capital, raw materials, product-mix, employment generation, value of production, sales turnover and net profit. The score value of each component has been secured on the basis of the growth percentage of each component. The growth percentage has been calculated on the basis of data pertaining to five year starting from 2000-01 to 2004-05 using the following formula.

$$\text{Growth percentage} = \frac{\text{Current (last) year value - Base (first) year value}}{\text{Base (first) year value}}$$

Table 4.1 explains the distribution of scores for ten growth factors. It is found from Table 4.1 that the percentage of growth and distribution of score values for the factors are: one for 0 to 10 per cent, 2 for 10 to 20 per cent, 3 for 20 to 30 per cent, 4 for 30 to 40 per cent, 5 for 40 to 50 per cent, 6 for 50 to 60 per cent, 7 for 60 to 70 per cent, 8 for 70 to 80 per cent, 9 for 80 to 90 per cent and 10 for 90 to 100 per cent. From the overall data, it is observed that, the percentage of growth factors individually is from one to ten. Therefore, the total score for the ten growth factors is 100.

(ii) Distribution of Scores for the Ten Components of Growth

Table 4.2 presents the distribution of scores for the ten growth factors.

According to Table 4.2, the distribution of scores for the ten growth factors ranges from one to ten, uniformly. The total score of all the ten components gives the level of entrepreneurship growth in tiny industrial units in Tirunelveli district.

(iii) Levels of Growth

The levels of growth have been determined by the total score values obtained from the identified ten components of growth. The levels of growth have been classified into three

Table 4.1: Percentage of Growth and Distribution of Scores for Ten Growth Factors

Sl. No.	*Growth Factors*	*0-10%*	*10-20%*	*20-30%*	*30-40%*	*40-50%*	*50-60%*	*60-70%*	*70-80%*	*80-90%*	*90-100%*
1.	Fixed Assets	1	2	3	4	5	6	7	8	9	10
2.	Owned Funds	1	2	3	4	5	6	7	8	9	10
3.	Borrowed Funds	1	2	3	4	5	6	7	8	9	10
4.	Working Capital	1	2	3	4	5	6	7	8	9	10
5.	Raw materials	1	2	3	4	5	6	7	8	9	10
6.	Product-mix	1	2	3	4	5	6	7	8	9	10
7.	Employment Generation	1	2	3	4	5	6	7	8	9	10
8.	Value of Production	1	2	3	4	5	6	7	8	9	10
9.	Sales Turn-over	1	2	3	4	5	6	7	8	9	10
10.	Net Profit	1	2	3	4	5	6	7	8	9	10
	Total	**10**	**20**	**30**	**40**	**50**	**60**	**70**	**80**	**90**	**100**

categories, namely low level, medium level and high level for analytical purposes. For this, arithmetic mean ($\bar{x}$) and standard deviation (SD) obtained have been used. The total score values above or equal to $\bar{x}$ + SD have been classified as indicating high level growth, the total score values equal to or less than $\bar{x}$ – SD have been classified as indicating low level growth and total score values between ($\bar{x}$ + SD) and ($\bar{x}$ - SD) have been classified as indicating medium level growth.

Table 4.2: Distribution of scores for ten growth factors

Sl. No.	*Growth Factor*	*Scores Range*
1.	Fixed assets	1-10
2.	Owned funds	1-10
3.	Borrowed funds	1-10
4.	Working capital	1-10
5.	Raw materials	1-10
6.	Product-mix	1-10
7.	Employment generation	1-10
8.	Value of production	1-10
9.	Sales turnover	1-10
10.	Net profit	10-100

(iv) Extent of Variation

The extent of variation in growth has been calculated with the following formula:

$$\text{Coefficient of variation (\%)} = \frac{\text{Standard Deviation (SD) of Growth scores}}{\text{Arithmetic Mean}} \times 100$$

(v) Multiple Regression Model

In order to identify the factors influencing the growth of entrepreneurship in tiny industrial units, a multiple regression of the following model was estimated:

$$\text{Log } Y = \beta_0 + \beta_1 \log X_1 + \beta_2 \log X_2 + \ldots\ldots\ldots \beta_7 \log X_7 + U$$

where,

Y = Total growth scale value for ten components (in numbers)

X_1 = Age of the units in years

X_2 = Capacity utilization in percentage

X_3 = Fixed investment (Rs. in lakhs)

X_4 = Working capital (Rs. in lakhs)

X_5 = Borrowed capital (Rs. in lakhs)

X_6 = Value of production (Rs. in lakhs)

X_7 = Sales turnover (Rs. in lakhs)

U = Disturbance term.

β_1, β_1, ... β_7 are the parameters to be estimated.

COMPONENT-WISE ANALYSIS

This section analyses the identified ten components of entrepreneurship growth in tiny industrial units during the period 2004-05 and measures their growth in terms of score values.

(i) Fixed Assets

The fixed capital investments of the entrepreneurs in tiny industrial units are met by owned funds and borrowed funds. Fixed assets of entrepreneurs comprise of land, buildings, plant and machinery, fixtures and fittings, tools, furniture and vehicles.

Table 4.3 shows the total amount of fixed assets in the selected tiny industries in the study area as on 2004-2005.

From Table 4.3, it is found that out of 250 tiny entrepreneurs selected for the study, 25 units are agro-based and food products units, 154 are textiles and garments units, 26 units are forest-based, 18 units are chemical based and 27 miscellaneous units. Among the 25 agro based and food products units, 9 (36 per cent) units have fixed assets worth Rs. 50000 to 75000. Only 4 (16 per cent) units have fixed assets worth above Rs. 1,00,000. Out of 154 textiles and garments units, 53 (34.42 per cent) units have fixed assets ranging between Rs. 25000 and 50000. 48 (31.17 per cent) units have fixed assets worth Rs. 50000 to Rs. 75000. 23 (14.94 per cent) units have more than Rs. 100000 worth of fixed assets. Among forest based units, 4 (15.38 per cent) out of 26 units have fixed assets worth less than Rs. 25,000. Chemical-based units have the lowest sample percentage. Among the 18 chemical-based units, a maximum 27.78 percentage units have fixed assets between Rs. 25000 and Rs. 50000. Whereas out of 27 miscellaneous category units, a maximum 37.04 percentage of units have fixed assets between Rs. 25000 – Rs. 50000. Thus, it is clear from the data that out of 250 units, 148 (59.20 per cent) units have fixed assets ranging from Rs. 25000 to Rs. 75000. Only 39 (15.60 per cent) units have fixed assets worth more than Rs. 1,00,000.

Table 4.3: Fixed Assets of the Selected Tiny Industries as on 2004-05

Sl. No.	*Fixed Assets (in Rs.)*	*Agro-based and Food Products*	*Textiles and Garments*	*Forest-based*	*Chemical-based*	*Miscella-neous*	*Total*
1.	Below 25000	4 (16)	9 (5.84)	4 (15.38)	2 (11.11)	3 (11.11)	22 (8.80)
2.	25000-50000	3 (12)	53 (34.42)	5 (19.23)	5 (27.78)	10 (37.04)	76 (30.40)
3.	50000-75000	9 (36)	48 (31.17)	6 (23.08)	4 (22.22)	5 (18.52)	72 (28.80)
4.	75000-100000	5 (20)	21 (13.63)	5 (19.23)	4 (22.22)	6 (22.22)	41 (16.4)
5.	Above 100000	4 (16)	23 (14.94)	6 (23.08)	3 (16.67)	3 (11.11)	39 (15.60)
	Total	**25 (100)**	**154 (100)**	**26 (100)**	**18 (100)**	**27 (100)**	**250 (100)**

Note: Figures in brackets are percentages.

(ii) Growth Scores for Fixed Assets

The calculated growth score values for fixed assets in the case of the selected tiny entrepreneurs are analysed and presented in Table 4.4.

Table 4.4: Score Values for Fixed Assets of the Selected Tiny Industries

Sl. No.	*Name of the Tiny Industry*	*Total Score Value*	*Average Score*
1.	Agro-based and food products	193	7.72
2.	Textiles and Garments	1261	8.19
3.	Forest-based	217	8.35
4.	Chemical-based	156	8.67
5.	Miscellaneous Industries	210	7.78
	Total	**2037**	**8.15**

It is observed from Table 4.4 that the average score of the fixed assets in the chemical based tiny industry is 8.67. Next to this, the forest based tiny industry's average score is 8.35. Agro based and food products average score is the lowest (7.72 per cent) among the selected tiny industries. The total average score of the selected entrepreneurs for fixed assets is 8.15. It is evident that the higher average scores are found among the chemical-based industries, forest based industries and the textiles and garments industry.

(iii) Own Funds

From the accounting point of view own funds means the amount invested by the entrepreneurs to commence business activities. When the business expands, they generate a surplus which is reinvested in business by the entrepreneurs.

Table 4.5 shows the amount of own funds used by the selected tiny entrepreneurs as on 2004-05.

Table 4.5 provides details regarding own fund used in the selected tiny industries. Out of 25 agro based and food products tiny industries, 11 (44 per cent) units have own funds ranging between Rs. 75000 and Rs. 100000. Only 4 (16 per cent) units have own funds less than Rs. 25000. Among the 154 textiles and garments based tiny industries, 51 (33.12 per cent) units have own funds ranging from Rs. 75000 to Rs. 100000 and 42 (27.27 per cent) units use own funds ranging between Rs. 50000 and Rs. 75000. Only 8 units have own funds less than Rs. 25000.

Table 4.5: Own Funds used in the selected Tiny Industries

Sl. No.	*Own Funds (in Rs.)*	*Agro-based and Food Products*	*Textiles and Garments*	*Forest-based*	*Chemical-based*	*Miscellaneous*	*Total*
1.	Below 25000	4 (16)	8 (5.19)	3 (11.54)	-	3 (11.11)	18 (7.20)
2.	25000-50000	3 (12)	24 (15.58)	4 (15.38)	6 (33.33)	5 (18.52)	42 (16.80)
3.	50000-75000	4 (16)	42 (27.27)	6 (23.08)	5 (27.78)	4 (14.81)	61 (24.40)
4.	75000-100000	11 (44)	51 (33.12)	10 (38.46)	3 (16.67)	12 (44.45)	87 (34.80)
5.	Above 100000	3 (12)	29 (18.84)	3 (11.54)	4 (22.22)	3 (11.11)	42 (16.80)
	Total	**25** **(100)**	**154** **(100)**	**26** **(100)**	**18** **(100)**	**27** **(100)**	**250** **(100)**

Note: Figures in brackets are percentages.

Among forest based industries, 10 (38.46 per cent) out of 26 units have own funds between Rs. 75000 and Rs. 100000 and only 3 (11.54 per cent) units use more than Rs. 100000 as own funds. Of the 18 chemical based industries, 6 (33.33 per cent) units make use of Rs. 25000 to Rs. 50000 from their own funds and 4 (22.22 per cent) units use more than Rs. 100000 as own fund. In the miscellaneous tiny units' category, 12 (44.45 per cent) units have Rs. 75000 to Rs. 100000 as their own fund. The above analysis reveals that 148 out of 250 tiny sector industrial units have own funds ranging between Rs. 50000 to 100000.

(iv) Growth Scores for Own Fund

Table 4.6 shows the growth scores for own funds in the case of the selected entrepreneurs in tiny industrial units.

Table 4.6: Score Values for Own Funds of the Selected Tiny Industries

Sl. No.	*Name of the Tiny Industry*	*Total Score Value*	*Average Score*
1.	Agro-based and food products	212	8.48
2.	Textiles and Garments	1241	8.06
3.	Forest-based	203	7.81
4.	Chemical-based	156	8.67
5.	Miscellaneous Industries	205	7.59
	Total	**2017**	**8.07**

It is observed from Table 4.6 that the tiny entrepreneurs of chemical based units have the maximum (8.67) average growth score as regards own fund. The average score forest based, textiles and garments and miscellaneous tiny unit is less than the overall average score of 8.07. On the whole, it is evident from Table 4.6 that the average score of own funds in the chemical based units and agro and food products units is more than the overall average score.

(v) Borrowed Funds

Entrepreneurs borrow funds from various sources such as friends, relatives, partners, money lenders, commercial organizations, banks, Government agencies and co-operative societies. The Government organizations like Small Industries Development Corporation, District Industries Centre, Tamil Nadu Industrial Investment Corporation too help the entrepreneurs to avail themselves of loans from banks.

Table 4.7 shows the distribution of selected tiny industrial units according to the amount borrowed as on 2004-05.

Table 4.7 shows the funds borrowed by the entrepreneurs of the selected tiny industries. In the agro based and food products category, 8 (32 per cent) units out of 25 have borrowed funds ranging from Rs. 75000 to Rs. 100000. Only 6 (24 per cent) units have borrowed funds more than Rs. 100000. As regards the textiles and garments category, 44 (28.57 per cent) out of 154 units have borrowed funds ranging from Rs. 50000 to Rs. 75000. 36 (23.38 per cent) units have borrowed funds ranging Rs. 75000 to Rs. 100000. 114 (74.03 per cent) out of 154 units have borrowed funds more than Rs. 50000.

Table 4.7: Funds Borrowed by Selected Entrepreneurs in Tiny Industrial Units as on 2004-05

Sl. No.	*Borrowed Funds (in Rs.)*	*Agro-based and Food Products*	*Textiles and Garments*	*Forest-based*	*Chemical-based*	*Miscella-neous*	*Total*
1.	Below 25000	2 (8)	15 (9.74)	–	–	1 (3.70)	18 (7.20)
2.	25000-50000	3 (12)	25 (16.23)	4 (15.38)	3 (16.67)	4 (14.81)	39 (15.60)
3.	50000-75000	6 (24)	44 (28.57)	5 (19.23)	6 (33.33)	10 (37.03)	71 (28.40)
4.	75000-100000	8 (32)	36 (23.38)	14 (53.85)	7 (38.89)	9 (33.35)	74 (29.60)
5.	Above 100000	6 (24)	34 (22.08)	3 (11.54)	2 (11.11)	3 (11.11)	48 (19.20)
	Total	**25 (100)**	**154 (100)**	**26 (100)**	**18 (100)**	**27 (100)**	**250**

Note: Figures in brackets are percentages.

Regarding forest based units, 14 (53.85 per cent) units have Rs. 75000 to Rs. 100000 as borrowed funds. Only 3 (11.54 per cent) units have more than Rs. 100000 as borrowed funds. 13 (72.22 per cent) chemical based units have borrowed funds ranging from Rs. 50000 to Rs. 100000. Only 2 (11.11 per cent) units have borrowed funds more than Rs. 100000. 19 (70.37 per cent) out of 27 miscellaneous tiny units have borrowed capital ranging between Rs. 50000 and Rs. 100000.

The above analysis reveals that on the whole 145 (58 per cent) out of 250 units, surveyed have borrowed funds between Rs. 50000 and Rs. 100000. Only 48 (19.20 per cent) units have more than Rs. 100000 as borrowed funds.

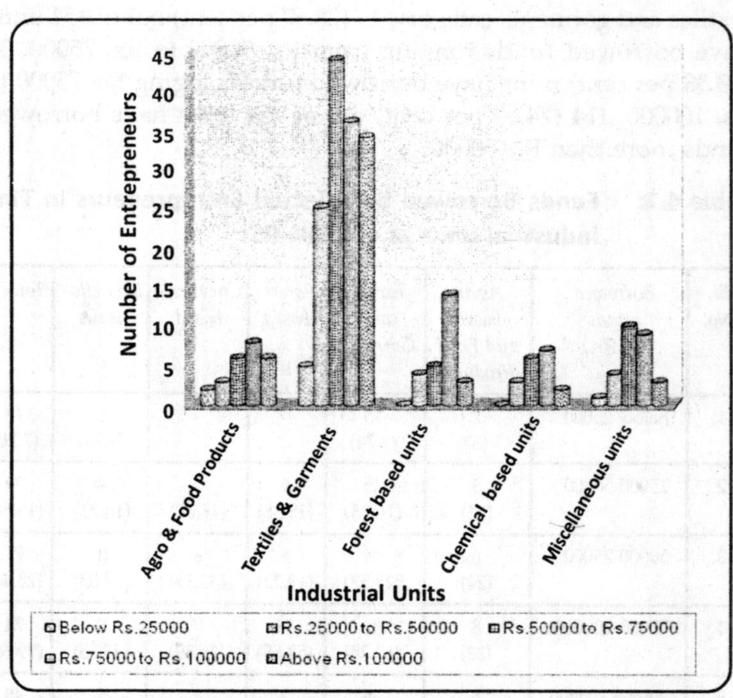

Fig. 4.1: Funds Borrowed by the Selected Tiny Industries as on 2004-05

(vi) Growth Scores for Borrowed Funds

Table 4.8 shows the growth scores for borrowed funds in the case of the selected entrepreneurs in tiny industrial units.

Table 4.8: Score Values for Borrowed Funds of the Selected Entrepreneurs

Sl. No.	*Name of the Tiny Industry*	*Total Score Value*	*Average Score*
1.	Agro-based and food products	184	7.36
2.	Textiles and Garments	1170	7.60
3.	Forest-based	236	9.08
4.	Chemical-based	146	8.11
5.	Miscellaneous Industries	216	8.00
	Total	**1952**	**7.81**

From Table 4.8, it is found that the average score for borrowed funds is 9.08 in the forest based tiny units category. Followed by the forest based units, the chemical based and miscellaneous category units have 8.11 and 8.0 as average scores for borrowed funds. The average scores for borrowed funds in the case of the agro and food products category and the textiles and garments category are less than the overall average score of 7.81.

The above analysis reveals that among the tiny industries selected for the study, the forest based units are using more borrowed funds than the other categories of tiny industries.

(vii) Working Capital

The entrepreneurs require working capital to meet their day-to-day operating expenses such as procurement of raw materials, payment of wages, electricity bills, rent, taxes, transport charges and marketing expenses.

Table 4.9 shows the distribution of entrepreneurs' selected tiny industries according to the working capital used in their units as on 2004-05.

Table 4.9 reveals that 9 (36 per cent) out of 25 agro based and food products tiny industries are using more than Rs. 100000 as working capital. Only 3 (12 per cent) units are using less than Rs. 25000 as working capital. On the whole, in the agro based and food products category 14 (56 per cent) units have more than Rs. 75000 as working capital. In the textiles and garments products category 45 (29.22 per cent) units are using more than Rs. 100000 as working capital. 85 (55.19 per cent) units have working capitals ranging between Rs. 50000 and Rs. 100000 in the textiles and garments category.

As regards the forest based tiny industries category 16 (61.54 per cent) out of 26 units have working capital more than Rs. 100000. 8 (44.44 per cent) out of 18 chemical based units are using more than Rs. 100000 as working capital. In the miscellaneous industries category 15 (55.55 per cent) units have more than Rs. 75000 as working capital. It is inferred from the above analysis that 121 (48.40 per cent) out of 250 units are using working capitals ranging between Rs. 50000 and Rs. 100000.

Table 4.9: Working Capital used in the Selected Tiny Industrial Units as on 2004-05

Sl. No.	Working Capital (in Rs.)	Agro-based and Food Products	Textiles and Garments	Forest-based	Chemical-based	Miscellaneous	Total
1.	Below 25000	3 (12)	3 (1.95)	4 (15.38)	3 (16.67)	3 (11.11)	16 (6.40)
2.	25000-50000	4 (16)	21 (13.64)	3 (11.54)	2 (11.11)	4 (14.82)	34 (13.60)
3.	50000-75000	4 (16)	43 (27.92)	3 (11.54)	3 (16.67)	5 (18.52)	58 (23.20)
4.	75000-100000	5 (20)	42 (27.27)	8 (30.77)	2 (11.11)	6 (22.22)	63 (25.20)
5.	Above 100000	9 (36)	45 (29.22)	8 (30.77)	8 (44.44)	9 (33.33)	79 (31.60)
	Total	**25 (100)**	**154 (100)**	**26 (100)**	**18 (100)**	**27 (100)**	**250 (100)**

Note: Figures in brackets are percentages.

(viii) Growth Scores for Working Capital

Table 4.10 shows the growth scores for the working capital in the case of selected tiny industries.

Table 4.10: Score Values for the Working Capitals of the Selected Tiny Industries

Sl. No.	Name of the Tiny Industry	Total Score Value	Average Score
1.	Agro-based and food products	182	7.28
2.	Textiles and Garments	1161	7.54
3.	Forest-based	201	7.73
4.	Chemical-based	159	8.83
5.	Miscellaneous Industries	216	8.00
	Total	**1919**	**7.68**

It is found from Table 5.10 that the average scores value for working capital of the chemical based units is higher (8.83 per cent) than that of the other industry categories. Next to chemical based industries, miscellaneous units have 8.0 as average score. It is evident from the above analysis that the score values of chemical based, miscellaneous industries and forest based units are more than the overall average score of 7.68.

(ix) Raw Materials Consumed

The value of raw materials used by the entrepreneurs of the selected tiny industrial units during the year 2004-2005 is presented in Table 4.11.

Table 4.11: Value of Raw Materials Used by the Entrepreneurs in Selected Tiny Industrial Units for the Year 2004-05

Sl. No.	*Raw Materials used (in Rs.)*	*Agro-based and Food Products*	*Textiles and Garments*	*Forest-based*	*Chemical-based*	*Miscellaneous*	*Total*
1.	Below 25000	4 (16)	10 (6.49)	3 (11.54)	2 (11.11)	2 (7.41)	21 (8.40)
2.	25000-50000	3 (12)	28 (18.18)	4 (15.38)	3 (16.67)	4 (14.81)	42 (16.80)
3.	50000-75000	7 (28)	40 (25.97)	5 (19.23)	4 (22.22)	8 (29.63)	64 (25.60)
4.	75000-100000	8 (32)	44 (28.57)	10 (38.46)	6 (33.33)	8 (29.63)	76 (30.40)
5.	Above 100000	3 (12)	32 (20.79)	4 (15.39)	3 (16.67)	5 (18.52)	47 (18.80)
	Total	25 (100)	154 (100)	26 (100)	18 (100)	27 (100)	250 (100)

Note: Figures in brackets are percentages.

Table 4.11 shows that 8 (32 per cent) units out of 25 coming under the agro based and food products tiny industries category are using Rs. 75000 to Rs. 100000 worth of raw materials in a year. Only 3 (12 per cent) units are spending more than Rs. 100000 for raw materials. On the whole 15 (60 per cent) out of 25 agro and food products units are spending Rs. 50000 to Rs. 100000 for raw materials. In the textiles and garments units, 44 (28.57 per cent) out of 154 units are using Rs. 75000 to Rs. 100000 for raw materials. 32 (20.79 per cent) units are consuming more than Rs. 100000 worth of raw materials. On the whole 84 (54.54 per cent) units are spending Rs. 50000 to Rs. 100000 for raw materials in a year in the textiles and garments category.

Among the forest based tiny industrial units, 10 (38.46 per cent) units are spending Rs. 75000 to Rs. 100000 for raw materials. 15 (57.69 per cent) out of 26 forest based units are using Rs. 50000 to Rs. 100000 worth of raw materials. 6 (33.33 per cent) out of 18 chemical based units are spending Rs. 75000 to Rs. 100000 on raw materials for production. On the whole 10 (55.55 per cent) units are using Rs. 50000 to Rs. 100000 worth of raw materials in the chemical based units. In the miscellaneous category 16 (59.26 per cent) out of 27 units are using Rs. 50000 to Rs. 100000 worth of raw materials. It is observed from the above analysis that 140 (56 per cent) units out of 250 surveyed are spending Rs. 50000 to Rs. 100000 for raw materials in a year.

(x) Growth Scores for Raw Materials

Table 4.12 shows the growth scores for raw materials used by the selected tiny industries.

Table 4.12: Score Values for Raw Materials used by the Selected Tiny Industries

Sl. No.	*Name of the Tiny Industry*	*Total Score Value*	*Average Score*
1.	Agro-based and food products	218	8.72
2.	Textiles and Garments	1356	8.81
3.	Forest-based	217	8.35
4.	Chemical-based	146	8.11
5.	Miscellaneous Industries	239	8.85
	Total	**2176**	**8.70**

Table 4.12 reveals that the average growth score for raw materials is higher (8.85) in the miscellaneous category. Next to this, the textiles and garments producing units have 8.81 as the average growth score.

It is also observed from Table 4.12 that the miscellaneous category units, Textiles and garments units and Agro and food based units have growth scores more than the overall growth score of 8.70.

(xi) Product-Mix

Entrepreneurs who manufacture multiple products may have to introduce a new product or withdraw an old one or modify the existing product. The set of all products offered for sale by an organization is called a product-mix[1].

Product-mix not only ensures higher production of goods, but also provides adequate scope to the entrepreneur to utilize the by products and produce ancillary components at a lower cost and enhance his profit margin. Product-mix also enables full utilization of production facilities and ensuring higher level of production[2].

Table 4.13 presents the number of products offered for sale by the entrepreneurs of the selected tiny industries.

Table 4.13 reveals that 14 (56 per cent) out of 25 agro and food based tiny units, offer 2 products for sale. 5 (20 per cent) units offer only one product. Among the 154 textiles and garments making tiny industries, 132 (85.72 per cent) units offer only one product for sale. 13 (50 per cent) forest based tiny units offer only one product. In the same category 9 units (34.62 per cent) offer two products. Among the chemical based tiny industries, 10 (55.55 per cent) out of 18 units offer only one product. In the miscellaneous category tiny industries 14 units (51.85 per cent) offer only one product.

The above analysis reveals that the majority (69.60 per cent) of the tiny units irrespective of the industry category offer only one product for sale.

Table 4.13: Product-Mix of the Selected Entrepreneurs in Tiny Industrial Units in the Year 2004-05

Sl. No.	*Product-Mix*	*Agro-based and Food Products*	*Textiles and Garments*	*Forest-based*	*Chemical-based*	*Miscellaneous*	*Total*
1.	One Product	5 (20)	132 (85.72)	13 (50)	10 (55.55)	14 (51.85)	174 (69.60)
2.	Two Products	14 (56)	10 (6.49)	9 (34.62)	5 (27.78)	10 (37.04)	48 (19.20)
3.	Three and above Products	6 (24)	12 (7.79)	4 (15.38)	3 (16.67)	3 (11.11)	28 (11.20)
	Total	**25 (100)**	**154 (100)**	**26 (100)**	**18 (100)**	**27 (100)**	**250 (100)**

Note: Figures in brackets are percentages.

(xii) Growth Score of Product-Mix

Table 4.14 presents the growth scores for product-mix in the case of selected tiny industries.

Table 4.14: Score Values for Product-Mix of the Selected Tiny Industries

Sl. No.	*Name of the Tiny Industry*	*Total Score Value*	*Average Score*
1.	Agro-based and food products	179	7.16
2.	Textiles and Garments	1264	8.21
3.	Forest-based	227	8.73
4.	Chemical-based	144	8.00
5.	Miscellaneous Industries	214	7.93
	Total	**2028**	**8.11**

It is evident from Table 4.14, that the average product-mix growth score is more (8.73 per cent) in the forest based tiny industries. Next to this, the textiles and garments making tiny industries have an average growth score of 8.21.

The above analysis reveals that the average product-mix growth scores of forest based tiny industries and textiles and garments making units are higher than the overall average growth score of 8.11.

(xiii) Employment Generation

In view of India's scarce capital resources and abundant labour, the most important argument advanced in favour of the tiny and small scale industries is that they have a potential to create immediate large scale employment opportunities. According to a study[3], while the output employment ratio is the lowest in the small and tiny sector, employment generating capacity of the small and tiny sector is eight times that of the large scale sector.

Table 4.15 presents details of employment provided by the entrepreneurs of the selected tiny industrial units.

Table 4.15: Number of Persons Employed by the Entrepreneurs in the Selected Tiny Industrial Units during 2004-05

Sl. No.	*Employment Generation (No. of Workers)*	*Agro-based and Food Products*	*Textiles and Garments*	*Forest-based*	*Chemical-based*	*Miscella-neous*	*Total*
1.	Below 5	8 (32)	58 (37.66)	12 (46.15)	6 (33.33)	12 (44.44)	96 (38.40)
2.	5-10	7 (28)	47 (30.52)	7 (26.92)	7 (38.89)	8(29.63) (30.40)	76
3.	11-15	6 (24)	48 (31.17)	4 (15.39)	3 (16.67)	5 (18.52)	66 (26.40)
4.	Above 15	4 (16)	1 (0.65)	3 (11.54)	2 (11.11)	2 (7.41)	12 (4.80)
	Total	25 (100)	154 (100)	26 (100)	18 (100)	27 (100)	250 (100)

Note: Figures in brackets are percentages.

It is found from Table 4.15 that less than 5 persons are working in 8 (32 per cent) out of the 25 agro and food based tiny industries. On the whole, in the agro and food products category

15 (60 per cent) units are employing less than 10 persons. Among the 154 textiles and garments unit, 58 (37.66 per cent) units are employing less than 5 persons in their units. On the whole, a majority of 105 units (68.18 per cent) are giving employment to not more than 10 persons. 12 (46.15 per cent) out of 26 forest based units are employing 1 to 5 persons in their units. Taking the forest based units as a whole, 19 (73.07 per cent) units are employing less than 10 persons.

Among the chemical based tiny industrial units 13 (72.22 per cent) out of 18 units employ not more than 10 persons. Similarly, a majority (74.07 per cent) of the miscellaneous category tiny units are also employing less than 10 persons in their unit. The above analysis reveals that most (68.80 per cent) of the units have less than 10 persons in their units irrespective of the nature of the industry.

(xiv) Growth Score of Employment Generation

Table 4.16 presents the growth scores for employment generation in the case of selected tiny industries.

Table 4.16: Score Values for Employment Generation by the Selected Tiny Industries

Sl. No.	*Name of the Tiny Industry*	*Total Score Value*	*Average Score*
1.	Agro-based and food products	181	7.24
2.	Textiles and Garments	1218	7.91
3.	Forest-based	231	8.88
4.	Chemical-based	144	8.00
5.	Miscellaneous Industries	213	7.89
	Total	**1987**	**7.95**

It is inferred from Table 4.16 that the forest based tiny units have the maximum (8.88 per cent) employment growth scores compared to the other tiny industries categories. Next to forest based industry, chemical based industry has a growth score of 8.0.

On the whole the average employment growth score of all the tiny industries selected for this study is 7.95. Comparing the average growth score with the individual industry growth score, the employment growth scores for forest and chemical based tiny industries are higher than the overall growth score of 7.95.

(xv) Value of Production

Production means conversion of raw materials into semi-finished and finished goods. Every entrepreneur strives to ensure maximum production in the best manner at the lowest cost and generate maximum profits.

During the years 2000-01 to 2004-05 the SSI sector registered continuous growth in production. The average annual growth in production at current and constant prices was 16.9 per cent and 10 per cent respectively during 2004-05 according to the Economic Survey 2005-06[4].

The following Table 4.17 presents the total value of goods produced by the entrepreneurs of the selected tiny industries.

Table 4.17: Value of Goods Produced by the Entrepreneurs of Selected Tiny Industries during 2004-05

Sl. No.	*Value of Production (in Rs.)*	*Agro-based and Food Products*	*Textiles and Garments*	*Forest-based*	*Chemical-based*	*Miscella-neous*	*Total*
1.	Below 25000	5 (20)	43 (27.92)	3 (11.54)	2 (11.11)	5 (18.52)	58 (23.20)
2.	25000-50000	8 (32)	38 (24.68)	6 (23.08)	4 (22.22)	6 (22.22)	62 (24.80)
3.	50000-75000	7 (28)	40 (25.97)	9 (34.08)	7 (38.89)	8 (29.63)	71 (28.40)
4.	75000-100000	3 (12)	20 (12.99)	4 (15.38)	3 (16.67)	5 (18.52)	35 (14.00)
5.	Above 100000	2 (8)	13 (8.44)	4 (15.38)	2 (11.11)	3 (11.11)	24 (9.60)
	Total	25 (100)	154 (100)	26 (100)	18 (100)	27 (100)	250 (100)

Note: Figures in brackets are percentages.

Table 4.17 shows that in 2004-05, 8 (32 per cent) out of 25 agro and food products tiny industries produced goods worth Rs. 25000 to Rs. 50000. Only 2 (8 per cent) units produced goods worth more than Rs. 100000. On the whole, 15 out of 25 agro and food based products produced goods worth Rs. 25000 to Rs. 75000.

Among 154 textiles and garments making industries, 78 (50.65 per cent) units produced goods worth Rs. 25000 to Rs. 75000. 43 (27.92 per cent) units produced less than Rs. 25000 worth of goods. 15 out of 26 forest based tiny units produced goods worth between Rs. 25000 to Rs. 75000. Similarly 11 (61.11 per cent) units out of 18 chemical based units also produced Rs. 25000 to Rs. 75000 worth of goods. In the miscellaneous tiny industries category, 14 (51.85 per cent) units had production ranging between Rs. 25000 to Rs. 75000 worth of goods.

It is evident from the above analysis that irrespective of the industry category the majority (53.20 per cent) of the units produced goods ranging from Rs. 25000 to Rs. 75000 in worth.

(xvi) Growth Scores for Value of Production

Table 4.18 presents the growth scores for value of production in the selected tiny industries.

Table 4.18: Score Values for Production in the Selected Tiny Industries

Sl. No.	*Name of the Tiny Industry*	*Total Score Value*	*Average Score*
1.	Agro-based and food products	178	7.12
2.	Textiles and Garments	1191	7.73
3.	Forest-based	211	8.12
4.	Chemical-based	156	8.67
5.	Miscellaneous Industries	241	8.93
	Total	**1977**	**7.91**

Table 4.18 reveals that the average growth score value for production is more (8.93 per cent) in the miscellaneous industry category. The chemical based units rank second in average growth score value (8.67 per cent).

On the whole the average growth score is 7.91. The miscellaneous category tiny units followed by chemical and forest based industries have registered average growth scores higher than this overall score.

(xvii) Sales Turnover

Sales turnover decides the ultimate industrial activity since the quantum of production is made for meeting the market needs. Sales turnover also indicates the market share of the product. If the market share increases, the scale of operation of the business expands showing the growth of the business. Hence sales turnover has been taken as one of the variables indicating growth of entrepreneurship in tiny sector industries.

Table 4.19 highlights the sales turnover of the selected tiny industries in the year 2004-05.

Table 4.19: Sales Turnover of the selected Tiny Industries during 2004-05

Sl. No.	*Sales Turnover (in Rs.)*	*Agro-based and Food Products*	*Textiles and Garments*	*Forest-based*	*Chemical-based*	*Miscella-neous*	*Total*
1.	Below 50000	4 (16)	14 (9.09)	3 (11.54)	1 (5.56)	2 (7.41)	24 (9.60)
2.	50000-75000	4 (16)	46 (29.87)	4 (15.38)	2(11.11) (11.11)	3 (23.60)	59
3.	75000-100000	8 (32)	34 (22.08)	8 (30.77)	6 (33.33)	7 (25.93)	63 (25.20)
4.	100000-125000	6 (24)	41 (26.62)	7 (26.92)	7 (38.89)	11 (40.74)	72 (28.80)
5.	Above 125000	3 (12)	19 (12.34)	4 (15.39)	2 (11.11)	4 (14.81)	32 (12.80)
	Total	**25 (100)**	**154 (100)**	**26 (100)**	**18 (100)**	**27 (100)**	**250 (100)**

Note: Figures in brackets are percentages.

Table 4.19 reveals that in 2004-05, eight (32 per cent) units out of 25 agro and food based tiny industrial units sold goods ranging between Rs. 75000 to Rs. 100000 in worth. Only 3 (12 per cent) units had a sales turnover more than Rs. 125000. On the whole, the sales turnover of 14 (56 per cent) units ranged from Rs. 75000 to Rs. 125000.

In the textiles and garments making tiny units 46 (29.87 per cent) out of 154 units had a sales turnover ranging from Rs. 50000 to Rs. 75000. On the whole the sales turnover of textiles and garments making units ranged between Rs. 50000 and Rs. 125000 in 121 (78.57 per cent) units. 8 (30.77 per cent) out of 26 units belonging to the forest based tiny units had a sales turnover ranging between Rs. 75000 and Rs. 100000. Taking all the forest based units together, the sales turnover varied from Rs. 75000 to Rs. 125000 in 15 (57.69 per cent) units.

Among the chemical based industries, 7 (38.89 per cent) units had a sales turnover ranging between Rs. 100000 and Rs. 125000. Among all the chemical based units 13 (72.22 per cent) out of 18 units had a sales turnover ranging between Rs. 75000 and Rs. 125000. The sales turnover of most (66.67 per cent) of the miscellaneous category tiny units ranges between Rs. 75000 and Rs. 125000.

It is evident from the above analysis that the sales turnover varies between Rs. 75000 and Rs. 125000 among all the selected tiny industries.

(xviii) Growth Scores for Sales Turnover

The calculated score values for sales turnover of the selected entrepreneurs in tiny industries are presented in Table 4.20.

It is observed from Table 4.20 that the growth score of sales turnover is high (8.94 per cent) in the chemical based tiny industry. Next to chemical based units, the miscellaneous category tiny units have a growth score of 8.19 for sales turnover.

The calculated average growth score for all the tiny industries is 7.64. The entrepreneurs of chemical, miscellaneous and forest based tiny industrial units have a growth score above the average score of 7.65. Among the top three tiny industry categories, the average growth score of the chemical based tiny units is the highest (8.94 per cent).

Table 4.20: Score Values for the Sales Turnover of the Selected Entrepreneurs in Tiny Industrial Units

Sl. No.	*Name of the Tiny Industry*	*Total Score Value*	*Average Score*
1.	Agro-based and food products	179	7.16
2.	Textiles and Garments	1142	7.42
3.	Forest-based	207	7.96
4.	Chemical-based	161	8.94
5.	Miscellaneous Industries	221	8.19
	Total	**1910**	**7.64**

(xix) Net Profit

Net profit is that part of gross profit arrived after adjusting for non operating expenses and incomes. It indicates the profitability of an industrial unit during a particular period. Moreover, net profit also enables an industrial unit to generate more funds internally avoiding the influence of any debt obligation in the day to day financial affairs of the industrial unit. Efficient industrial units will have a higher net profit. Further an increase in net profit results from an increase in sales, production and the like. So, net profit has been recognized as an indicator of growth of entrepreneurship in tiny sector industries.

Table 4.21 shows the amount of net profit earned by the entrepreneurs in the year 2004-05 in different categories of tiny industries.

It is inferred from Table 4.21 that 7 (28.00 per cent) out of 25 entrepreneurs of agro and food products tiny industries have earned a net profit of Rs. 50000 to Rs. 75000. On the whole 13 (52.00 per cent) units have a net profit ranging between Rs. 50000 and Rs. 100000. Of the 154 textiles and garments making units, 95 (61.69 per cent) units have earned Rs. 50000 to Rs. 100000 as net profit. Only 32 (20.77 per cent) units have a net profit of more than Rs. 100000.

Table 4.21: Net Profit Earned by the Entrepreneurs of the Selected Tiny Industries during 2004-05

Sl. No.	*Net Profit (in Rs.)*	*Agro-based and Food Products*	*Textiles and Garments*	*Forest-based*	*Chemical-based based*	*Miscella-neous*	*Total*
1.	Below 25000	3 (12)	7 (4.55)	3 (11.54)	2 (11.11)	3 (11.11)	18 (17.2)
2.	25000-50000	4 (16)	20 (12.99)	4 (15.38)	2 (11.11)	4 (14.81)	34 (13.60)
3.	50000-75000	7 (28)	57 (37.01)	8 (30.77)	5 (27.78)	7 (25.93)	84 (33.60)
4.	75000-100000	6 (24)	38 (24.68)	5 (19.23)	6 (33.33)	8 (29.63)	63 (25.20)
5.	Above 100000	5 (20)	32 (20.77)	6 (23.08)	3 (16.67)	5 (18.52)	51 (20.40)
	Total	**25 (100)**	**154 (100)**	**26 (100)**	**18 (100)**	**27 (100)**	**250 (100)**

Note: Figures in brackets are percentages.

Regarding forest based tiny industries, 8 (30.77 per cent) units out of 26 have a net profit ranging between Rs. 50000 and Rs. 75000. Among the chemical based tiny units 11 (61.11 per cent) out of 18 units have earned a net profit of Rs. 50000 to Rs. 100000. 15 (55.56 per cent) units belonging to the miscellaneous category have earned a net profit ranging between Rs. 50000 and Rs. 100000.

The above analysis reveals that 147 out of 250 tiny units selected for the study have a net profit ranging between Rs. 50000 and Rs. 100000.

(xx) Growth Scores for Net Profit Earned

Table 4.22 presents the net profit score values for net profit earned by the selected entrepreneurs in different categories of tiny industries.

Table 4.22: Net Profit Score Values for Net Profit Earned by the Selected Entrepreneurs in Tiny Industrial Units

Sl. No.	*Name of the Tiny Industry*	*Total Score Value*	*Average Score*
1.	Agro-based and food products	182	7.28
2.	Textiles and Garments	1156	7.51
3.	Forest-based	203	7.81
4.	Chemical-based	156	8.67
5.	Miscellaneous Industries	228	8.44
	Total	**1928**	**7.71**

From Table 4.22 it is observed that the entrepreneurs of chemical based tiny units have a high (8.67 per cent) growth score compared to other categories of tiny industrial units. The miscellaneous category tiny units rank second having a net profit growth score of 8.44.

The calculated average growth score for all the categories of tiny units is 7.71. Among the three tiny industry categories namely, forest based, chemical based and miscellaneous industries whose average growth scores are higher than the average growth score of 7.71, the chemical based units have the highest growth score of 8.67 for net profit.

LEVELS OF GROWTH

The entrepreneurs of the selected tiny industrial units have been classified into three categories namely those having high, medium and low levels of growth on the basis of growth scores obtained by using the Scaling Technique. For this, arithmetic mean ($\bar{X}$) and Standard Deviation (SD) for the score values were computed. While the score values $\geq (\bar{X} + SD)$ have been classified as indicative of high level growth, the score values ≤ ($\bar{X}$ – SD) indicate low level growth and the score values between ($\bar{X}$ + SD) and ($\bar{X}$ – SD) have been classified as indicating medium level growth.

($\bar{X}$ + SD) i.e. 79.80 + 7.49 = 87.29 [High level growth]

($\bar{X}$ – SD) i.e. 79.80 - 7.49 = 72.31 [Low level growth]

Between ($\bar{X}$ + SD) and ($\bar{X}$ – SD) i.e. 72.31 and 87.29 [medium level growth].

Table 4.23 presents the different levels of growth of the selected 250 entrepreneurs in Tamil Nadu state.

Table 4.23: Levels of Growth of the Selected Entrepreneurs in Tiny Industrial Units

Sl. No.	*Level of Growth*	*Number of Units*	*Percentage*
1.	High	41	16.40
2.	Medium	132	52.80
3.	Low	77	30.80
	Total	**250**	**100.00**

From Table 4.23, it is clear that out of 250 entrepreneurs, 41 (16.40 per cent) come under high level growth; 132 entrepreneurs (52.8 per cent) under medium level growth and 77 entrepreneurs (30.80 per cent) under low level growth. It is evident from the analysis that 69.20 per cent of the units have attained a satisfactory level of growth in the study area. 77 (30.80 per cent) units need to improve their performance to achieve a higher level growth.

Extent of Variation in Growth

Table 4.24 shows the mean, standard deviation and coefficient of variations which help to study the extent of variation in growth levels.

Table 4.24: Mean ($\bar{x}$), Standard Deviation (SD) and Coefficients of Variation (C.V.) of the Score Values in the Levels of Growth of the Entrepreneurs

Sl. No.	Level of Growth	Number of Units	Total Score	$\bar{X}$	S.D.	C.V. (%)
1.	High	41	3342	81.50	7.42	9.10
2.	Medium	132	10563	80.02	7.86	9.82
3.	Low	77	6045	78.51	8.37	10.66
	Total	**250**	**19950**	**79.80**	**7.49**	**9.39**

It is observed from Table 4.24 that the coefficient of variation is 9.10 per cent for high level growth, 9.82 per cent for medium level growth and 10.66 per cent for low level growth. It indicates that the entrepreneurs with low level growth have more variation in growth scores compared to the other two levels. It is inferred that the high level growth units are very consistent in growth, followed by medium level growth units.

RELATIONSHIP BETWEEN SOCIO-ECONOMIC FACTORS AND LEVELS OF GROWTH

In this section an attempt has been made to analyse the relationship between the levels of growth of tiny sector industries and relevant socio-economic factors.

Age and the Level of Growth

Age and levels of growth of the entrepreneurs are given in Table 4.25.

Table 4.25 reveals that out of 41 entrepreneurs with high levels of growth, a majority of 16 (39.02 per cent) fall under the age group between 30 and 40 years. In the same high growth category, 28 (68.29 per cent) entrepreneurs come under the age group of 30 to 50 years. Among the 132 entrepreneurs with the medium level of growth 66 (50 per cent) entrepreneurs belong to the age group of 41 to 50 years. In this category, 99 (75 per cent) entrepreneurs belong to the age group of 30 to 50 years.

Table 4.25: Age and the Level of Growth

Sl. No.	*Age*	*Level of Growth*			*Total*
		High	*Medium*	*Low*	
1.	Less than 30	3 (7.32)	12 (9.09)	22 (28.57)	37 (14.80)
2.	30-40	16 (39.02)	33 (25.00)	27 (35.06)	76 (30.40)
3.	41-50	12 (29.27)	66 (50.00)	13 (16.88)	91 (36.40)
4.	Above 50	10 (24.39)	21 (15.91)	15 (19.08)	46 (18.40)
	Total	**41 (100)**	**132 (100)**	**77 (100)**	**250 (100)**

Among the 77 entrepreneurs with a low level growth, 27 (35.07 per cent) come under the age category of 30 to 40 years. 28 (35.96 per cent) entrepreneurs belong to the age group of above 40 years. Here a null hypothesis has been formulated that the age of the entrepreneurs and the level of their growth are two independent attributes. To test the null hypothesis that there is no relationship between age and the level of growth, the chi-square test has been applied.

The results of the chi-square test are furnished below:

Calculated value (C.V.) = 32.8528

Table value at 5 per cent level of significance (T.V.) = 12.592

Degrees of freedom = 6

Inference = Significant

As the calculated chi-square value is greater than the table value at 5 per cent level of significance, the null hypothesis is rejected. It is concluded that the age of the respondents has influenced the level of their growth as entrepreneurs.

Educational Status and the Level of Growth

Education is considered to be an important factor which influences the growth of entrepreneurs in the successful management of the enterprise. Details regarding education status and level of growth are given in Table 4.26.

Table 4.26: Educational Status and the Level of Growth

Sl. No.	Status of Education	Level of Growth			Total
		High	Medium	Low	
1.	School Level	15 (36.59)	38 (28.79)	8 (10.39)	61 (24.40)
2.	College Level	15 (36.59)	64 (48.48)	64 (83.12)	143 (57.20)
3.	Technical	11 (26.82)	30 (22.73)	5 (6.49)	46 (18.40)
	Total	**41 (100)**	**132 (100)**	**77 (100)**	**250 (100)**

Table 4.26 reveals that out of 41 high growth achievers an equal number of 15 (36.59 per cent) entrepreneurs have school and college level education. Among the 132 medium growth achievers, 64 (48.48 per cent) have college level education. Among the low level growth achievers, 64 (83.12 per cent) out of 77 entrepreneurs have college level education. On the whole 132 (52.8 per cent) entrepreneurs irrespective of their educational status have achieved medium growth.

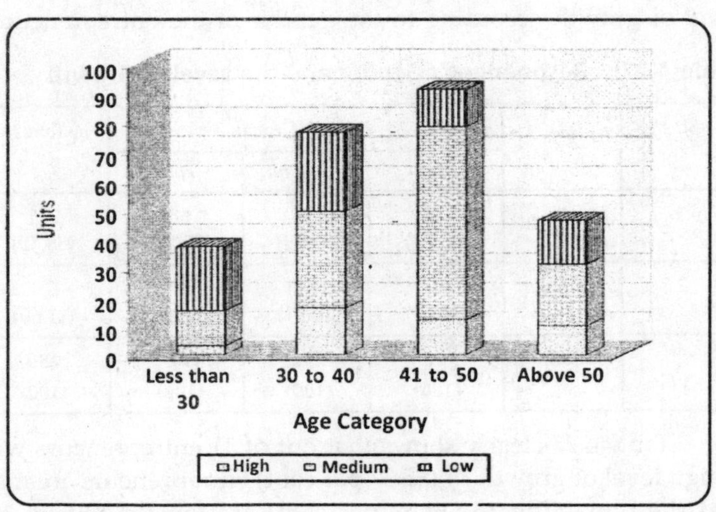

Fig. 4.2: Age and the Level of Growth

For further analysis a null hypothesis has been formulated that the level of growth is independent of the educational status of the respondents. In order to test the null hypothesis that there is no relationship between the educational status and the level of growth, the chi-square test has been applied and the results are furnished below.

The results of the chi-square test:

Calculated value (C.V.)	=	32.1723
Table value at 5 per cent level of significance (T.V.)	=	9.488
Degrees of freedom	=	4
Inference	=	Significant

As the calculated chi-square value is greater than the table value at 5 per cent level of significance, the null hypothesis is rejected. Thus it may be concluded that there exists a relationship between the educational status of the respondents and their growth level as entrepreneurs.

Level of Growth and the Respondent's Gender

Gender is another important factor which may influence the growth of entrepreneurship. The following table presents the level of growth according to the gender of the entrepreneur.

Table 4.27: Respondent's Gender and the Level of Growth

Sl. No.	*Sex*	*Level of Growth*			*Total*
		High	*Medium*	*Low*	
1.	Male	35 (85.37)	118 (89.39)	68 (88.31)	221 (88.40)
2.	Female	6 (14.63)	14 (10.61)	9 (11.69)	29 (11.60)
	Total	**41 (100)**	**132 (100)**	**77 (100)**	**250 (100)**

Table 4.27 clearly shows that out of 41 entrepreneurs with a high level of growth 35 (85.37 per cent) entrepreneurs are male and the remaining 16 (14.63 per cent) are female. Out of 132 entrepreneurs with a medium level of growth 118 (89.39 per cent)

are male and the rest (10.61 per cent) are female. Among the 77 entrepreneurs with a low level of growth, 68 (88.31 per cent) are male and the remaining 9 (11.69 per cent) are female.

In order to analyse further, a null hypothesis has been formulated that there is no relationship between the sex of the entrepreneurs and the level of their growth. To test the relationship, the chi-square test has been applied and the results are given below:

Calculated value (C.V.)	=	0.5123
Table value at 5 per cent level of significance (T.V.)	=	5.991
Degrees of freedom	=	2
Inference	=	Not significant

As the calculated chi-square value is less than the table value at 5 per cent level of significance, the null hypothesis is accepted. It is said that level of growth and the sex of the respondents are independent attributes. Hence there is no relationship between the level of growth and the sex of the respondents.

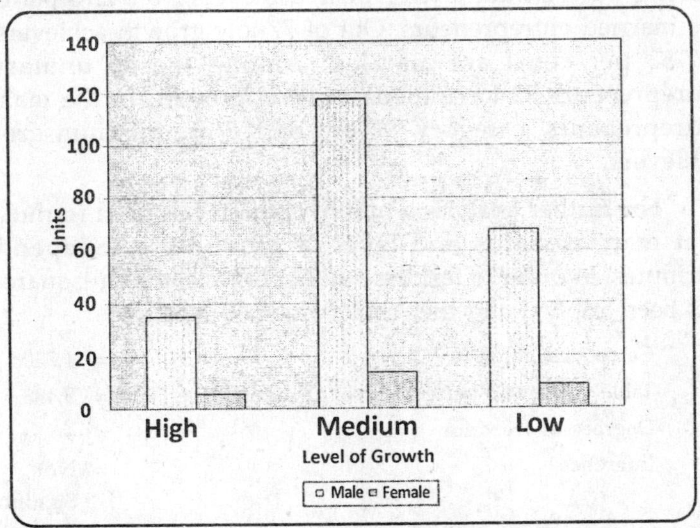

Fig. 4.3: Respondents' Gender and Level of Growth

Marital Status and the Level of Growth

Table 4.28 presents the marital status of the tiny entrepreneurs and the level of their growth as entrepreneurs.

Table 4.28: Marital Status and the Level of Growth

Sl. No.	*Marital Status*	*Level of Growth*			*Total*
		High	*Medium*	*Low*	
1.	Unmarried	7 (17.07)	22 (16.67)	17 (22.08)	46 (18.40)
2.	Married	30 (73.17)	96 (72.73)	52 (67.53)	178 (71.20)
3.	Widow/Widower	4 (9.76)	14 (10.60)	8 (10.39)	26 (10.40)
	Total	**41 (100)**	**132 (100)**	**77 (100)**	**250 (100)**

Table 4.28 shows that among the 41 entrepreneurs who have achieved a high level growth, 30 (73.17 per cent) are married. Among the medium level growth achievers, 96 (72.73 per cent) are married entrepreneurs. Out of 77 low growth achievers, 52 (67.53 per cent) are married. Among the 46 unmarried entrepreneurs 22 have medium level growth. In the married entrepreneurs' category, 96 out of 178 are medium growth achievers.

For further analysis a null hypothesis has been formulated that marital status and level of growth are independent attributes. In order to test the null hypothesis, the chi-square test has been applied and the results are shown below:

Calculated value (C.V.) = 1.7208
Table value at 5 per cent level of significance (T.V.) = 9.488
Degrees of freedom = 4
Inference = Not Significant

As the calculated chi-square value is less than the table value at 5 per cent level of significance, the null hypothesis is accepted. It is concluded that the level of growth and marital status are independent attributes. Hence there exists no relationship between marital status and the level of growth of the entrepreneurs.

Technical Knowledge and the Level of Growth

Technical knowledge of the entrepreneurs is an important factor influencing the level of growth of the entrepreneur. A two way table has been prepared to test the relationship between technical knowledge and the level of growth. Table 4.29 shows the relationship between the technical knowledge of the tiny entrepreneurs and their level of growth.

Table 4.29: Technical Knowledge and the Level of Growth

Sl. No.	*Technical Knowledge*	*Level of Growth*			*Total*
		High	*Medium*	*Low*	
1.	With technical knowledge	27 (65.85)	12 (9.09)	7 (9.09)	46 (18.4)
2.	Without technical knowledge	14 (34.15)	120 (90.91)	70 (90.91)	204 (81.6)
	Total	**41 (100)**	**132 (100)**	**77 (100)**	**250 (100)**

Table 4.29 shows that out of 41 entrepreneurs with high level of growth, a majority of 27 (65.85 per cent) have some technical knowledge and the remaining 14 (34.15 per cent) do not have any technical knowledge. Out of 132 entrepreneurs with medium level of growth, 120 (90.91 per cent) do not have any technical knowledge. The rest (9.09 per cent) of them have some technical knowledge. Table 4.29 shows that out of 77 entrepreneurs with a low level of growth, 7 (9.09 per cent) have some technical knowledge and the rest (90.91 per cent) do not have any technical knowledge.

In order to test the null hypothesis that there exists no relationship between technical knowledge and the level of growth, the chi-square test is used and the results are given below.

Calculated value (C.V.) = 67.6627

Table value at 5 per cent level of significance (T.V.) = 5.991

Degrees of freedom = 2

Inference = Significant

As the calculated value is more than the table value, the two attributes are not independent. So the null hypothesis is rejected. Hence, there exists a relationship between technical knowledge and the level of growth.

Family Size and the Level of Growth

Growth level of tiny entrepreneurial units according to the family size of the entrepreneurs is presented in Table 4.30.

Table 4.30: Family size and the Level of Growth

Sl. No.	*Family Size*	*Level of Growth*			*Total*
		High	*Medium*	*Low*	
1.	Below 3	5 (12.20)	24 (18.18)	18 (23.38)	47 (18.80)
2.	3-5	25 (60.98)	65 (49.25)	36 (46.75)	126 (50.40)
3.	Above 5	11 (26.83)	43 (32.57)	23 (29.87)	77 (30.80)
	Total	**41 (100)**	**132 (100)**	**77 (100)**	**250 (100)**

Table 4.30 indicates that out of 41 high growth achievers, 25 (60.98 per cent) have 3-to 5 dependent persons. Among the medium growth achievers, a majority (49.25 per cent) come under the 3 to 5 family size. Similarly in the category of low growth achievers too, a majority (46.75 per cent) have 3 to 5 dependents.

For further analysis a null hypothesis has been formulated that family size and the level of growth are two independent attributes. The null hypothesis has been tested by applying the chi-square test and the result is given below.

Calculated value (C.V.)	=	3.8073
Table value at 5 per cent level of significance (T.V.)	=	9.49
Degrees of freedom	=	4
Inference	=	Not significant

As the calculated value is less than the table value at 5 per cent level of significance, the null hypothesis is accepted. It is seen that family size and the level of growth are independent attributes. Hence, there exists no relationship between the family size and the level of growth of the entrepreneurs.

Nature of Family and the Level of Growth

The nature of family is an important factor for running a venture and also for becoming an entrepreneur. Family is the primary group wherein every member is directly associated with its activities. It is the family where socialization directs and guides the behaviour of its members. The nature and size of the family determines the extent to which an entrepreneur can take decisions by himself or herself and not depend upon others[5].

Entrepreneurs from joint families experience lower stress than those belonging to nuclear families. In the joint family, there is an advantage of support from others, thereby giving the entrepreneur freedom from family responsibilities. On the other hand in a nuclear family the entrepreneur is motivated to create a decent standard of living, hence they employ servants to look after children and thereby the freedom needed for concentrating on the enterprise is assured.

It is inferred from the above table that out of 41 entrepreneurs with high level of growth, a majority of 21 (51.22 per cent) belong to joint families and 20 (48.78 per cent) belong to nuclear families. Out of 132 entrepreneurs with medium level of growth, a majority of 79 (59.85 per cent) belong to nuclear families and 53 (40.15 per cent) belong to joint families. It is also seen that out of 77 entrepreneurs with a low level of growth, a majority of 72 (93.51 per cent) belong to nuclear families and 5 (6.49 per cent) belong to joint families.

Table 4.31 reveals the relationship between the nature of family and the level of growth of entrepreneurs.

Table 4.31: Nature of Family and the Level of Growth

Sl. No.	*Nature of Family*	*Level of Growth*			*Total*
		High	*Medium*	*Low*	
1.	Nuclear Family	20 (48.78)	79 (59.85)	72 (93.51)	171 (68.40)
2.	Joint Family	21 (51.22)	53 (40.15)	5 (6.49)	79 (31.60)
	Total	**41** **(100)**	**132** **(100)**	**77** **(100)**	**250** **(100)**

A null hypothesis has been formulated that the nature of family and the level of growth are two independent attributes. To test this null hypothesis, the chi-square test is used and the results are given below.

Calculated value (C.V.)	=	33.2925
Table value at 5 per cent level of significance (T.V.)	=	5.991
Degrees of freedom	=	2
Inference	=	Significant

As the calculated value is greater than the table value at 5 per cent level of significance, the nature of family and the level of growth are not independent attributes. So the null hypothesis is rejected. Hence there exists a relationship between the nature of family and the level of growth of entrepreneurs.

Occupational Background and the Level of Growth

The entrepreneurs are classified according to their occupational background namely, agricultural labourer, farmer, non-agricultural labourer, government employee, private employee and micro entrepreneurs. The entrepreneurs hailing from a family with industrial or business background are able to manage their business efficiently. The experience gained from their family becomes the basis for the present business. It has been ascertained that the occupational background of the family of the entrepreneurs has a close relationship with the growth of the tiny entrepreneurs. So it has been taken as one of the variables and its significance has to be tested. Table 4.32 presents the occupational background and the level of growth of entrepreneurs.

Table 4.32: Occupational Background and the Level of Growth

Sl. No.	*Occupational Background*	*Level of Growth*			*Total*
		High	*Medium*	*Low*	
1.	Agricultural Labourers	6 (14.63)	10 (7.58)	10 (12.99)	26 (10.40)
2.	Farmers	18 (43,90)	52 (39.39)	20 (25.97)	90 (36.0)
3.	Non-agricultural labourers	5 (12.20)	15 (11.36)	12 (15.58)	32 (12.80)
4.	Government employees	2 (4.88)	11 (8.33)	2 (2.60)	15 (6.0)
5.	Private employees	5 (12.20)	14 (10.61)	18 (23.38)	37 (14.80)
6.	Micro-entrepreneurs	5 (12.20)	30 (22.73)	15 (19.48)	50 (20.0)
	Total	**41 (100)**	**132 (100)**	**77 (100)**	**250 (100)**

Table 4.32 reveals that out of 41 entrepreneurs with a high level of growth, a majority of 18 (43.90 per cent) are farmers. 6 (14.63 per cent) entrepreneurs are agricultural labourers. Out of 132 entrepreneurs with medium level of growth, a majority of 52 (39.39 per cent) are farmers. 30 (22.73 per cent) are micro entrepreneurs. Out of 77 entrepreneurs with a low level of growth, a majority of 20 (25.97 per cent) are farmers. 18 (23.38 per cent) entrepreneurs are private employees and 15 (19.48 per cent) are micro-entrepreneurs.

For further analysis a null hypothesis has been formulated that the occupational background and the level of growth are two independent attributes. This null hypothesis has been tested by applying the chi-square test. The results of the chi-square test are presented below:

Calculated value (C.V.) = 16.8129

Table value at 5 per cent level of significance (T.V.) = 18.307

Degrees of freedom = 10

Inference = Not Significant

As the calculated value is less than the table value, the null hypothesis is accepted. Hence there exists no relationship between occupational background and the level of growth.

FACTORS INFLUENCING THE GROWTH OF ENTREPRENEURS

In order to find the factors which influence the growth of entrepreneurs, multiple linear regression was estimated by the method of least squares. The computed results are given in Table 4.33.

It is found from Table 4.33 that the coefficient of multiple determinations R^2 was 0.6314 indicating 63.14 per cent variation in the growth of entrepreneurs of high level growth, associated with independent variables included in the regression model. Four out of seven variables, namely, capacity utilization, fixed investment, working capital and sales turnover are statistically significant at 5 per cent level and they are positively related to the growth of entrepreneurs in the high level category. It indicates that one per cent increases in these four variables could increase the growth scale by 0.2916 per cent, 0.1052 per cent, 0.2813 per cent and 0.2016 per cent respectively. Among the significant variables, capacity utilization had a greater influence on growth scale followed by working capital. As per the F-value given in Table 5.33, the fitted regression model is found to be significant at 5 per cent level.

In the case of medium level growth category, the value R^2 indicates 61.73 per cent variations in the growth scale. The regression coefficient of capacity utilization, fixed investment working capital and value of production are found to be significant at 5 per cent level and positively related. It means that an additional one per cent of each of these variables is capable of increasing the growth scale by 0.2813 per cent, 0.2016 per cent, 0.1942 per cent and 0.3144 per cent respectively. The variable, value of production, had a greater influence on the growth scale in the case of medium level growth category of entrepreneurs, followed by capacity utilization. The F-value indicates that the model fitted is statistically significant at 5 per cent level.

Table 5.33: Estimated Regression Results of Factors Influencing the Growth of Entrepreneurs

Variable	*Parameter Estimate*		
	High Level	*Medium Level*	*Low Level*
Intercept	1.7841	2.1071	1.9721
Log X_1	0.0814 (0.1041)	0.0914 (0.0614)	0.0072 (0.0041)
Log X_2	0.2916* (3.1471)	0.2813* (3.1471)	0.1911* (2.7142)
Log X_3	0.1052* (2.3147)	0.2016* (2.7196)	0.1141 (0.0971)
Log X_4	0.2813* (2.7214)	0.1972* (2.7612)	0.3011* (2.7231)
Log X_5	0.0811 (0.0671)	0.0196 (1.0141)	0.0179 (1.0147)
Log X_6	0.0804 (0.0611)	0.3114* (3.4776)	0.2117* (3.1011)
Log X_7	0.2016* (3.1172)	0.1042 (1.2167)	0.0541 (1.1216)
R^2	0.6314	0.6173	0.6276
F-value	32.47	38.72	41.36
Number of Observations	41	132	77

Figures in brackets are the t-values.

* Indicates that the co-efficient are statistically significant at 5 per cent level.

All the seven variables included in the regression model for the low level growth category of entrepreneurs are jointly responsible for about 62.76 per cent variation in the growth scale. Out of seven variables, three variables namely, capacity utilization, working capital and value of production are statistically significant at 5 per cent level and they are positively related to the growth scale. One per cent increase in these variables may lead to 0.1911 per cent, 0.3011 per cent and 0.2117 per cent increase respectively in the growth scale of the low growth level category of entrepreneurs. Working capital had a greater influence on growth scale followed by value of production. The F-value shows that the regression model fitted is statistically significant at 5 per cent level.

Thus, it may be concluded that four variables each in the case of high and medium level growth categories and three variables in the case of low level growth category have significant influence on the growth scale of the entrepreneurs. But capacity utilisation, value of production and working capital have greater influence on the growth scale in the case of high, medium and low level growth category of entrepreneurs.

SUMMARY

In this chapter, the measurement of growth, the contribution of each component towards the development of entrepreneurs in tiny industrial units, the extent of variation and the levels of growth of the 250 tiny entrepreneurs have been discussed. Ten components have been identified to measure the growth. A scoring technique has been evolved to measure each component. With the help of the scoring technique, the growth level has been measured. The growth score has enabled the researcher to identify high, medium and low level growth units.

The distribution of scores for the ten growth factors ranges from 1 to 10. In the case of growth factors such as fixed assets, own funds, working capital, sales turnover and net profits, the total average score values are 8.15, 8.08, 7.69, 7.65 and 7.71 respectively and the maximum average score is found in the chemical-based industries, whereas in the case of growth factors like borrowed funds, product-mix and employment generation, the total average scores are 7.82, 8.12 and 7.95 respectively and the maximum average score is found in the forest-based industries.

The remaining factors of growth such as value of raw materials and value of production have a total average score value of 8.72 and 7.92 respectively and their maximum average scores are found among the miscellaneous industries. Most of the growth factors are found among the chemical-based industries.

Moreover, from the analysis it is found that in the case of the sample entrepreneurs, the maximum fixed assets are in the range Rs.25000 to Rs.75000, own funds range between Rs.50000 and Rs.100000, borrowed funds are between Rs.50000 and Rs.100000 and working capital funds are above Rs.50000. The value of raw materials ranges between Rs.50000 and Rs.100000. Only one product is being offered by a majority (69.60 per cent) of the units. Less than 10 persons are employed in the tiny units. The value of production ranges between Rs.25000 and Rs.75000. Sales turnover is above Rs.75000 and the net profits range between Rs.50000 and Rs.100000. Most of the tiny industrial units employ below 10 workers and they concentrate on single products.

The levels of growth of entrepreneurs are categorized into high, medium and low on the basis of the total scores obtained from the growth scale of the entrepreneurs. Out of 250 entrepreneurs, 41 (16.40 per cent), 132 (52.8 per cent) and 77 (30.80 per cent) are in the category of high, medium and low level respectively. Regarding the extent of variation, the low level category has more inconsistency compared to the other two categories. The high level category is found to be more consistent than the other two categories.

The analysis of the chi-square tests to examine the relationship between the level of growth and the socio-economic factors of the respondents indicated that age, educational status, technical knowledge and nature of family have influenced the level of growth.

The regression results indicate that capacity utilisation, value of production and working capital are the most influencing variables in the case of high, medium and low level categories respectively.

REFERENCES

1. William J. Stanton, Michael, J. Etzel and Bruce J. Walker, 1994. *Fundamentals of Marketing,* Mc Graw Hill International Edition, p. 238.

2. Vasant Desai, 2004. *Management of a Small Scale Industry,* Mumbai: Himalaya Publishing House, pp. 227.

3. Venkataraman, R. Quoted by Rudder Dutt and Sundaram, K.P.M. 1993. *Indian Economy,* New Delhi: S.Chand & Company Ltd., p. 565.

4. http://indiabudget.nic.in.

5. Takshak, Renu, 1990. *Credit Procurement and Utilization by Entrepreneurs,* Haryana Agricultural University, Hisar.

5

Problems Faced by Tiny Sector Entrepreneurs in Tirunelveli District

INTRODUCTION

The growth of an entrepreneur is invariably linked with the problems faced by him. The problems differ from place to place and between one industrial group and another. The problems may relate to marketing, finance, raw material, labour, power, technical and managerial guidance. All these problems ultimately affect the overall performance of a unit particularly the tiny sector. The better performance leads to higher growth in terms of investment and employment and this depends on the capacity of the unit. In other words, the unutilized capacity of a unit is an index of its problems. Hence, an attempt has been made in this chapter to analyse capacity under-utilization of the sample tiny sector entrepreneurs, and the problems encountered by them. For better exposition, the analysis has been divided under three heads, namely:

(i) Capacity underutilization;

(ii) Problems faced by the tiny sector entrepreneurs; and

(iii) Relationship between the level of growth and problems faced by the entrepreneurs.

CAPACITY UNDERUTILIZATION

As capacity underutilization has been the yard stick to measure the magnitude of the problems faced by the sample tiny sector entrepreneurs, this section attempts to analyse the problems and the reasons for underutilization.

Distribution of Average Unutilized Capacity

Table 5.1 shows the distribution of the unutilized capacity of selected tiny industries.

Table 5.1: Unutilized Capacity of Selected Tiny Industries

Sl. No.	*Annual Average Unutilized Capacity (%)*	*Agro-based and Food Products*	*Textiles and Garments*	*Forest-based*	*Chemical-based*	*Miscella-neous*	*Total*
1.	Below 25	2 (8)	24 (15.58)	2 (7.69)	-	3 (11.11)	31 (12.40)
2.	25-50	7 (28)	41 (26.62)	8 (30.77)	2 (11.11)	8 (29.63)	66 (26.40)
3.	51-75	11 (44)	64 (41.56)	11 (42:31)	13 (72.22)	11 (40.74)	110 (44.00)
4.	Above 75	5 (20)	25 (16.24)	5 (19.23)	3 (16.67)	5 (18.52)	43 (17.20)
	Total	**25 (100)**	**154 (100)**	**26 (100)**	**18 (100)**	**27 (100)**	**250 (100)**

Note: Figures in brackets are percentages.

It is inferred from Table 5.1, that 11 (44.00 per cent) out of 25 agro and food based units are having 51 to 75 per cent unutilized capacity. Only 2 (8 per cent) are utilizing more than 75 per cent capacity. In the textiles and garments based tiny units, 64 (41.56 per cent) units have unutilized capacity ranging between 51 to 75 per cent. Only 24 (15.58 per cent) units are utilizing more than 75 per cent capacity. Among the forest based tiny units, 11 (42.31 per cent) units are having 51 to 75 per cent unutilized capacity and only 2 (7.69 per cent) units utilize more than 75 per cent installed capacity.

Regarding the chemical based industrial units, 13 (72.22 per cent) units are not utilizing 51 to 75 percentage of the installed capacity. In the miscellaneous products industry category also 11 (40.74 per cent) out of 27 tiny units are keeping 51 to 75 percentage of the installed capacity unutilized. The above analysis reveals that a majority (44 per cent) of the tiny units are having unutilized capacity ranging from 51 to 75 per cent.

Mean Unutilized Capacity

Table 5.2 presents the mean unutilized capacity of the selected tiny industries.

Table 5.2: Mean unutilized capacity of Selected Tiny Industries

Sl. No.	*Industry Group*	*Average Age of the Units (in Years)*	*Mean Unutilized Capacity (per cent)*	*Total Units*
1.	Agro-based and food products	7.4	48.35	25
2.	Textiles and Garments	6.5	54.26	154
3.	Forest-based	7.6	50.19	26
4.	Chemical-based	6.8	44.18	18
5.	Miscellaneous Industries	5.4	41.24	27
	Overall	6.7	47.64	250

It is clear from Table 5.2 that the forest-based industries are the oldest (7.6 years) followed by agro and food products industries (7.4 years). The average age of the chemical-based industries, textile and garments industries and miscellaneous group industries is 6.8 years, 6.5 years, and 5.4 years respectively.

It is also observed that the highest percentage of mean unutilized capacity is found among the textile and garments units (54.26 per cent), followed by forest-based industries (50.19 per cent). Thus, it is clear from the overall analysis that the textile-based industries are the oldest, followed by agro-based and food products industries. The textile and garments industries have the highest percentage of mean unutilized capacity followed by forest-based industries. It is to be noted that the miscellaneous units which are the fifth in average age utilize maximum capacity compared to other industries. The forest-based units which are the oldest stand second in mean unutilized capacity. The agro-based food products units which are the second oldest stand third in mean unutilized capacity.

Reasons for Underutilization of Capacity

As all the problems of the sample tiny units are ultimately connected with capacity underutilization, the key to solve such problems may be found in unearthing the reasons for underutilization. Since the present study deals with units of heterogeneous character scattered all over the district, the units' own evaluations of the reasons is taken into account. The units were asked to rank the reasons for under utilization as number one, two, and three and weighted scores were given as under: 3 for number one, 2 for number two and 1 for number three. Finally, rating of the reasons and ranking on the basis of weighted scores were undertaken. Table 5.3 presents the reasons for capacity underutilization, their weighted scores, their ratings and ranking on the basis of weighted scores.

According to Table 5.3, all the 250 entrepreneurs marked the first reason for underutilization. 86 respondents marked the second reason and only 38 respondents marked the third reason. The responses were converted into weighted scores by using the weights allotted to each response. Later the weighted scores were ranked in the ascending order. Among the various reasons for underutilization, 'competition' ranked first securing 25.83 per cent of the total weighted scores. Followed by this, 'other reasons' ranked second. Scarcity of raw material ranked third. The problems such as lack of skilled workmen, lack of full time concentration and power failure appear to be matters of no major concern since their rating are insignificant. The most frequently cited reason among 'other reasons' is mechanical breakdown.

Table 5.3: Reasons for Underutilization of Capacity

Sl. No.	*Reason*	*Units' Ranking of Reasons*			*Weighted Score*	*Rating*	*Rank*
		Number 1	*Number 2*	*Number 3*			
1.	Scarcity of raw material	42	14	-	154	16.04	3
2.	Competition	71	13	9	248	25.83	1
3.	Slackness of demand	24	14	4	104	10.83	4
4.	Shortage of finance	24	5	8	90	9.38	5
5.	Lack of full time concentration	11	4	-	41	4.27	7
6.	Lack of skilled workmen	7	16	4	57	5.94	6
7.	Power Failure	5	4	4	27	2.81	8
8.	Other reasons*	66	16	9	239	24.90	2
9.	Number of units not specifying the reason	-	164	212	-		
	Total	**250**	**250**	**250**	**960**	**100**	

* Includes product acceptability, litigation, seasonal demand, mechanical breakdown, natural calamities and transport bottlenecks.

PROBLEMS FACED BY THE TINY SECTOR ENTREPRENEURS

Having identified the causes for underutilization of capacity in the previous section, it is proposed to analyse the problems currently faced by the sample entrepreneurs in order to evaluate the magnitude and intensity of the problems. For this, the entrepreneurs' self-assessment of the problems as done in the case of reasons for underutilization of capacity are taken into consideration. The entrepreneurs were asked to sort out the problems faced by them relating to marketing, finance, raw material, labour, power, technical and management guidance. Further, if the problem was related to raw materials, then they were asked to clearly specify whether it was a problem of scarcity, high prices, low quality, transport or something related. The same technique has been adopted to analyse other problems as well.

Major Problems Faced by Tiny Sector Entrepreneurs

Table 5.4 shows the major problems encountered by the sample tiny entrepreneurs at present in different tiny industries.

It is inferred from Table 5.4 that out of 250 sample units 151 (60.4 per cent) are facing marketing problems and the remaining 99 (39.6 per cent) units are not facing any marketing problem. Among the various tiny industry groups, marketing problems are experienced more (35.6 per cent) by units belonging to the textile and garments industry. Finance problems are encountered by 139 (55.6 per cent) units and the remaining 111 (44.4 per cent) units are not facing any finance problem. Among the industries facing finance problems the textile and garments making industry has more (34.04 per cent) number of units.

Problems related to raw materials are faced by 130 (52.0 per cent) units and the remaining 120 (48.0 per cent) units are not facing such problems. The textile and garments units are facing this type of problem more. As regards labour problems 70 (28.0 per cent) units are experiencing them and the remaining 180 (72.0 per cent) units are not facing such problems. Out of these 180 units 133 (53.2 per cent) units making textiles and garments do not have labour problems.

Table 5.4: Major problems encountered by tiny industries

Sl. No.	Industry Group	Marketing		Finance		Raw Material		Labour		Power		Technical Managerial Guidance		Total
		FP	NFP	FP	NFP	FP	NFP	FP	NFP	FP	NFP	FP	NFP	
1.	Agro and food product industries	22 (8.8)	3 (1.2)	14 (5.6)	11 (4.4)	19 (7.6)	6 (2.4)	14 (5.6)	11 (4.4)	17 (6.8)	8 (3.2)	3 (1.2)	22 (8.8)	25 (10)
2.	Textiles and garments industries	89 (35.6)	65 (26.0)	86 (34.4)	68 (27.2)	74 (29.6)	80 (32.0)	21 (8.4)	133 (53.2)	5 (2)	149 (59.6)	3 (1.2)	151 (60.4)	154 (61.6)
3.	Forest-based industries	11 (4.4)	15 (6.00)	14 (5.6)	12 (4.8)	17 (6.8)	9 (3.6)	12 (4.8)	14 (5.6)	15 (6.0)	11 (4.4)	11 (4.4)	15 (6.00)	26 (10.4)
4.	Chemical-based industries	9 (3.6)	9 (3.6)	10 (4.00)	8 (3.2)	9 (3.6)	9 (3.6)	9 (3.6)	9 (3.6)	10 (4.0)	8 (3.2)	3 (1.2)	15 (6.00)	18 (7.2)
5.	Miscellaneous	20 (8.00)	7 (2.8)	15 (6.0)	12 (4.8)	11 (4.4)	16 (6.4)	14 (5.6)	13 (5.2)	8 (3.2)	19 (7.6)	5 (2)	22 (8.8)	27 (10.8)
	Total	**151 (60.4)**	**99 (39.6)**	**139 (55.6)**	**111 (44.4)**	**130 (52.0)**	**120 (48.0)**	**70 (28.0)**	**180 (72.0)**	**55 (22.0)**	**195 (78.0)**	**25 (10.0)**	**225 (90.0)**	**250 (100)**

Note: Figures in brackets are percentages.

FP – Facing Problem, NFP – Not Facing Problem.

The problem of lack of power supply is encountered by 55 (22.0 per cent) units and the remaining 195 (78.0 per cent) units do not have this problem. Among the 55 units which experience this power supply problem, 17 units come under the agro and food based industry. Problems related to technical and managerial guidance are faced by only 25 (10.0 per cent) units and the remaining 225 (90.0 per cent) units do not have such problems. Among the 25 problem facing units, 11 units come under the forest based industry.

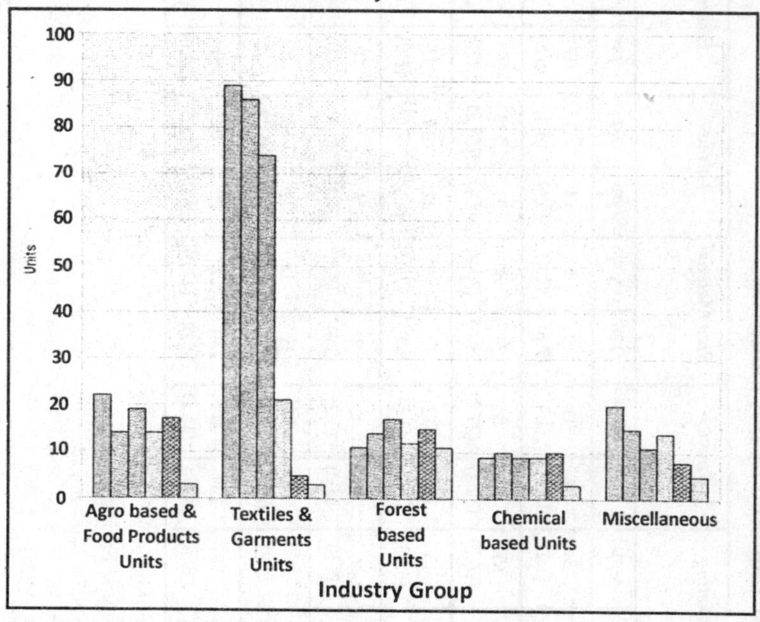

Fig. 5.1: Major Problems Encountered by the Tiny Industries

Problems of Marketing

Marketing is one of the major stumbling blocks for tiny entrepreneurs. Tiny industries do not have any marketing organization. In consequence, their products compare unfavourably with the quality of the products of large scale industries. They suffer from comparative disadvantages vis-à-vis large scale units. In this study the tiny entrepreneurs were asked to mark the first two most important marketing problems faced by them. The first two marketing problems as stated by the tiny entrepreneurs are shown in Table 5.5.

Table 5.5: Problems of Marketing Encountered by Tiny Industries

Sl. No.	*Problem*	*Number of Entrepreneurs Facing the problem of Marketing*	
		Number One	*Number Two*
1.	Competition from Small Units	72	7
2.	Competition from Large Units	21	5
3.	Slackness in Demand	7	4
4.	Other Problems*	51	3
5.	Number of Units not specifying the problem	–	132
	Total	**151**	**151**

* Include transport bottlenecks and seasonal demand.

Out of 250 tiny entrepreneurs 151 (60.4 per cent) have marketing problems as shown in Table 5.5. Among the entrepreneurs who have marketing problems, 72 say that the competition from small units is the most important problem. For 21 entrepreneurs, competition from large scale units is the major problem. Other problems like transport bottlenecks and seasonal demand are the major problems of 51 entrepreneurs. Among the 151 entrepreneurs who have marketing problem, only 19 have reported the second major marketing problem. Out of these 19 entrepreneurs, 7 say that competition from small units is the second major marketing problem. For the remaining 12 competition from small and large scale units is the second major problem.

The above analysis reveals that among the various marketing problems, competition from small and large scale units is considered to be the most important problem faced by tiny entrepreneurs.

Problems of Marketing Encountered by the Tiny Industries

The marketing problems encountered by the industries are presented in Table 5.6.

Table 5.6: Industry Wise Distribution of Marketing Problems

Sl. No.	*Industry Group*	*Number one Difficulty*				*Total Units*
		Competition from Small Units	*Competition from Large Units*	*Slackness in demand*	*Other problems*	
1.	Agro-based and food products	6 (3.97)	9 (5.96)	1 (0.66)	6 (3.97)	22 (14.57)
2.	Textiles and Garments	53 (35.10)	4 (2.65)	3 (1.99)	29 (19.20)	89 (58.94)
3.	Forest-based	–	3 (1.99)	3 (1.99)	5 (3.31)	11 (7.28)
4.	Chemical-based	4 (2.65)	3 (1.99)	–	2 (1.32)	9 (5.96)
5.	Miscellaneous Industries	9 (5.96)	2 (1.32)	–	9 (5.96)	20 (13.25)
	Total	**72 (47.68)**	**21 (13.91)**	**7 (4.64)**	**51 (33.76)**	**151 (100)**

Note: Figures in brackets indicate percentage.

Table 5.6 shows the distribution of tiny industries in relation to the marketing problems faced by them. Out of the 151 tiny industries which are facing marketing problems, 22 (14.57 per cent) are agro-based food products units, 89 (58.54 per cent) are textiles and garments making units, 11 (7.28 per cent) are forest based units, 9 (5.96 per cent) are chemical based units and 20 (13.25 per cent) units come under the miscellaneous industries category.

As regards competition from small units, it is most significant (35.10 per cent) in the textiles and garments industry. Compared to other industry groups, the agro and food based industry is facing more (5.96 per cent) competition from large units. Slackness in demand is experienced by the textiles and garments group and forest based industries. The other problems like transportation bottlenecks and seasonal demand are experienced by 51 (33.77 per cent) of the units. The majority among these 51 units are the textiles and garments industries.

Finance

Finance, which has been aptly described as the "life-blood" of industry, is a pre-requisite for the mobilization of real resources to organize production and marketing. Table 5.7 highlights the problems of finance encountered by tiny industries.

From Table 5.7, it is found that 139 entrepreneurs specified their number one difficulty and 76 reported their number two difficulty in the area of finance. A majority of 54 entrepreneurs mentioned meagre assistance from Government agencies as their number one difficulty and 33 entrepreneurs mentioned it as number two difficulty.

It is also observed that the second ranking number one difficulty mentioned by 41 entrepreneurs is shortage of working capital. 4 entrepreneurs have mentioned it as their number two difficulty. 28 entrepreneurs have stated credit sales and delayed settlement of account to be their number one difficulty and 16 entrepreneurs have mentioned them as number two difficulty. The problem of high rate of interest is the number one problem for 16 entrepreneurs and the same problem is reported by 9 entrepreneurs as number two problem. Moreover, it is also observed that shortage of fixed capital and procedural stagnation in Government agencies are not number one problem at all; instead, they have been mentioned as number two problem by 3 entrepreneurs and 11 entrepreneurs respectively. Thus, it is clear from the table that the problem of meagre assistance from Government agencies and the shortage of working capital are the major problems of finance encountered at present by the tiny entrepreneurs.

Table 5.7: Problems of Finance Encountered by Tine Industries

Sl. No.	*Problem*	*Number of Units for whom it is difficult*	
		Number One	*Number Two*
1.	Shortage of Working Capital	41	4
2.	Shortage of Fixed Capital	–	3
3.	High rate of interest	16	9
4.	Procedural Stagnation in Government Agencies	–	11
5.	Meagre Assistance from Government Agencies	54	33
6.	Other Difficulties*	28	16
7.	Number of Units not specifying the difficulty	–	63
	Total	**139**	**139**

* Include repayment and high instatement.

Problems of Finance Encountered by the Tiny Industries

Table 5.8 presents the distribution of problems of finance encountered at present by the various tiny industry groups.

It is noticed from Table 5.8 that 139 units out of the 250 sample units are facing finance problems. Among them 14 (10.07 per cent) are agro and food based units, 86 (61.87 per cent) are textiles and garments making units, 14 (10.07 per cent) come under forest based industry, 10 (7.19 per cent) are chemical based units and 15 (10.79 per cent) units come under the miscellaneous industries group. Out of 139 units which face finance problems, 41 (29.50 per cent) units are facing the working capital shortage problem. The problem of shortage of working capital is significant in the textiles and garments industry. The problem of high rate of interest is faced by 16 (11.51 per cent) units. Among them the problem is significant (4.31 per cent) in the textiles and garments industry. The problem of meagre government assistance is encountered by 54 (38.85 per cent) units. This problem is mostly felt in the textiles and garments industry. Other problems such as frequency of repayment and high instalment rates are experienced by 28 (20.15 per cent) units. Problems relating to repayment are significant in the textiles and garments industry.

Table 5.8: Industry Wise Distribution of Finance Problems

Sl. No.	*Industry Group*	*Number One Difficulty*				*Total Units*
		Shortage of Working Capital	*High Rate of Interest*	*Meagre Assistance*	*Other problems*	
1.	Agro-based and food products	3 (2.16)	–	3 (2.16)	8 (5.76)	14 (10.07)
2.	Textiles and Garments	29 (20.87)	6 (4.31)	41 (29.50)	10 (7.20)	86 (61.87)
3.	Forest-based	2 (1.44)	3 (2.16)	6 (4.32)	3 (2.16)	14 (10.07)
4.	Chemical-based	2 (1.44)	4 (2.88)	2 (1.44)	2 (1.44)	10 (7.19)
5.	Miscellaneous Industries	5 (3.60)	3 (2.16)	2 (1.44)	5 (3.60)	15 (10.79)
	Total	**41 (29.50)**	**16 (11.51)**	**54 (38.85)**	**28 (20.15)**	**139 (100)**

Note: Figures in brackets indicate percentage.

Initial Capital

Initial capital is very essential for starting an industry. It is the fund at the disposal of the entrepreneurs for establishing the enterprise in the first instance. Table 5.9 analyses the major sources of initial capital for the entrepreneurs.

Table 5.9: Major Sources of Initial Capital

Sl. No.	*Major Sources*	*Number of Units*	*Percentage*
1.	Income from agriculture	8	3.20
2.	Income from trade	3	1.20
3.	Income from manufacturing	7	2.80
4.	Savings from salary	3	1.20
5.	Borrowings from friends and relatives	7	2.80
6.	Other sources*	222	88.80
	Total	**250**	**100.00**

* Include borrowings from wife, sale proceeds of agricultural land.

Table 5.9 shows that 88.80 per cent of the respondents entered the industry by using their income from other sources, such as borrowings from wife and sale proceeds of agricultural land. It is also evident that the use of the five specific sources is very meagre (11.20 per cent). Thus, it is inferred that a majority of the respondents have entered the industries using the borrowings from wife or the sale proceeds of agricultural land.

Term Loans

The shortage of funds is compensated by raising term loans from various financial institutions which lend money. Different sources used by the entrepreneurs are presented in Table 5.10.

Table 5.10: Sources of Term Loans

Sl. No.	*Sources*	*Number of Units*	*Percentage*
1.	Tamil Nadu Industrial Investment Corporation (TIIC)	160	64.00
2.	Commercial Banks	59	23.60
3.	Small Industries Development Bank of India (SIDBI)	31	12.40
	Total	**250**	**100.00**

As found in Table 5.10, term loans are raised mostly from Tamil Nadu Industrial Investment Corporation (64.00 per cent). Commercial banks (23.66 per cent) and SIDBI (12.40 per cent) have proved to be the other sources for term loans. Therefore, it can be inferred that a majority of the tiny industry groups have got term loans from Tamil Nadu Industrial Investment Corporation (TIIC). TIIC has been more beneficial and accessible to the entrepreneurs in various fields for raising term loans.

Proportion of Working Capital borrowed from Commercial Banks

The working capital need of a concern depends on the nature of the organization, scale of operation, mode of payment and the work force used. For meeting the working capital need, entrepreneurs borrow funds from commercial banks or from other sources. The details of working capital borrowed by the sample entrepreneurs are presented in Table 5.11.

Table 5.11: Proportion of Working Capital Raised from Commercial Banks

Sl. No.	*Proportion (in percentage) of amount borrowed*	*Number of Units*	*Percentage*
1.	Nil	32	12.80
2.	Up to 50	11	4.40
3.	51-75	42	16.80
4.	76-90	148	59.20
5.	Above 90	17	6.80
	Total	**250**	**100.00**

It is evident from Table 5.11 that 148 (59.20 per cent) out of the 250 sample entrepreneurs have borrowed 76-90 per cent of their working capital from commercial banks. 42 (16.80 per cent) units have borrowed 51-75 per cent of their working capital from commercial banks. 17 (6.80 per cent) units have borrowed more than 90 per cent of their working capital from commercial banks. It is also observed from Table 5.11 that 32 (12.80 per cent) units have not borrowed any amount from commercial banks for their working capital needs.

Raw Materials

The major problems relating to raw materials arise due to scarcity, high and uncertain prices, low quality, transport and seasonal supply of raw materials.

Table 5.12 presents the problems related to raw materials encountered by the sample entrepreneurs.

Table 5.12: Problems of Raw Material Encountered by Tiny Industries

Sl. No.	*Problem*	*Number of Entrepreneurs Facing Problems*	
		Number One	*Number Two*
1.	Scarcity	64	10
2.	High Price	27	9
3.	Low Quality	13	4
4.	High Transport Cost	7	3
5.	Other Problems*	19	3
6.	Number of entrepreneurs not specifying the problems	–	101
	Total	130	130

* Include uncertain prices, seasonal supply of raw materials, Government restrictions, and lack of storage facilities etc.

Table 5.12 shows that 130 out of the 250 tiny entrepreneurs are experiencing problems related to raw materials. Among the 130 entrepreneurs who have encountered the raw materials problem, 64 are facing the problem of raw materials scarcity. Next to the scarcity problem, comes the problem of high price of the raw materials. Only 7 out of the 130 tiny entrepreneurs have expressed that the problem of high transportation costs is their number one problem regarding the availability of raw materials. As regards the number two problem, the response was given by only 29 out of 130 entrepreneurs who are facing the problem of getting raw materials. Among them, 10 entrepreneurs have indicated that the scarcity of raw materials is their problem.

Problems Relating to Raw Materials Encountered by the Tiny Industries

Table 5.13 shows the problems relating to raw materials encountered by the tiny industries:

Table 5.13: Problems Relating to Raw Materials Encountered by Tiny Industries

Sl. No.	*Industry*	*Number One Difficulty*					*Total Units*
		Scarcity of raw material	*High Prices*	*Low Quality*	*Transport*	*Other Problems*	
1.	Agro-based and food products	7 (5.38)	6 (4.61)	1 (0.77)	2 (1.54)	3 (2.31)	19 (14.61)
2.	Textiles and Garments	42 (32.31)	14 (10.77)	7 (5.38)	3 (2.30)	8 (6.15)	74 (56.92)
3.	Forest-based	5 (3.85)	5 (3.85)	2 (1.54)	2 (1.54)	3 (2.31)	17 (13.08)
4.	Chemical-based	3 (2.31)	1 (0.77)	2 (1.54)	–	3 (2.31)	9 (6.93)
5.	Miscellaneous Industries	7 (5.38)	1 (0.77)	1 (0.77)	–	2 (1.54)	11 (8.46)
	Total	**64 (49.23)**	**27 (20.77)**	**13 (10.0)**	**7 (5.38)**	**19 (14.62)**	**130 (100)**

Note: Figures in brackets represent percentage.

It is inferred from Table 5.13 that 64 (49.23 per cent) units are facing the problem of raw materials scarcity. The problem is significant (32.31 per cent) in the textiles and garments industry. The problem of high price is experienced by 27 (20.77 per cent) units. Among these 27 units, 14 come under the textiles and garments industry. The problem of high price is comparatively less in other tiny industries. The problem of low quality of raw material is faced by 13 (10.0 per cent) units. Among them, 7 units come under the textiles and garments industry. Transportation problems connected with the procurement of raw materials are experienced by 7 (5.38 per cent) units. Among the 7 units, 3 are from the textiles and garments industry.

Other problems like uncertain prices, seasonal supply of raw materials, government restrictions and lack of storage facilities are faced by 19 (14.62 per cent) units. Among them, 8 (6.15 per cent) units come under the textiles and garments industry. In the case of problems relating to transport, it is significant for the textiles and garments industry (2.30 per cent) alone and insignificant for the rest of the industries.

Thus, it can be inferred from the overall data, that the problem of scarcity, high prices, transport and other problems such as uncertain prices and seasonal supply of raw materials are the major problems. Raw material is the number one problem for agro-based and food products industries and the problem of low quality is the number one problem for forest based industries.

Labour

Table 5.14 highlights the number one and number two labour problems encountered by the entrepreneurs at present.

Table 5.14: Labour Problems Encountered by Tiny Industries

Sl. No.	Problem	Number of Entrepreneurs	
		Number One	Number Two
1.	Scarcity of skilled labour	40	5
2.	High wages	21	3
3.	Turnover	3	2
4.	Absenteeism	6	2
5.	Number of entrepreneurs not specifying the problems	–	58
	Total	**70**	**70**

It is observed from Table 5.14 that 70 entrepreneurs are facing labour problems. Among them, 40 (57.41 per cent) entrepreneurs are experiencing scarcity of skilled labourers as number one problem. The problem of high wages is experienced by 21 (30 per cent) entrepreneurs.

It is also noted from Table 5.14 that among the 70 entrepreneurs who are facing labour problems, only 12 entrepreneurs have mentioned their number two problem. Among the number two problems specified by these 12 entrepreneurs, scarcity of skilled labour is the problem of 5 (41.67 per cent) entrepreneurs.

Power Supply

Power supply is another major problem encountered by the entrepreneurs at present. Details are given in Table 5.15.

Table 5.15: Power Problems Encountered by Tiny industries

Sl. No.	*Problem*	*Number of Units*	*Percentage*
1.	High Cost	24	43.64
2.	Power Failure	20	36.36
3.	Low Voltage	5	9.09
4.	Other Problems*	6	10.91
	Total	**55**	**100.00**

* Include problems in getting additional transformers for additional power, the uneconomical nature of installing a generator and the product coming under excise duty if produced with power.

Table 5.15 reveals that 55 entrepreneurs are facing power problems in their units. Among them, 24 (43.64 per cent) say that the power tariff rates are very high. Power failure problem is encountered by 20 (36.36 per cent) entrepreneurs. It is evident from Table 5.15 that among the various power problems, the high cost of power and power failure affect the tiny entrepreneurs much.

Technical and Managerial Guidance

Table 5.16 gives various reasons expressed by the entrepreneurs for not using technical and managerial guidance.

Table 5.16 reveals that out of 25 tiny entrepreneurs who are not making use of technical and managerial guidance, 12 (48 per cent) say that it is not convenient for them to use technical and managerial guidance. 5 entrepreneurs say that technical and managerial guidance is not useful to them.

Table 5.16: Reasons for not Using Technical and Managerial Guidance

Sl. No.	*Reasons*	*Number of Units*	*Percentage*
1.	Expensive	4	16.00
2.	Inconvenient	12	48.00
3.	Not useful	5	20.00
4.	Not aware	4	16.00
	Total	25	100.00

RELATIONSHIP BETWEEN LEVEL OF GROWTH AND PROBLEMS FACED BY THE ENTREPRENEURS

In this section an attempt has been made to examine the level of growth vis-a-vis problems faced by the tiny entrepreneurs. For this, chi-square test of the following formula has been used.

$$\text{Chi-Square } (\chi^2) = \sum \frac{(O - E)^2}{E} \text{ with (r-1) (c-1) degrees of freedom}$$

O = Observed frequency

E = Expected frequency

$$E = \frac{\text{Row total} \times \text{Column total}}{\text{Grand total}}$$

c = Number of columns, r = Number of rows

Relationship Between Unutilized Capacity and Growth Level

The relationship between unutilized capacity and level of growth is given in Table 5.17.

Table 5.17 reveals that out of 41 high level growth achievers 14 (34.15 per cent) have unutilized capacity of below 25 per cent. It means they are using about 75 per cent capacity annually. 12 (29.27 per cent) entrepreneurs who have achieved high growth are not using more than 75 per cent installed capacity. Among the medium level growth achievers, 65 (49.24 per cent) entrepreneurs have 51-75 per cent unutilized capacity. Only 10 (7.58 per cent) entrepreneurs are using more than 75 per cent capacity. As regards low growth achievers a majority of 38 (49.36 per cent) entrepreneurs have 51-75 per cent unutilized capacity. In this category only 7 out of 77 entrepreneurs are using more than 75 per cent capacity.

Table 5.17: Capacity Utilization and level of growth

Sl. No.	*Annual Average Unutilized Capacity (in %)*	*Level of Growth*			*Total*
		High	*Medium*	*Low*	
1.	Below 25	14 (34.15)	10 (7.58)	7 (9.09)	31 (12.40)
2.	25-50	8 (19.51)	46 (34.85)	12 (15.58)	66 (26.40)
3.	51-75	7 (17.07)	65 (49.24)	38 (49.36)	110 (44.00)
4.	Above 75	12 (29.27)	11 (8.33)	20 (25.97)	43 (17.20)
	Total	**41 (100)**	**132 (100)**	**77 (100)**	**250 (100)**

For further analysis a null hypothesis has been formulated that unutilized capacity and level of growth are two independent attributes. To test the null hypothesis that there is no relationship between unutilized capacity and level of growth, chi-square test has been applied.

The results of the chi-square test are furnished below:

Calculated value (C.V.) = 50.8289

Table value at 5 per cent level of significance (T.V.) = 12.592

Degrees of freedom = 6

Inference = Significant

As the calculated chi-square value is greater than the table value at 5 per cent level of significance, the null hypothesis is rejected. It is concluded that the unutilized capacity in the units of the respondents has influenced the level of growth of entrepreneurs.

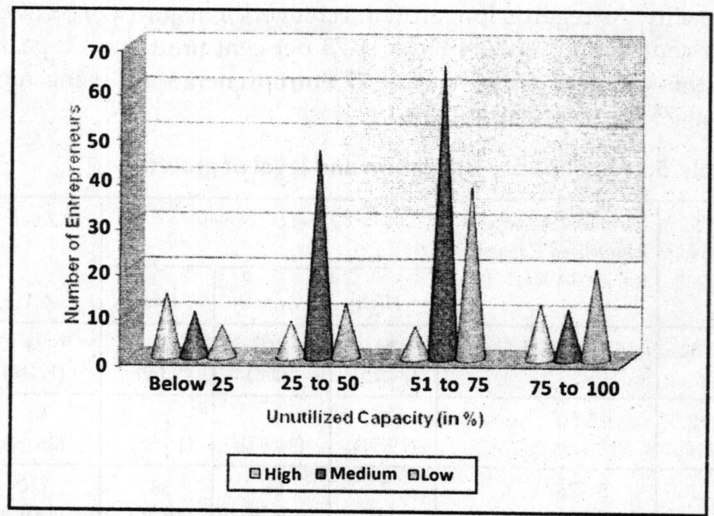

Fig. 5.2: Relationship Between Unutilized Capacity and Level of Growth

Relationship Between Marketing Problems and Growth Level

Marketing problems faced by the tiny entrepreneurs and their level of growth are presented in Table 5.18.

Table 5.18: Marketing Problems and Level of Growth

Sl. No.	*Problems*	*Level of Growth*			*Total*
		High	*Medium*	*Low*	
1.	Competition from small units	6 (27.27)	41 (53.95)	25 (47.17)	72 (47.68)
2.	Competition from large units	1 (4.55)	5 (6.58)	15 (28.30)	21 (13.91)
3.	Slackness in Demand	1 (4.55)	3 (3.95)	3 (5.66)	7 (4.64)
4.	Other problems*	14 (63.64)	27 (35.53)	10 (18.87)	51 (33.77)
	Total	**22 (100)**	**76 (100)**	**53 (100)**	**151 (100)**

* Include transport bottlenecks and seasonal demand.

Table 5.18 reveals that among the entrepreneurs, who are facing marketing problems, 22 have high growth, 76 have medium growth and 53 have low growth. In the high growth achievers category a majority (63.64 per cent) have expressed that they are having transportation problems and their products are having seasonal demand only. Among the medium growth achievers 41 (53.95 per cent) entrepreneurs have said that they are facing competition from small units. In the low growth achievers category also the tiny entrepreneurs are facing competition from small units.

In order to test the null hypothesis that there is no relationship between the marketing problems and level of growth, chi-square test has been applied.

The results of the chi-square test are furnished below:

Calculated value (C.V.)	=	26.7695
Table value at 5 per cent level of significance (T.V.)	=	12.592
Degrees of freedom	=	6
Inference	=	Significant

As the calculated chi-square value is greater than the table value at 5 per cent level of significance, the null hypothesis is rejected. Thus it is concluded that there exists a relationship between the marketing problems faced by the entrepreneurs and their growth level.

Relationship Between Financial Problems and Growth Level

Table 5.19 exhibits the relationship between financial problems and the level of growth achieved by the tiny entrepreneurs.

Table 5.19 shows that among the 139 tiny entrepreneurs, who have financial problems, 18 have achieved high growth, 75 have medium growth and 46 have achieved low growth. Among the high growth achievers 33.33 percentage of tiny entrepreneurs are facing shortage of working capital. 40 per cent of the medium growth achievers have expressed that Government assistance is inadequate. Low level growth achievers are facing shortage of working capital and they have also expressed their dissatisfaction about inadequate Government assistance.

Table 5.19: Financial problemS and level of growth

Sl. No.	*Problems*	*Level of Growth*			*Total*
		High	*Medium*	*Low*	
1.	Shortage of working capital	6 (33.33)	16 (21.33)	19 (41.30)	41 (29.50)
2.	High rate of interest	5 (27.78)	4 (5.33)	7 (15.22)	16 (11.51)
3.	Meagre assistance from Government agencies	5 (27.78)	30 (40.00)	19 (41.30)	54 (38.85)
4.	Other difficulties*	2 (11.11)	25 (33.33)	1 (2.17)	28 (20.14)
	Total	**18 (100)**	**75 (100)**	**46 (100)**	**139 (100)**

* High instalment and repayment problems.

For further analysis a null hypothesis has been formulated that there is no relationship between financial problems and level of growth. In order to test the null hypothesis, chi-square test has been applied and the result furnished below.

Calculated value (C.V.)	=	21.6704
Table value at 5 per cent level of significance (T.V.)	=	12.592
Degrees of freedom	=	6
Inference	=	Significant

As the calculated chi-square value is greater than the table value at 5 per cent level of significance, the null hypothesis is rejected. It is concluded that the level of growth and financial problems are dependent attributes. Hence some relationship exists between the level of growth and the financial problems of the respondents.

Relationship between Problems Relating to Raw Materials and Level of Growth

The details about problems relating to raw materials of the tiny entrepreneurs and their level of growth are furnished in Table 5.20.

Table 5.20: Problems relating to Raw materials and level of growth

Sl. No.	*Problems*	*Level of Growth*			*Total*
		High	*Medium*	*Low*	
1.	Scarcity	6 (31.58)	52 (72.22)	6 (15.38)	64 (49.23)
2.	High price	7 (36.84)	7 (9.72)	13 (33.33)	27 (20.77)
3.	Low quality	2 (10.53)	3 (4.17)	8 (20.51)	13 (10.00)
4.	High transport cost	2 (10.53)	2 (2.78)	3 (7.69)	7 (5.38)
5.	Other problems*	2 (10.53)	8 (11.11)	9 (23.00)	19 (14.62)
	Total	**19 (100)**	**72 (100)**	**39 (100)**	**130 (100)**

* Seasonal supply, Government restriction, lack of storage facilities.

Table 5.20 reveals that among the 130 tiny entrepreneurs who are facing problems regarding raw materials, 19 have achieved high growth, 72 have reached medium growth and the remaining 39 entrepreneurs have low level growth. Among high level achievers 36.84 per cent of the entrepreneurs have expressed that high price is their major problem regarding raw materials. A majority (72.22 per cent) of the medium growth achievers is facing the problem of raw materials scarcity and 33.33 per cent of the low growth achievers have said that high price is their major problem regarding raw materials.

In order to test the established null hypothesis that there is no relationship between the problems relating to raw materials and level of growth, chi-square test is used and the result is given below:

Calculated value (C.V.) = 21.6704

Table value at 5 per cent level of (T.V.) significance = 12.592

Degrees of freedom = 6

Inference = Significant

As the calculated value is more than the table value at 5 per cent level of significance the null hypothesis is rejected. It is proved that problems relating to raw materials and level of growth are dependent attributes. Hence there exists a relationship between the problems relating to raw materials and the level of growth of the entrepreneurs.

Relationship Between Labour Problems and Level of Growth

The relationship between labour problems and the level of growth of the entrepreneurs in tiny sector is presented in Table 5.21.

Table 5.21: Labour problems and level of growth

Sl. No.	*Problems*	*Level of Growth*			*Total*
		High	*Medium*	*Low*	
1.	Skilled labour scarcity	8 (50.00)	20 (55.56)	12 (66.67)	40 (57.14)
2.	High wages	6 (37.50)	12 (33.33)	3 (16.67)	21 (30.00)
3.	Labour Turnover	1 (6.25)	1 (2.78)	1 (5.55)	3 (4.29)
4.	Absenteeism	1 (6.25)	4 (11.11)	2 (11.11)	6 (8.57)
	Total	**16 (100)**	**36 (100)**	**18 (100)**	**70 (100)**

Table 5.21 shows that out of 70 tiny entrepreneurs who are facing labour problems, 16 have achieved a high level of growth, 36 entrepreneurs have reached a medium level of growth and the remaining 18 have achieved low growth. Among the high growth achievers 50 per cent of the entrepreneurs are facing scarcity of skilled labour. The scarcity of skilled labour problem is experienced by 55.56 per cent of the medium growth achievers too. Among the low level growth achievers, 12 (66.67 per cent) entrepreneurs are facing the skilled labour scarcity problem. It is also evident from Table 5.21 that irrespective of the level of growth, the scarcity of skilled labour problem is experienced by a majority of the tiny entrepreneurs. For further analysis a null

hypothesis has been formulated that labour problems and level of growth are two independent attributes. In order to test the null hypothesis, chi-square test has been applied and the result is shown below:

Calculated value (C.V.)	= 0.5925
Table value at 5 per cent level of significance (T.V.)	= 12.592
Degrees of freedom	= 6
Inference	= Not significant

As the calculated chi-square value is less than the table value at 5 per cent level of significance, the null hypothesis is accepted. It is derived that labour problems and level of growth are independent attributes. Hence there exists no relationship between labour problems and the level of growth of the entrepreneurs.

Relationship Between Power Supply Problem and the Level of Growth

The problem of power supply vis-à-vis the level of growth of the entrepreneurs in tiny sector is given in Table 5.22.

Table 5.22: Problems of power supply and level of growth

Sl. No.	*Problems*	*Level of Growth*			*Total*
		High	*Medium*	*Low*	
1.	High cost	5 (41.67)	10 (38.46)	9 (52.94)	24 (43.64)
2.	Frequent power failure	5 (41.67)	10 (38.46)	5 (29.41)	20 (36.36)
3.	Low voltage	1 (8.33)	3 (11.54)	1 (5.88)	5 (9.09)
4.	Other problems*	1 (8.33)	3 (11.54)	2 (11.77)	6 (10.91)
	Total	**12 (100)**	**26 (100)**	**17 (100)**	**55 (100)**

* Include problems in getting additional transformers for additional power, the uneconomical nature of installing a generator and the product coming under excise duty if produced with power.

It is evident from table 5.22 that 55 tiny entrepreneurs are facing power problem. Among them, 12 have achieved high level growth, 26 entrepreneurs have reached medium level growth and the remaining 17 tiny entrepreneurs have achieved low growth. Among the high level growth achievers, 41.67 per cent of entrepreneurs are experiencing frequent power failures and 41.67 per cent of entrepreneurs of the same category say that the power tariff is high. In the medium and low level growth categories also, high power tariff and frequent power failure are indicated as problem by a good number of tiny entrepreneurs.

In order to examine the formulated null hypothesis that there is no relationship between problem in power supply and level of growth, chi-square test has been applied.

The computed results are given below:

Calculated value (C.V.)	=	3.0234
Table value at 5 per cent level of significance (T.V.)	=	12.592
Degrees of freedom	=	6
Inference	=	Not significant

Since the calculated value is less than the table value at 5 per cent level of significance, the formulated null hypothesis is accepted. Hence there is no relationship between problems in power supply and the level of growth of entrepreneurs in the study area.

Relationship between Level of Growth and Managerial Guidance

Table 5.23 shows the level of growth of entrepreneurs vis-a-vis technical guidance.

It is inferred from Table 5.23 that out of 41 entrepreneurs with high level growth, 30 (73.17) are utilizing technical and managerial guidance and the remaining 11 (26.83 per cent) are not utilizing any technical and managerial guidance. Out of 132 entrepreneurs with medium level growth, a majority (90.91 per cent) is utilizing technical and managerial guidance and only 9.09 per cent are not utilizing. Among the 77 entrepreneurs with low level growth, 67 (87.01 per cent) are utilising technical and managerial guidance and 10 (12.99 per cent) are not making use of any technical and managerial guidance. It is also evident from Table 5.23 that the majority (90 per cent) of the tiny entrepreneurs are making use of technical and managerial guidance, though their growth level varies.

Table 5.23: Technical and Managerial Guidance and Level of Growth

Sl. No.	*Use of technical and managerial guidance*	*Level of Growth*			*Total*
		High	*Medium*	*Low*	
1.	Utilized technical and managerial guidance	30 (73.17)	120 (90.91)	67 (87.01)	225 (90.00)
2.	Not utilized technical and managerial guidance	11 (26.83)	12 (9.09)	10 (12.99)	25 (10.00)
	Total	**41 (100)**	**132 (100)**	**77 (100)**	**250 (100)**

To examine the formulated null hypothesis that the level of growth is independent of utilization of technical and managerial guidance, chi-square test was applied. The results of the chi-square test are given below:

Calculated value (C.V.) = 14.217

Table value at 5 per cent level of (T.V.) significance = 5.991

Degrees of freedom = 2

Inference = Significant

As the calculated value is greater than the table value at 5 per cent level of significance, the formulated null hypothesis is rejected. Thus it is concluded that technical and managerial guidance has influenced the level of growth of entrepreneurs.

SUMMARY

This chapter has analysed the various problems faced by the entrepreneurs and the reasons for the underutilization of capacity. It is found that the annual average unutilized capacity was 51 to 75 per cent and the highest mean unutilized capacity was found among textiles and garments industries, followed by forest based industries. Competition among the entrepreneurs is the reason for underutilization of capacity.

The major problems faced by the entrepreneurs are related to marketing, finance and raw materials. Among 151 entrepreneurs who face marketing problem, 72 are affected by competition from small units. The competition from small units is more (35.10 per cent) in the textiles and garments industry. Out of 139 tiny entrepreneurs who face problems relating to finance, 54 say that Government assistance is very meagre. 41 entrepreneurs are facing working capital shortage. Both these finance problems are more in the textiles and garments industry. 88.8 per cent of the surveyed units are using borrowings from wife or the sale proceeds of agricultural lands as initial capital investment. A majority (64 per cent) of the entrepreneurs are raising term loans through Tamil Nadu Industrial Investment Corporation. 59.20 per cent of the sample units are using the commercial banks for meeting the 76 to 90 per cent of the working capital needs.

Out of 130 tiny entrepreneurs, who are facing problems relating to raw materials, 64 are experiencing raw materials scarcity. The problem of raw materials scarcity is significant (32.31 per cent) in the textiles and garments industry. Labour problems are experienced by 70 sample units, among them 40 units are facing the problem of scarcity of skilled labour. Among the 55 sample units which encounter power supply problems, 24 say that the power tariff is high. Frequent power failure is experienced by 20 units. Among the 250 sample units only 25 units are not using technical and managerial guidance.

Chi-square results show that unutilized capacity and problems relating to marketing, finance, raw materials and technical and managerial guidance are influencing the growth of tiny entrepreneurs.

6

Summary of Findings Suggestions and Conclusion

INTRODUCTION

The tiny sector industries have an important role to play in achieving the plan objectives of increasing industrial production, dispersal of industries, utilizing local available resources, generating additional employment and reducing regional imbalance in growth. The tiny sector industries have over the years developed as an important constituent of the Indian economy in terms of their share in employment, output and exports. These are the main reasons that the Government of India had stressed in its industrial policy to promote tiny sector industries widely distributed in rural areas and small towns. In pursuance of this policy, a programme was evolved for setting up the District Industries Centre (DIC) as an effective nodal agency for the development of tiny sector industries.

Most of the districts in Tamil Nadu are backward districts. In order to solve the unemployment problem and to have an equitable growth of small and tiny industries in developed and backward areas, the District Industries Centres were formed in most of the districts in Tamil Nadu. Many programmes have been launched in order to alleviate poverty and to choose self-employment through the District Industries Centre. Hence the present study entitled "Entrepreneurship in Tiny Sector Industries - an Indian Scenario" has been undertaken to analyse the forces behind entrepreneurial development, the growth of tiny sector industries, their level of growth and the factors influencing their growth and the problems faced by the entrepreneurs.

For the purpose of analysis, 250 tiny sector industries were selected by the probability random sampling method. The sample tiny sector industries were grouped in to five categories, namely:

(i) Agro and Food Products;

(ii) Textiles and Garments;

(iii) Forest based;

(iv) Chemical based; and

(v) Miscellaneous industries.

The present study is based on both primary and secondary data. The personal interview method was adopted to collect primary data with a well designed and pre-tested interview schedule. The secondary data were collected from the published as well as unpublished reports, records, action plan and the like. The data related to the growth components of tiny industries were obtained for a period of five years. The primary data were collected from October 2005 to March 2006. The major findings, conclusions and suggestions are presented in this chapter.

SUMMARY OF FINDINGS

The work done and its findings are summarized in this section to draw specific inferences and suggestions for improving the tiny sector.

Forces Behind Entrepreneurial Development

In the third chapter forces behind entrepreneurial development in tiny sector industries have been discussed.

Socio-economic Profile of the Respondents

It has been found that 36.40 per cent of the respondents belong to the age group of 41-50 years followed by the age group

30-40 years which constitutes 30.40 per cent. It has been observed that the sample respondents are well educated and 57.20 per cent of the selected tiny entrepreneurs have college level education and 18.40 per cent of them possess technical education. Among the respondents, 88.40 per cent are male and the remaining 11.60 per cent are female. The majority of the respondents, about 55 per cent, belong to backward/most backward communities, whereas only 13.60 per cent and 31.20 per cent belong to schedule caste and forward communities respectively.

A maximum of 68 per cent of the total respondents belong to the nuclear family system. 71.20 per cent of the total respondents are married and 18.40 per cent are unmarried. 50.40 per cent of the total respondents have a family size of 3 to 5 members and 30.80 per cent have more than 5 family members. Among the respondents, those who have only one earning member in the family constitutes 56.40 per cent and 26.40 per cent of the respondents have two earning members in their families.

The occupational background among the respondents is mainly farming. This section constitutes 36 per cent. Out of the 250 respondents, 34.80 per cent have material possession worth Rs. 100000 to Rs. 200000. 31.20 per cent of them have material possession worth more than Rs. 200000. 31.60 per cent of respondents have a monthly income ranging between Rs. 2,001 and Rs. 3,000. Only 17.20 per cent of respondents have earnings more than Rs. 4,000 per month. It is observed that 39.60 per cent of the respondents have a family income of Rs. 3,001 to Rs. 5,000 per month, whereas 36.40 per cent have more than Rs. 5,000 as family income per month

40.40 per cent of the total respondents spend Rs. 3001-4000 on their monthly family expenditure. Nearly 36.40 per cent of the total respondents have no savings. 31.20 per cent of the total respondents have monthly savings less than Rs. 1000.

Personality Traits of the Tiny Entrepreneurs

The analysis of personality traits revealed that the average personality traits score is 2.66. The number of respondents who have a personality index of above 60 constitute 36.80 per cent. 34 per cent of the respondents have a personality index ranging between 41 and 60.

Entrepreneurship Index

The average scores are high in the entrepreneurship variables namely individuality, risk taking, profit orientation, time management and creativity. The mean score values of these entrepreneurship variables are 3.69, 3.53, 3.46, 3.45 and 3.41 respectively. The overall average of entrepreneurship variables among the entrepreneurs is 2.8845.

An analysis of entrepreneurship index among the respondents revealed that a maximum of 34.40 per cent have an index of 41-60. 28.80 per cent have an index ranging between 61 and 80. The respondents who have an entrepreneurship index of above 60 constitute 37.20 per cent.

Association Between Socio-economic Variables and Entrepreneurship Index

An analysis of the association between entrepreneurship and socio-economic variables revealed that there is an association between entrepreneurship and some profile variables, namely age, education, family size, earning members in the family, occupational background, monthly income and family income since the chi-square values are significant at 5 per cent level.

Correlation between Personality Traits and Entrepreneurship

The correlation analysis revealed that a significant correlation exists between entrepreneurship and personality traits variables, namely decision making ability, economic motivation, managerial ability, problem recognition and risk taking willingness. Their correlation co-efficients are statistically significant at 5 per cent level.

Factors Influencing Tiny entrepreneurs to start or to manage the enterprise

The principal factor analysis method with orthogonal varimax rotation is used to identify the significant set of influencing factors. Twenty variables were included in the factor analysis. The result showed that four important factors influence the respondents to start or manage the tiny enterprises, namely: *(i)* achievement and support factor; *(ii)* interest factor; *(iii)* traditional status factor; and *(iv)* economic necessity factor. The communality value indicates the power of the variable to explain the factors altogether. By communality values, the important variables which influence the respondents to start and/or manage an enterprise are economic independence, self interest and self prestige since their communality values are 0.8532, 0.8113 and 0.7156 respectively.

The higher Eigen value shows the higher intensity of the factor explaining the variables altogether. By Eigen values, the most important factors that influence the respondents to start and/or manage the enterprises are the achievement and support factor and the interest factor since their Eigen values are 4.2377 and 3.4929 respectively.

Analysis of the Growth of Entrepreneurship in Tiny Sector Industries

In the fourth chapter, an attempt has been made to analyse the growth of entrepreneurship in tiny sector industries.

The total sample of tiny sector industrial units selected for the study was 250 units. Among the 250 units, 25 units come under agro-based and food products industries, 154 units are grouped under textiles and garments industries, 26 units belong to forest based industries, 18 units belong to chemical-based industries, and the remaining 27 sample units come under the miscellaneous groups of industries.

To measure the growth of the tiny sector industries, ten growth factors were identified by the researcher. It was found that 148 (59.20 per cent) units have fixed assets ranging from Rs. 25,000 to Rs. 75,000. Only 39 (15.60 per cent) units have fixed assets worth more than Rs. 1,00,000. The total average growth score of the selected industrial units for the fixed assets was estimated to be 8.15.

More number of units belonging to agro-based and food products industries, textiles and garments industries, forest based and miscellaneous group of industries have employed their own funds amounting to Rs. 75,000 to Rs. 1,00,000. The highest growth score in the case of industries having their own fund was found among the units of the chemical-based industry. The average growth score of the selected industries for own fund was estimated to be 8.07.

It could be observed from the analysis that more number of units of the agro-based and food products industries, forest based and chemical-based industries have employed borrowed funds ranging from Rs. 75,000 to Rs. 1,00,000. The highest growth score in the case of the units with borrowed funds was 9.08 and the lowest growth score was 7.36. The average growth score worked out to be 7.81.

It could be seen that the highest percentage of the selected tiny sector industrial units, in the agro-based and food products industry, textiles and garments industry, chemical-based and miscellaneous group of industries have used more than Rs. 1,00,000 as working capital. The maximum growth score for working capital was found among the units of the chemical-based industries.

It is observed from the analysis that more number of units of the selected tiny industries use Rs. 75,000 to Rs. 1,00,000 worth of raw material for their production. The average growth score for the value of raw material for the selected tiny sector industries was estimated to be 8.70 and the maximum growth score was found among the units of the miscellaneous category industries followed by the units of textiles and garments industries.

A majority of the units coming under the agro and food products industry and the forest based industry offer two products as their product mix. Most of the units belong to the textiles and garments industry, chemical based and miscellaneous category industries offer only one product. The average growth score for product mix was estimated as 8.11. The forest based tiny units have the highest growth score as regards product mix.

In the case of employment generation, the units of the textiles and garments industry, forest based and miscellaneous group of industries employ less than 5 workers in their operations, whereas the agro and food products units and chemical based units employ 5 to 10 workers. The average growth score for employment was estimated as 7.95 and the maximum growth score is found among forest based units.

The value of goods produced by the tiny industrial units ranges between Rs. 50,000 and Rs. 75,000 among the forest based, chemical based and miscellaneous category industries. Regarding production, the highest growth score (8.93) was found among the units of the miscellaneous group of industries. The units of chemical-based industries have an average growth score 8.67. The average growth score for all the industries is 7.91.

The sales turnover ranges between Rs. 1.00,000 and Rs. 1,25,000 among a majority of the units belonging to chemical based and miscellaneous category industries. As regards the agro and food products units and forest based units the sales turnover varies between Rs. 75,000 and Rs. 1,00,000. The average growth score is 7.64. The maximum growth score (8.94) is found among the chemical based units.

Most of the units belonging to chemical and miscellaneous industries earn a net profit between Rs. 75.000 and Rs. 1,00,000. The net profit varies between Rs. 50,000 and Rs. 75,000 among the agro and food products, textiles and garments and forest based units. The highest (8.67) growth score is found among the chemical based units. The average growth score for all the selected industries is only 7.71.

Regarding levels of growth, the analysis reveals that out of the 250 selected units 132 units are under the category of medium level of growth, 77 units are under the category of low level of growth and the remaining 41 units come under high level of growth.

An analysis of the co-efficient of variation indicates that the units which recorded medium-level of growth are more consistent in their growth performance compared to the other two categories, namely, the high level and the low level growth performances.

To test the relationship between socio-economic factors and the different levels of growth, the chi-square test was applied. It revealed that age, educational status, technical knowledge and nature of family have influenced the level of growth of entrepreneurship in tiny sector industries.

The estimated results of the multiple-linear regression model used for identifying the factors which influence the growth of tiny sector industrial units reveal that among the significant variables, capacity utilization has a greater influence on high level of growth of the tiny industrial units in the study area.

As regards the medium level of growth units, value of production has a greater influence on the growth of the tiny sector industrial units. In the case of the low level growth units category, among the various significant variables, working capital is found to have a greater influence on the growth of tiny sector industries.

It might be concluded from the analysis that the growth of the units of the chemical-based industries in terms of the ten identified growth factors is remarkable. The variables, namely capacity utilization, value of production and working capital have greater influence on the growth scale in the case of high, medium and low level growth category of tiny sector industrial units in the study area.

Problems Faced by the Tiny Sector Entrepreneurs

The fifth chapter attempts to analyse the problems faced by tiny sector entrepreneurs. The problems faced by the tiny sector entrepreneurs are summarized and presented below.

It was found that the annual average unutilized capacity was between 51 and 75 per cent and the mean unutilized capacity was found to be the highest among the units of the textiles and garments (54.26 per cent) industries, followed by forest based industries (50.19 per cent). The major reasons for the unutilized capacity are competition (71 units) followed by the other reasons (66 units).

As far as the problems other than capacity utilization faced by the tiny sector industrial units are concerned, it could be observed that most of the units are facing marketing, finance and raw material problems. All these problems are found mostly among the textiles and garments industries.

Out of 151 tiny entrepreneurs who face marketing problem 72 (47.68 per cent) experience competition from small units and this problem is more among the units of the textiles and garments industry. Finance problem is encountered by 139 tiny entrepreneurs. Among them 54 (38.85 per cent) respondents say that the Government assistance to the tiny sector is very meagre.

It is observed that 88.8 per cent of the sample tiny entrepreneurs use the borrowings from wife and sale proceeds of agricultural land as the major source of initial capital for starting their enterprises. As regards term loans, 64 per cent of the tiny entrepreneurs utilize the term loan facilities of the Tamil Nadu Industrial Investment Corporation. For meeting the working capital needs, the tiny entrepreneurs borrow funds from commercial banks. The study reveals that 76-90 per cent of the working capital needs of a majority (59.20 per cent) of the respondents are met by the borrowings from commercial banks.

Problems relating to raw material are encountered by 130 tiny entrepreneurs. 49.23 per cent of the respondents experience the problem of raw material scarcity and most of them own units belonging to the textiles and garments industry and miscellaneous category industries.

Labour problems are encountered by 70 sample tiny entrepreneurs. Among the various labour problems, the scarcity of skilled labour is experienced by 57.14 per cent of the respondents. Power supply is another major problem and it is experienced by 55 tiny entrepreneurs and 43.64 per cent of these respondents say that the cost of power is high. 36.36 per cent respondents face power failure. 25 sample entrepreneurs use no technical and managerial guidance. Among them, 12 respondents say that it is not convenient for them to use technical and managerial guidance.

Relationship Between Level of Growth and Problems Faced by the Entrepreneurs

The chi-square test was used to examine the relationship between growth level and the problems faced by the entrepreneurs. The computed results of the chi-square test showed that the problems namely unutilized capacity, marketing, finance, raw material and technical and managerial guidance have affected the level of growth.

SUGGESTIONS

In the changed environment, the tiny sector needs to integrate itself with the overall domestic economy and global marketing by gearing itself to greater independence and by networking and sub contracting. Building competitive strengths, introducing technology upgradation and quality improvement are the vital issues which need to be addressed in order to build the capability to withstand emerging pressures and to ensure sustained growth. An analysis of issues which can contribute to the competitive advantage of the sector has been attempted in the following sections.

1. Suggestions to overcome underutilization

The study clearly points out underutilization of the installed capacities in tiny sector industries. On an average, the mean unutilized capacity ranges between 41 and 54 per cent. The study also reveals that the mean unutilized capacity is more in the textiles and garments industry. The most cited reason for underutilization of capacity is competition.

As a measure to overcome the problem of underutilization of installed capacity, the tiny industrial units can take sub contract from the larger counterparts by ensuring quality and timely supply. The unutilized capacity could also be leased to other prospective entrepreneurs who can use the unutilized capacity productively to avoid keeping the unutilized capacity idle and thus to earn additional income.

As the concept of outsourcing is gaining considerable momentum among large scale industries and multinational corporations, the tiny industries could capitalize on this opportunity by taking orders from the, outsourcing enterprises and ensuring the quality of the products. This will help the tiny entrepreneurs utilize the idle capacity productively.

2. Suggestions to overcome marketing problems

According to the present study, most of the tiny industrial units are facing marketing problems. Their major marketing problem is the competition from the other small industrial units. Competition from small industrial units could be avoided through product differentiation, enriching quality, exploring new markets, sub contracting, creating regional network of distributors and retailers. The massive growth of Self Help Groups throws another viable marketing opportunity which could be explored and used optimally. By networking with local NGOs, the products could be distributed through the SHG members of the NGOs. For their services SHGs could be offered sales commission. The SHG members could also be motivated by offering additional incentives based on sales. Being an income generating activity this work could be taken up by the SHGs.

Exhibition cum sales could also be arranged frequently in different parts of the district by the District Industries Centre in collaboration with the tiny associations during festivals and other special occasions. A consortium of tiny entrepreneurs can also be formed to promote export and to fix a uniform price to avoid competition among the small and tiny entrepreneurs. New marketing techniques and innovative marketing methods like direct marketing, multilevel marketing could be used to increase sales turnover. Training programmes in modern methods of marketing could help the tiny entrepreneurs in upgrading their marketing technology on modern lines.

3. Suggestions to overcome finance problems

Financial inadequacy is also reported to be one of the most important causes leading to sickness of tiny industrial units. Though the tiny sector was created through the Industrial Policy Resolution of 1977 to meet the aspirations of tiny entrepreneurs, till today it is treated as a small scale sector. Because of this the problem of tiny entrepreneurs cannot be addressed properly. The separate legislation to protect the genuine interests of tiny entrepreneurs should be given due priority by the Government by creating an Apex Finance Institution or Bank solely devoted to the needs of the tiny industries in the country. Such an institution will address some hitherto unknown difficulties of the sector and come out with remedial measures to improve the health of the weaker tiny industrial units. Apart from providing financial assistance the proposed Bank/Apex Finance Institution may also provide expertise in guiding tiny entrepreneurs in their financial management problems and offer preventive assistance to them in case when sickness is anticipated.

4. Suggestions to overcome raw materials problems

If raw materials are not available no enterprise can be established and in the absence of enterprises entrepreneurs cannot emerge. The lack of raw materials is normally the greatest economic barrier for the growth of entrepreneurship. The shortage of the right type of raw material has affected a majority of the tiny industrial units. Because of their weak financial position, the tiny entrepreneurs have had to utilize the services of middlemen to get raw materials on credit. Such arrangement, however, results in higher cost. The meagre resources induce the tiny entrepreneurs to use cheap and inferior materials, which naturally affect the quality of their finished products. Moreover the irregular supply of certain raw materials adversely affects their production programmes.

The Government can initiate some steps to make raw materials available to the tiny industrial units. The Government could utilize the services of the existing Government departments to ensure a regular supply of raw materials. If the Government intervenes in the supply of raw material, the role of the unscrupulous middlemen will be reduced and this will reduce the cost of production.

Agro based and food products tiny industrial units are affected by the seasonal nature of the material and failure of monsoon. The inadequate working capital restricts the tiny entrepreneurs to stock the material during season. This could be reduced by extending liberal working capital credit at very low interest rates as available to the agricultural sector.

5. Suggestions to overcome labour problems

Handling labour, which is a major contributor to industrial production, is one of the most difficult tasks of the tiny entrepreneurs because of the human element involved in it. It is observed from the study that a majority of entrepreneurs are experiencing scarcity of skilled labourers and high cost of labour. The scarcity of skilled labour could be reduced by organizing systematic training programmes by the Government through the Small Industries Service Institute (SISI) or the District Industries Centre (DIC).

The tiny enterprises can also give on the job training to the newly recruited persons to impart the adequate skill required for performing the operation before giving placement. The fresher from the formal and non-formal technical training institutes could be given apprenticeship training and the successful trainees may be inducted into regular employment. For the semi-skilled labourers category, the unskilled labourers may be given training to impart the skill required. The high cost of labour could be compensated through increased labour productivity.

6. Suggestions to overcome power supply problems

The tiny entrepreneurs in the study area reported that they are affected by high power tariff rates and power failure. The high cost of power can be reduced by extending the power tariff concession and offering subsidies to the tiny entrepreneurs irrespective of the type of products produced and the purpose for which they are used. Power failure could be avoided by installing transformers with sufficient capacity.

7. Suggestions to overcome the problems of upgradation of technology

Notable technological innovations and changes are taking place all over the world. The tiny entrepreneurs should also correspondingly respond to the changes by upgrading their technology. As a number of tiny entrepreneurs have to compete with small and large industries in a number of common product areas, upgradation of technology becomes inevitable. There is a misconception regarding modernization and upgradation of technology among the tiny entrepreneurs. Modern technology need not necessarily mean adopting automation in every case. In the case of tiny industries, the process of modernization and upgradation of technology could be undertaken in phases depending upon the resources available with the units.

While the Government is dereserving a sizeable number of products from the list of reserved items for manufacture in the small scale sector, it should provide sufficient guidance for the upgradation/modernization of tiny industries to compete with their larger counterparts in the common products categories. At present dereservation has created a tough competition between the tiny sector and their well equipped larger counterparts.

To overcome this problem, the Small Industries Service Institute (SISI) may be geared up to provide the necessary guidance to the tiny entrepreneurs. SISI can form suitable committees to identify the upgradation/modernization needs of all the tiny sector industries and come up with a suitable modernization package with liberal long term credit at zero rate of interest with tax holidays for the loan period.

Modernization would need higher and better skills to operate, maintain and run modern plant facilities to get maximum productivity. While upgrading technology proper training need to be given to the existing personnel. On the other hand it would create opportunities for many skilled and educated operators, technicians and engineers in future tiny industries.

8. Suggestions to the policy makers/Government

The new Micro, Small and Medium Enterprises Development Act, 2006 came into force on 2nd October 2006. Parliament could now introduce amendments to create an Apex Financing Institution or Bank solely to look into the needs of the tiny sector industries and to provide suitable assistance packages.

According to the Third All India Census of Small Scale Industries the number of tiny industries among the SSI was estimated as 97.9 per cent. As the dominant tiny sector was included in the SSI sector, no proper attention was given exclusively to assist the tiny sector industries. Although the investment limits have been defined properly and revised from time to time from the inception of the tiny sector through the Industrial Policy Resolution of 1977, no separate Board in the lines of the Small Scale Industries Board (SSIB) has been set up so far to streamline the tiny sector industries and to address the peculiar problems of the tiny sector industries.

The Government of India, under the Ministry of Industries, could establish a Tiny Industries Board and initiate a Package Scheme of Incentives for tiny sector industries. At present the assistance extended by the Ministry of Industries to the small-scale sector industries are enjoyed only by a very meagre percentage of small scale industries. The financially weak tiny enterprises are not able to take advantage of the assistances extended to the small scale sector.

Although the Central Government incentives and subsidies assist the growth of enterprises, it is the State Government incentives which attract entrepreneurs to set up their enterprises in a particular state. So the State Government has to play a vital role in providing assistance and facilities to allure and motivate tiny entrepreneurs to locate their ventures in the state. The State Government assistance must be so devised as to synchronize the assistance with social returns in an efficient, cost effective manner that will simultaneously promote moral imperatives.

The State Directorate of Industries while providing assistance to the small and tiny sector industries could maintain a separate set of registers for reference by and exclusive assistance for the tiny sector industries. At present the tiny sector industries are clubbed with the small scale sector for the purpose of policy decisions and assistance.

The State Government should enroll all the tiny industries separately through the District Industries Centre and offer assistance packages after assessing the exact needs of the tiny sector industries. The District Industries Centre should encourage the tiny entrepreneurs to form an association for tiny industrial units and facilitate the members of the association to meet at regular intervals to share their experiences and the problems encountered by them. This forum will help the tiny entrepreneurs to lobby effectively with the Government, to negotiate with the District Industries Centre to implement necessary assistance schemes and to represent their genuine problems.

At regular intervals the District Industries Centre could organize district level workshops to enlighten the tiny entrepreneurs about recent developments in technology and to infuse professionalism among the entrepreneurs.

Just like the Handicrafts Marketing and Service Extension Centre which help the promotion of Handicrafts, the State Government could set up a Tiny Industries Marketing and Service Extension Centre or create a separate section in the Small Industries Service Institute to assist exclusively the tiny entrepreneurs in training, development and marketing.

Though a separate cell has been created in the District Industries Centre to assist the entrepreneurs to promote export, no special initiative has been taken to achieve the objectives. The export promotion cell of the District Industries Centre could organize regular workshops to encourage the tiny entrepreneurs about their export potentials and to assist in fulfilling the export-import formalities.

CONCLUSION

The small and tiny sector is considered as an ideal nursery for the rapid growth and development of entrepreneurship. The need of the hour is the growth of entrepreneurship in the country to accelerate the process of economic growth. From the point of view of long-term perspective, however, the capacity of tiny manufacturers to become economically viable, technically progressive and efficient and to develop competitive strength shall be the only justification for their continuance. In the present study an attempt has been made to assess the entrepreneurial traits, growth of entrepreneurship and the problems faced by the tiny entrepreneurs in Tamil Nadu.

The present study will help the planners and the decision makers who are involved in the development of tiny entrepreneurs to review the existing policies and to make suitable suggestions to amend the provisions of the Act which governs the tiny sector industries. Based on the experience of the researcher the following important issues have been identified for an in depth study. The researcher will feel amply rewarded if the present study helps to undertake similar studies in the areas suggested below.

1. A study on the impact of Government assistance to the tiny sector industries.
2. An analysis of the factors responsible for the slow growth of tiny sector industries.
3. A study of the factors causing sickness in tiny sector industries.
4. An analysis of the challenges faced by the tiny entrepreneurs in the present global economic scenario.

The problems of the dominant tiny sector are multi-dimensional. These can be solved by the coordinated efforts of the entrepreneurs, coordinated functioning of promotional agencies and Governmental assistance. The need of the hour is an appropriate industrial policy exclusively for accelerating growth.

Bibliography

BOOKS

Agarwal, V.K. 1975. *Initiative, Enterprise and Economic Choices in India*, New Delhi: Munshiram Manoharlal.

Benjamin, Fruther, 1976. *Introduction of Factor Analysis*, New Delhi: Affiliated East-West Press.

Drucker, P.F. 1985. *Innovation and Entrepreneurship Practices and Principles*,London: Heinemann.

Durariraj, N., and M. Soundara Nageswaran, 1988. *Entrepreneurship in Small-scale Industries in Paramakudi Taluk*, Tirunelveli: Doss Printers.

Edwards, A.L. 1969. *Techniques of Attitude Scale Constructions*, Bombay: Vilkils, Feffer and Simons Private Limited.

Ellis Albert, 1962. *Reasons and Emotions in Psychology: Secaus*, New Jersey: Lyle Stuart.

Fred N. Kerlenger, 1973. *Methods of Factor Analysis, Foundations of Behavioural Research*, Newyork: Holt Rinchart and Winston Inc.

Glasser William, 1975. *Reality Therapy*, New York: Harper and Row.

Goldan, B.N. 1986. *Productivity Growth in Indian Industry*, New Delhi: Allied Publishers.

Goyal, S.K. 1984. *Small Scale Sector and Big Business,* New Delhi: Indian Institute of Public Administration.

Harry H. Harman, 1967. *Modern Factor Analysis,* Chicago: The University of Chicago Press.

Ian D. Little, 1987. *Small Manufacturing Enterprises, A Comparative Study of India and Other Countries,* New York: Oxford University Press.

Kalchetty Eresi, 1989. *Management of Finance in Small Scale Industries,* Allahabad: Vohra Publishers and Distributors.

Kopardekar, D. 1974. *Small Scale Industries,* Pune: G.Y. Rane Prakasham.

Mansfield, Richard, S. Mc Cleveand, D.C., Spenser Lyle and Santiago Jose, 1987. *The Identification and Assessment of Competencies and Other Personal Characteristics of Entrepreneurs in Developing Countries,* Boston: Mc Ber & Company.

Nanjundan, S. 1980. *Changing Role of Small-scale Sector in India's Economic Policies,* (1947-77), New Delhi: Allied Publishers Pvt. Limited.

Nandapurkar, G.G. 1982. *Small Farmers - A Study of their Entrepreneurial Behaviour,* New Delhi: Metropolitan Book Company Private Limited.

Perumalsamy, S. 1985. *Economic Development of Tamil Nadu,* New Delhi: S. Chand and Company.

Puhazhenthi, V, and Satyasai, K.S.S. 2000. *Micro Finance for Rural People,* Mumbai: Department of Economic Analysis and Research, National Bank for Agriculture and Rural Development.

Ramesh P. Sinha, 1985. *Some Problems of Small Scale Industries,* New Delhi: Janak Prakashan.

Rao, V.K.R.V. 1965. *Small Scale and Cottage Industries,* Allahabad: Chaitanya Publishing House.

Rogers, Carl, R. 1961. *On Becoming: A Person Loughton,* Miffin.

Sharma, R.A. 1980. *Entrepreneurial Change in Indian Industry,* New Delhi: Sterling Publishers Private Limited.

Skinner, B.F. 1973. *About Behaviourism,* New York: Knopf.

Thanulingam Nadar, N. 1985. *Small-scale Industry Inter-Relationship with Large-scale Industry,* Coimbatore: Rainbow Publications.

Thurstone, L. and Chava, E. 1929. *The Measurement of Attitude,* Chicago: University of Chicago Press.

Desai Vasant, 2004. *Management of a Small Scale Industry,* Mumbai: Himalaya Publishing House.

Velmani, K.S.K. 2002. *Gazetteers of India, Tamil Nadu State,* Chennai: Tiruneveli District, Government of Tamil Nadu Commissioner of Archives and Historical Research.

Venkataraman, R. quoted by Rudder Dutt and Sundaram K.P.M. 1993. *Indian Economy,* New Delhi: S. Chand & Company Limited.

William J. Stanton, Michael, J. Etzel and Bruce J. Walker, 1994. *Fundamentals of Marketing,* Mc Graw Hill International Edition.

THESIS

Arulappan, A. 1996. *A Study of Entrepreneurship in Small Scale Industries in North Arcot Ambadkar District-Tamil Nadu,* Ph.D., Thesis, Madras University, Madras.

Campbell Mc Connel and W.C. Peter 1963, *Research Activity, Product Diversification and Product Differentiation by Small Manufacturer in Nebraska,* Nebraska: University of Nebraska.

Jeyakumar, 1995. *An Economic Study of Entrepreneurial Performance in Small Scale Industries in Madurai District,* Ph.D., Thesis, Madurai Kamaraj University, Madurai.

Kanchana,T. 2001. *The Study of Entrepreneurship in Sivakasi Region,* Ph.D., Thesis, Madurai Kamaraj University, Madurai.

Knight, A. John, 1973. "*A Study on Relative Effectiveness of Three Modes of Presentation, Preference, Listening and Post Listening Behaviour of Farm Broadcast Listeners*", Unpublished Thesis, Division of Agricultural Extension, I.A.R.I., New Delhi.

Lingasamy, 1997. *Enrepreneurship in Small Scale Industries in Kamarajar District*, Ph.D., Thesis, Madurai Kamaraj University, Madurai.

Meera, M.J. 2001. "*Performance Analysis of Samatha Self-Help Groups in the Empowerment of Rural Women in Panchayats*", Unpublished Thesis, KAU Vellayani.

Mohan, R. 1996. *Innovation and Small Scale Entrepreneurship in Madurai District*, Ph.D., Thesis, Madurai Kamaraj University, Madurai.

Moorthy, G.K. 1980. *Financing of Small Scale Industries in Rayalaseema Region*, Ph.D., Thesis, Andhra Pradesh, Waltair.

Noor Jahan, A.K.A.H. "*A Critical Analysis of Technological Gaps in Adoption of Pest Management Practices in Rice*", Unpublished Thesis ,Tamil Nadu Agricultural University, Madurai.

Paulraj, L.R. "*Profile and Role Performance of FDG Conveners*", Unpublished Thesis, Tamil Nadu Agricultural University, Madurai.

Seema, 1999. "*Marketing Behaviour of Coconut Growers in Andaman and Nicobar Islands*", Unpublished Thesis, Tamil Nadu Agricultural University, Madurai.

Selvarani, 2001. Women Entrepreneurship and Venture Management - A Study in Virudhunagar District, Ph.D., Thesis, Madurai Kamaraj University, Madurai.

Shamboo Prasad, 1981. *Role of Small Scale Industries in a Developing Region with Special Reference to Bihar*, Magadh University, Bihar.

Sounthara Pandian, 1992. *Growth of Entrepreneurship in Small Scale Industry*, Ph.D., Thesis, Madurai Kamaraj University, Madurai.

Supe, S.V. "*Factors Related to Different Degrees of Rationality in Decision Making among Farmers*", Unpublished Thesis, Division of Agriculture, I.A.R.I., New Delhi.

Takshak, Renu, 1990. *Credit Procurement and Utilization by Entrepreneurs,* Haryana Agricultural University, Hisar.

Trivedi,G. "*Measurement and Analysis of Socio-Economic Status of Farm Families*", Unpublished Thesis, I.A.R.I., New Delhi.

Venkatesan, S. "*Performance of Leadership Roles: Farmer Discussion Group Conveners of Madurai District*", Unpublished Thesis, Tamil Nadu Agricultural University, Madurai.

JOURNALS

Advani, A.H. March 2-15, 1981. "Small Scale Sector Cracking Up", *Business India*, No. 78.

Anita, H.S. and A.S. Laxinisha, June 1999. "Women Entrepreneurship in India", *Southern Economist*, Vol. 31, No. 9.

Ayda Eradyin, Bilge Armatli-Koroglu, July 2005. "Innovation, Networking and the New Industrial Clusters: The Characteristics of Networks and Local Innovation Capabilities in the Turkish Industrial Clusters", *Entrepreneurship & Regional Development*, Vol. 17, No. 4.

Balasubrahmany, M.H. October-December, 1999-2000. "India's Small Industry Policy in the 90's: Waning Protectionism", *The Indian Economic Journal*, Vol. 47, No. 2.

Basavaraja, M.G. June 1999. "Role of SSIs: Study of Karnataka", *Southern Economist*, Vol. 38, No. 4.

Chandra, J. Narayana Rao V. and Visweswara Rao, K. November 1993. "Small Scale Sector- Prospects and Problems", *Business Spectrum*.

Duane Ireland, R. Michael A.Hitt, David G.Sirmon, 2003. "A Model of Strategic Entrepreneurship: The Construct and its Dimensions", *Journal of Management*, Vol. 29, No. 6.

Edapen, Mridul, 1984. "Structure of Manufacturing Workforce, A Preliminary Analysis of Emerging Tendencies", *Economic and Political Weekly*, Vol. 19.

Gangadharan, S. May 1989. "Textile Industry— Modernisation Pace and Crisis Deepening", *The Economic Times*, Research Bureau.

Kashyap, S.P. April - June 1995. "Emerging Industrial Policy Reforms: Implication for Small Size Enterprises", *Productivity*, Vol. 36, No. 1.

Indian Institute of Public Opinion Economic Unit, December 1999. "Export Potentiality and Small Scale Industries", *Monthly Public Opinion Surveys*, Vol. XLV, No. 3.

John B. Miner, 2000. "Testing a Psychological Typology of Entrepreneurship Using Business Founders", *The Journal of Applied Behavioral Science*, Vol. 36, No. 1.

Joseph Andrew Kuzilwa, 2005. "The Role of Credit for Small Business Success: A Study of the National Entrepreneurship Development Fund in Tanzania", *The Journal of Entrepreneurship*, Vol. 14, No. 2.

Kamalanabhan, T.J. 2006. "Evaluation of Entrepreneurial Risk-taking Using Magnitude of Loss Scale" *Journal of Entrepreneurship*, Vol. 15, No. 1.

Madhu Murthy, K. December 2003. "Entrepreneurs: Evaluation of the Concept and Characteristics", *Sedme*, Vol. 29, No. 4.

Mahajan,V.S. October 2, 1980. "Small and Tiny Units", *Economic Times*.

Nag, A. 1978. "Growth of the Small-scale Sector: An Assessment", *Yojana*.

Nair, K.R.G. 2006. "Characteristics of Entrepreneurs: An Empirical Analysis", *Journal of Entrepreneurship*, Vol. 15, No. 1.

Nandi, A. 1973. "Motives, Modernity and Entrepreneurial Competence", *The Journal of Social Psychology*, Vol. 31, No. 2.

Nanjundan, January 1996. "Economic Reforms and SSI Units", *Economic and Political Weekly*, Vol. XXXI, No. 5.

Nasser Ahmed and Kakoly, H.N. 1993. "Determinants of Agricultural Entrepreneurial Success", *Indian Journal of Social Science Research*, 34 (2).

Neelamegam, R. January 3, 1990. "Small Business Financing", *The Economic Times.*

Patel, M.M. 1995. "Role of Entrepreneurship in Agricultural Development", *Kurukshetra,* Vol. 43, No. 3.

Prasad Kumar M. and Narayanan, S.K. 1995. "Industrial Sickness: A Case Study of Small Scale Engineering Units in Coimbatore", *Journal of Accounting and Finance,* Vol. 9, No. 1.

Rajendran, December 1998. "Small Scale Industrial Policies", *Southern Economist,* Vol. 37, No. 17.

Reddy, P.N. July 1997. "Small Scale Industry: Moving Towards Viability", *Business Line.*

Robin Mukherjee, Pranab Kumar Das and Uttam Kumar Bhattacharya, November 1999. "Small Scale Industries in West Bengal 1971-97: Data Analysis for Study of Growth", *Economic and Political Weekly,* Vol. 36, No. 48.

Rolland LeBrasseur, Louis Zanibbi, Terrence J.Zinger, 2003. "Growth Momentum in the Early Stages of Small Business Start-Ups", *International Small Business Journal,* Vol. 21, No. 3.

Sandesara, J.C. November 27, 1982. "Incentives and their Impact on Small Industries", *Economic and Political Weekly,* Vol. 17, No. 48.

Sandesara, J.C. February 6, 1993."Modern Small Industry 1972 and 1987-88: Aspects of Growth and Structural Change", *Economic and Political Weekly,* Vol. XXVIII. No. 5

Sidharthan, N. May 1998. The Budget and Industrial Development, *Economic and Political Weekly,* Vol. XXXIII, No. 18.

Srinivasalu Bayineni, M. May 1996. "Development of Small Scale Industries", *Third Concept,* Vol. 1, No. 7.

Sue Marlow, 2001."Investigating the Use of Emergent Strategic Human Resource Management Activity in the Small Firm", *Journal of Vocation Marketing,* Vol. 7, No. 2.

Sunday L.Owualah, 1999. "Tackling Youth Unemployment through Entrepreneurship", *International Small Business Journal*, Vol. 17, No. 3.

Swamy, T.L.N. April-June 1995. "Eighth Five Year Plan - Role of Small Industry", *Productivity*, Vol. 36, No. 1.

Thomas M. Hult, Charles C.Snow, Destan Kandemir, 2003. "The Role of Entrepreneurship in Building Cultural Competitiveness in Different Organisational Types", *Journal of Management*, Vol. 29, No. 3.

Tripta and Kaushik, April - June 2002. "Impact of Financial Assistance Schemes on the Economic Empowerment of Women", *Indian Journal of Social Research*, Vol. 43, No. 2.

Venkata Ramaiah, P. 1993. "Entrepreneurial Behaviour of Farmers", *Indian Journal of Extension Education*, Vol. 9, No. 1.

Vijay Vayas, 2005. "Imitation Incremental Innovation and Climb Down: A Strategy for Survival and Growth of New Ventures", *The Journal of Entrepreneurship*, Vol. 14, No. 2.

Vaidyanathan, A. June 16, 1991. "Cottage and Small Industries: Policy and Performance", *Fortune India*.

Vikram Chadha, May 1999. "Financing the Modernisation of Small Industries in India: Opportunities and Constraints", *Southern Economist*, Vol. XXXVIII, No. 2.

REPORTS

Annual Plan, 2005-06. Directorate of Industries and Commerce, Chennai.

Annual Report, 2005-06. Ministry of Small Scale Industries, Government of India, New Delhi.

Annual Report, 2005-06. Credit and Fiscal Concession to Small Scale Industries Sector, Ministry of Small Scale Industries, Government of India, New Delhi.

Annual Report, Small Industries Development Organization, 1998.

Annual Report, 1999-2000. Reserve Bank of India.

Census of India, 2001. Primary Census, Government of India, New Delhi.

District Statistical Handbook, 2003-04. Statistical Department, Government of Tamil Nadu.

Economic Survey, 1984-85. Ministry of Finance, Government of India, New Delhi.

Economic Survey, 1985-86. Ministry of Finance, Government of India, New Delhi.

Economic Survey, 2005-06. Ministry of Finance, Government of India, New Delhi.

Industrial Statistics, 2003. Department of Statistics, Tamil Nadu.

Report of the Director, Geological Survey of India, Tamil Nadu and Pondicherry, Madras.

Report of the Working Group on Small Scale Sector, 1969. Administrative Reforms Commission, The Government of India Press, Simla.

WEBSITES

www.nellai.tn.nic

www.tanstia-fnt.com

www.nisiet.org

www.tn.gov.in.

www.laghu-udyog.com

www.ssi.nic.in

www.techsmall.com

www.indianhandicrafts.org.in

www.smallindustryindia.com

www.tamilnaduindcom.org

www.census.tn.nic.in

www.indiastat.com

www.joe.sagepub.com

www.entrepreneurshipgenius.com

www.ccsbe.org

www.sba.muohio.edu

www.papers.ssrn.com

www.ediindia.org

www.mplew-jena.mpg.de/esi/disscussion

Index

G

H

I

J

K

❑❑❑

❑❑❑